The DNA of *Successful* Leaders

Tapping *Your Natural Power* to
Win Friends and Influence Others

Troy L. Tate

Cumulatius Publishing,
31726 Rancho Viejo Road Suite 222
San Juan Capistrano, CA 92675

Library of Congress Cataloging-in-Publication Data

Tate, Troy L.

The DNA of Successful Leaders:
Tapping Your Natural Power to
Win Friends and Influence Others
Troy L. Tate

ISBN 0-9768154-0-0 (hardcover)

1. Leadership 2. Personality Types 3. Influencing Others in Workplace

Library of Congress Control Number 2005904230

Cover and interior design
by www.KarenRoss.com

THE DNA OF SUCCESSFUL LEADERS:

*Tapping Your Natural Power
to Win Friends
And Influence Others*

Cumulatius Publishing
San Juan Capistrano, CA

The DNA of Successful Leaders

Acknowledgements

This book is the fruit of so much effort over the last several years. Despite my dream to write this book and all that I have done to move it along, I would not have completed it and understood its concepts and principles without the contribution of key people, for which I wish to express acknowledgement and appreciation.

Thanks to Terry Hart, whose experience, wisdom and contributions to the book at a critical stage, fostered in me the confidence not only that I could complete it but also that it would benefit many in the business world and beyond.

Thanks to Patience Jarolimek, whose encouragement, support, ideas and enthusiasm have motivated me to move ahead with my book and my business.

Thanks to Sidra Gaines, Kevin Miller, Dan Lamont, Steve Faught, Rose Brown, and Craig Georgianna for their excellent input and suggestions on earlier drafts. Thanks to Karen Ross for her jacket and interior layout design.

Thanks to Dianne Yancey for sharing her wisdom with me regarding different personality groups, particularly the Yellow that she so wonderfully embodies.

Thanks to Craig Georgianna also for all that he taught me as we trained companies years ago on the different personalities. His wisdom and shared experiences have inspired me in many ways.

Thanks to my brother Wynn for his example of persistence and to my sister Lauri for her friendship and encouragement. Thanks to Alph for his support.

Thanks to my mother, who saw qualities in me I could not see in myself and who has never wavered in her love and encouragement to be the best "Troy" I could be. I will be forever grateful.

Thanks to my daughters Natalie, Marisa, Emily and Savannah, who have brightened up my life in so many ways, each being their own unique personality and bringing so many gifts and so much joy to my life. We have all the DNA colors in our home, which has made it a wonderful research laboratory.

Most important of all, words can't begin to express my gratitude to Laura, my wife, whose love, encouragement, humor, wisdom, faith and patience have given me the courage and determination to write this book and to test uncharted waters in my life. She offered me great insights on earlier drafts of my book. It is to Laura and our children that I dedicate this book with all my love and appreciation.

Table of Contents

The DNA of Successful Leaders

Tapping Your Natural Power to Win Friends and Influence Others

The DNA of Successful Leaders

SECTION I.

Opening

C H A P T E R   1

"Be yourself. Everybody else is already taken."

Being the Best You, You Can Be:
A Quick Look at the Big Picture

Human beings are remarkable creatures. As the most intelligent animals on the planet, we know how to send people into space, harness the power of the sun, heal the sick, and create great literature, music, and art. The list goes on and on.

But, the one thing that appears the easiest for us to know, the thing that is the most important for us to know, is the one thing that the vast majority of us don't know—who we really are. We often don't understand why we react the way we do to certain circumstances. (Have you ever thought: "Why did I do that!? What was I thinking!?") We frequently don't take advantage of the unique, natural strengths we're born with, and too often find ourselves in situations where we have to rely on our weaknesses to reach our goals - and we don't even realize it's happening. Many of us have spent years underachieving, and not living the rich and fulfilling lives that we're capable of, and entitled to.

Others of us have accomplished wonderful things, but have not yet tapped a natural power source that could magnify those achievements many times over. All of us have "blind spots" that have sabotaged or hurt key relationships. As a result, we're often oblivious to what we cause, convinced that those around us are to blame for less than successful results. When you do discover and use your natural powers, you'll not only eliminate those "blind spots" and increase the level of success and happiness in your own life and career, but also understand how to motivate others to give the best of their innate strengths toward a common purpose.

Most all of us are capable of achieving and enjoying more in our careers, jobs, businesses or relationships. The overwhelming cause of unfulfilled dreams isn't due to lack of talent or skill - it's because people either don't recognize and use their natural aptitudes and strengths, or recognize and manage around their natural weaknesses or both. If you're not as happy or successful as you want to be, it's not because you're not capable; it's because you've yet to become the best and most influential "you", you can be.

Do You Play the Violin or Trumpet?

Would you pay the legendary violinist Itzak Perlman $100,000 to perform in concert and then, just before the curtain rises, take away his violin, hand him a trumpet and tell him to go for it? If you did, would you then be shocked that he didn't render a *virtuoso* performance?

It sounds silly on the surface, but we frequently do that to ourselves, and then feel shocked or disappointed that we're not getting the results we desire. Are you struggling to play the trumpet harder and louder in your business, career or job when you're naturally gifted at the violin? Is the whole undertaking burning you out?

Henry David Thoreau said that the mass of men lead lives of quiet desperation and go to the grave with their song still inside. Have you lived your whole life not playing your unique composition on the instrument you were born to play?

Simply stated, if you don't recognize what your natural, God-given talents and aptitudes are, you're going into your everyday life battles, big and small, at an extreme disadvantage. And you're doing a disservice to yourself and everyone around you

There's no reason to accomplish less than your maximum potential in your career, relationships, and life. You're about to learn how to recognize your natural aptitudes—your natural talents and strengths—and how to use those aptitudes to your fullest advantage. You'll discover where your weaknesses lie (everyone has them), and how to avoid situations where they can hold you back.

Drives, Needs and Aptitudes

Becoming a successful leader is all about: (1) knowing your "DNA" and the "DNA" of those you lead, and (2) applying this knowledge to influence others effectively.

What is "DNA"? It's the drives, needs, talents and strengths you're born with and use to function in life. Think of it like the operating system for your soul—the system and filters through which you experience, interpret and respond to what happens to you. Your "DNA" governs how you process what you experience with your five senses and influences what you enjoy and what you don't like doing.

DNA stands for **Drives**, **Needs** and **Aptitudes**. You're about to learn what your DNA is and what to do with it to become a successful leader. You'll also learn how to determine the DNA of others, and how to use that knowledge to have a more powerful and enduring influence with those you lead.

Learning "the DNA skill" isn't as difficult as going into space, healing the sick, or creating great works of art. In fact, the most important thing for you to know will turn out to be easier and more enjoyable to apply than you thought possible. Understanding "DNA" will open you up to a whole new world of influence.

Your Drives — The "D" of DNA

Have you ever wondered why some people react to the same event so differently than you do? Sometimes you think they're "out to lunch", or "off the wall", or both. But in reality, they're seeing and reacting to what happens to them through a different set of filters than you. Their filters block out or disregard some things your filters let in and deem important and vice versa.

Every person is born with one or two drives. You're no exception. Your innate drives are pivotal to your success as a leader because they strongly influence how you interpret and respond to what happens to you, including how you relate to other personalities in all types of situations. The key for you is to understand "what makes you tick" and "what makes others tick you off" so you can take advantage of (instead of getting frustrated by) the differences.

Your Needs — The "N" of DNA

Everyone has a set of needs that are hard-wired at birth. Ask any parent who has two or more children and they'll tell you that not one of their children is exactly the same. Even before they were born, one was punching and kicking to get out, while another enjoyed the aquatic environment and didn't mind staying there until he or she was "induced" to leave. Your natural needs flow from your drives; those needs, in turn, strongly influence what your natural aptitudes (and weaknesses) will be. We devote most of our time and energy in life to fulfilling those needs, so it's important to be aware of what they are and how we satisfy them.

Your Aptitudes — The "A" of DNA

You've been blessed with natural strengths, talents, and skills — "aptitudes"—that can be used to lead effectively. Maybe you're good at communicating and motivating people. Maybe you have a natural ability with budgeting and forecasting. Possibly you have a skill at organizing, or figuring out a logical approach to solving a problem creatively. Or maybe your strength is logistics—effectively carrying out someone else's strategy. What are your natural strengths and assets and are you using them when you lead others?

The Price We Pay For Ignoring Our DNA

People in business often struggle with not knowing, let alone taking advantage of, their DNA. This is just as true for the entrepreneur as it is for the executive or employee. Many ignore their natural aptitudes and strengths to land a job that pays the bills, but dread going back to work each Monday morning. Other professionals stay stuck for years or even decades in a career that they were never cut out for so they can maintain the lifestyle that comes with it. Many entrepreneurs feel like they're a prisoner in their own businesses. They devote countless hours to what they're _not_ naturally good at and their business ends up with incremental gains, treading water, or sinking into oblivion. When mediocre to poor results occur, such people don't change their direction; they just work harder at creating the same limited outcomes.

When we start a new business, job or career, we often venture into uncharted waters without the compass and rudder that keeps us on course towards the desired destination—knowing our God given strengths and weaknesses and focusing the vast majority of our time and energy on where we float, not where we sink. We may spend our entire adulthood "making a living" instead of passionately pursuing what we're naturally good at and reaping the rewards of our excellence.

> *Mark Twain told about a man who died and met Saint Peter at the pearly gates. Realizing Saint Peter was wise and knowledgeable the man asked, "Saint Peter, I have been interested in art for many years. Tell me, who was the greatest artist of all time?"*
>
> *Saint Peter quickly responded and pointed, "Oh, that's a simple question. It's that fellow right over there."*
>
> *"You must be mistaken," replied the man, "I knew that man on earth, and he was a common laborer."*
>
> *"That's right, my friend," replied Saint Peter. "But he would have been the greatest artist of all time...if he had been an artist."*

Nobody's Perfect — Manage Around Your Weaknesses

Being the best "you", you can be is about identifying and embracing your natural   aptitudes and then stretching to build new and complimentary strengths.   But it's also about recognizing your weaknesses. *The DNA of Successful Leaders* will enable you to see what your natural weaknesses are, and what brings them into play.   Instead of dwelling on them or struggling to eliminate them without success, you'll recognize them and avoid situations, jobs, responsibilities where those weaknesses will be exposed and magnified. You can find others whose strengths offset your weaknesses. Everyone has weaknesses, but when dealt with properly, they'll stop being obstacles to your success and happiness.

Thomas Edison was almost deaf. But he didn't waste valuable time trying to teach himself to hear. Instead, he concentrated on the things he did best: thinking, organizing, and creating.

> *Toward the end of his life, George Bernard Shaw was asked, "You have known some of the most famous people of your time. You're on a first-name basis with royalty, world-renowned authors, artists, teachers, and dignitaries from every part of the world. If you had your life to live over again and could be anyone you've ever known, who would you want to be?"*
>
> *"I would choose," Shaw replied, "to be the man George Bernard Shaw could have been, but never was."*

In 2003, a British study conducted by Tulip Financial Research revealed that successful business people are surprisingly likely to suffer from dyslexia and other learning disorders. About 40 percent of the 300 subjects studied had been diagnosed with the condition – 4 times the rate of the general population.

Psychologists speculated that dyslexics compensate for their difficulty with details by learning to grasp the bigger picture and producing original ideas.   For instance, Sir Richard Branson, the billionaire founder of Virgin Records and Virgin Atlantic Airways, is dyslexic and admitted that he didn't understand the difference between net and gross profits until it was explained to him - **when he was fifty years old**! A dyslexic business owner lacking an understanding of basic accounting might seem destined for failure but look what Branson built—a business empire. Branson knew what he was good at and magnified it a thousand fold instead of dwelling on or trying to remove his weaknesses. His dyslexia and failure to understand financial complexities became irrelevant to his achieving success.

Uncovering Who You Are

Yes, humans are complex animals, but surprisingly we can be divided into just four basic groups.

Thousands of years ago, Hippocrates came up with four general personality groups or temperaments. Today, we have hundreds, perhaps thousands, of personality paradigms, which use animals, shapes, adjectives, directions, colors, acronyms (e.g., "ENTF") and other symbols to categorize personalities. Most are derived in whole or in part from Hippocrates' original work. The *DNA Torque™ Personality Profile*, the personality profiling tool in Chapter 2, is no exception. However, I believe you'll find it shines brightly above the rest in its simplicity and effectiveness.-

There are infinite variations of personalities within these four broad personality groups. But you, me and everyone we know or ever come in contact with, has a drive or drives that literally "color" how we see and react to the people and world around us — so I have chosen to categorize these groups by colors.

Colors influence how we feel and react. Our drives do also. Colors are more neutral than other devices or gimmicks to categorize personalities. The most powerful reason for using colors here is that each personality group identifies easily, even emotionally, with the color chosen for it. I've not yet encountered an exception to this rule.

The Four Personality Groups

Each personality color has its **D**rives, **N**eeds, and **A**ptitudes, and its way of communicating with and relating to others. The four color/personality groups are Red, Aqua, Yellow, and Blue. Sometimes each personality group will be identified by using a trait that typifies that group: **Powerful Red, Peaceful Aqua, Optimistic Yellow** and **Personable Blue**. Such traits are not intended to specifically and solely embody each of the personality groups. Rather, having the accompanying adjective tends to make it easier for some to remember.

REDS have **high energy** and are **driven** to **make things happen** and to **secure power**. (Have you ever noticed that power neckties are . . . red?) Reds need **to achieve, to be right** and **to be respected**. Reds' aptitudes include **initiative, focus, confidence, leadership, risk taking** and **decisiveness**.

AQUAS, akin to **calm seas**, are driven to seek **peace** and **balance** in their lives. Aquas need **tranquility** and **independence**. They love to **reflect** and "**go with the flow**"—as long as it's at their own pace and in their own way. Aquas' aptitudes include **objectivity, diplomacy, kindness, clarity**, and **openness to new ideas and strategies**.

YELLOWS are of **sunny disposition** and **optimistically embrace life**. Yellows are driven to **have fun** and to **feel happy**. Yellows need **freedom** and **social acceptance**. Yellows' aptitudes include **resilience, spontaneity**, and **out of the box creativity**. Yellows are also **naturally warm** and **forgiving of others.**

BLUES thrive on **order** and **structure** and love to **relate** to others on a **deep** level. Blues are driven to **do things perfectly** and to **connect with others deeply**. Blues need **security, order** and **understanding from others**. Blues' aptitudes include **discipline, loyalty, team building, sensitivity**, and **quality workmanship.**

Most of us are blends of two or more DNA colors, and therefore, may share a few of the needs and aptitudes (but not the drives) of a second DNA color.

So what color is your DNA and what is your secondary DNA color? You'll find out once you take the *DNA Torque Personality Profile* in Chapter 2, and tally the results.

You Influencing Them

No one operates and succeeds in a vacuum. Your success depends on others, and the four basic temperaments that you're going to learn won't only enable you to manage your own aptitudes and weaknesses, but also will allow you to see the aptitudes and weaknesses in those around you - the people you work for and with, plus friends and family members. You'll then use that information to gain friends and draw out the support and commitment from all those around you.

Great leaders know themselves and play to their strengths, while managing around their weaknesses. And they know the same about those with whom they work and apply that knowledge for the success and benefit of all.

If you read this book and apply what it teaches, will you be able to figure out and influence every person with whom you come in contact? Probably not. Human beings are complex and many have neuroses and psychoses that make reading their DNA difficult and influencing them even harder. But you will better understand more people than you ever have before and your influence with them will flourish.

Those who are intent on getting things done learn to recognize that people are not objects to control through intimidation or to manipulate to get the desired results. Using those tactics produce results that are weak and short lived. Yet people welcome influence that benefits them in their lives.

A leader who treats others as <u>she</u> wants to be treated will learn that it doesn't work for those who experience life through a different set of filters. In this situation, The Golden Rule needs to be slightly revised—do unto others as **they** would have you do unto **them**. Your drives and needs are not necessarily theirs. You need to communicate to those you lead <u>in their language</u> so that <u>their needs</u> are being addressed and met.

> *"The most effective leader is the one who satisfies the psychological needs of his followers."*
> *– David Ogilvy*

The Payoff of Knowing Your DNA and the DNA of Others

The *DNA Torque™ Personality Profile* in Chapter 2 is designed to uncover the personality group to which you belong and to ferret out any false identities you've assumed along the way in an attempt to be valued, happy and successful. It detects incongruity between your natural drives and learned behaviors. **It gives you a better sense of who you were born to be so that you can be clear and focused on where you want to go.** Finally, it helps you to magnify the natural aptitudes that you were blessed with rather than tossing them aside because you've been misled along the way as to their true value. The *DNA Torque™ Personality Profile* can set you on the path to be the best "you", you can be by getting back in touch with who you are.

When that happens, you'll see that there is great power in being genuine. You have nothing to spin. You are who you are, warts and all. It's massively liberating not to have to create and sustain a self image that isn't you.

I guarantee that this process for growth will be fruitful and that any attempt to skirt your identity either consciously or unconsciously to "be like Mike" (or anyone else) will inevitably sabotage your success as a leader, husband, wife, father, mother, friend or team member.

What would it be like if you and your salespeople understood your clients, customers and prospects better than they understand themselves? You'll learn here to understand what drives them, what their specific needs are and how they express them. If you give voice and put words to what they sense or struggle with, but can't quite explain, you're building an immovable foundation for a long term recurring revenue channel. These clients and customers will come back to you again and again because they will identify with your sales representatives and understand how your products and services truly meet their individual needs.

If you want to be in the upper echelon of leaders who create results that make a difference in the lives of your employees, vendors, customers and shareholders, *The DNA of Successful Leaders* will help you get there. If you want to understand how to be more effective in positively influencing the thoughts and behaviors of others, you've come to the right place. If you just want to better understand who you are and what makes you tick so you can best deploy your strengths and manage around your weaknesses, then you'll get the answers you need.

The foundation for any sustained success in life — in your marriage, family, organization or business — is to know who you are, to embrace the gifts you naturally were blessed with and then to let the natural weaknesses that otherwise limit your growth fade into the background. Simply stated, be who you are and learn to bring into your life the gifts that others embody—gifts that compliment what you already have.

Some people will get more out of this book than others. If you're curious about looking at yourself and others in a new way or if you're open to doing things differently to improve the results you want in your life, then you'll probably get far more out of this book than you otherwise would. If you're sure you know yourself, including all your blind spots, and that you're a master at influencing others, then you can't learn what you're already convinced you don't need to know. However, I suggest you check out whether your colleagues, subordinates, clients and/or bosses agree with your presumed mastery over yourself and others. You might have blind spots that you never knew were there.

Elie Wiesel has said that when we die and meet our maker, we're not going to be asked why we didn't find a cure for cancer, or solve world peace. Instead, we will be asked, "Why didn't you become you?"

Something wonderful is about to happen...
You're going to become the best "you", you can be.

C H A P T E R   2

Taking the DNA
Torque Personality Profile

The *DNA Torque™ Personality Profile* is designed to reveal the "DNA" you were born with. You now understand why I use the term "DNA" but what about "Torque"? "**Torque**" is a common term in the auto racing world used to describe **the force that causes the wheels to rotate.** Engineers design the engines in the racing cars to generate maximum torque within the parameters prescribed by the governing racing association because increased "**torque**" translates to a faster car.

In the business world, "**torque**" **is the power or force that propels effective human performance**. Think about the business you own or that employs you. Businesses and organizations want their hiring and training to generate the most "torque" out of their employees from the time, energy and money they invest in them.

If the *DNA Torque™ Personality Profile* and the principles taught in this book can help you to hire people who are the best fit for the job openings you need to fill and if those hired are trained according to how they best learn and are motivated by you according to what their "**DNA**" is, then you'll get more "**torque**" out of your workforce and increase your company's bottom line profitability. Your team will have a strategic advantage over your competitors because they will generate more revenue per employee at less cost; your competition won't know how to get similar "**torque**" out of their workforce.

Have fun with this profile. Be as honest as possible with your answers and the traits you identify—both strengths and weaknesses. If you mark the traits in Section 1 based on how you think you should respond, then this profile won't do you a lot of good. It'll reflect back to you the image you want others to see rather than who you really are. You can't be happy and influence others for the better being someone you're not.

Use a pencil and have an eraser handy. Don't be afraid to go back and change an answer if it seems more accurate upon further reflection. If you aren't sure the personality group it identifies as your primary DNA color is accurate, get another family member (preferably sibling or parent) to fill it out based on how they see you (rather than themselves). Then compare the answers and the scores. This profile is going to reveal your DNA color, which opens the door to your being the best you, you can be.

THE DNA TORQUE™ PERSONALITY PROFILE
SECTION 1
NATURAL TRAITS

Directions: In each of the following forty rows, place a check next to the one trait you are naturally most prone to display if you made no effort to control, hide or change it. Looking back as far as possible to your behavior as a child will help you most accurately determine which of the four traits is most natural (versus which is most accurate presently). Positive and negative traits are listed, so be candid as to both types of traits. <u>Pick one (and only one) trait in each row</u> so that you end up picking forty (40) traits overall. See Appendix 1 on page 192 for further definition of any of the traits listed.

1.	___Animated	___Outspoken	___Pleasant	___Sensitive
2.	___Competitive	___Disciplined	___Easy-going	___Playful
3.	___Mediator	___Sociable	___Strong-willed	___Well-mannered
4.	___Considerate	___Patient	___Persuasive	___Tenacious
5.	___Even tempered	___Refreshing	___Resourceful	___Respectful
6.	___Analytical	___Charismatic	___Confident	___Dry Humor
7.	___Funny	___Focused	___Nurturing	___Self-governing
8.	___Adaptable	___Scheduled	___Decisive	___Spontaneous
9.	___Assertive	___Deliberate	___Kind	___Optimistic
10	___Planner	___Promoter	___Satisfied	___Self-starter
11.	___Diplomatic	___Forgiving	___Self-reliant	___Sympathetic
12.	___Cheerful	___Detail-oriented	___Open-minded	___Risk-taker
13.	___Contemplative	___Independent	___Inspiring	___Intuitive
14.	___Committed	___Consistent	___Demonstrative	___Positive
15.	___Creative	___Innovative	___Inventive	___Productive
16.	___Conversationalist	___Faithful	___Tolerant	___Future-focused
17.	___Energetic	___Leader	___Listener	___Loyal
18.	___Engaging	___Mover	___Orderly	___Steady
19.	___Daring	___Informal	___Resilient	___Self-sacrificing
20.	___Gentle	___Precise	___Powerful	___Storyteller
21.	___Ambivalent	___Bossy	___Rebellious	___Overly Cautious
22.	___Obnoxious	___Distant	___Moody	___Abrasive
23.	___Impatient	___Undependable	___Resentful	___Reluctant
24.	___Fearful	___Distracted	___Blunt	___Fussy
25.	___Absent-minded	___Insecure	___Haphazard	___Head Strong
26.	___Indecisive	___Insensitive	___Unpredictable	___Worrier
27.	___Interrupter	___Hard-to-please	___Argumentative	___Quiet
28.	___Indifferent	___Arrogant	___Permissive	___Pessimistic
29.	___Aimless	___Inflexible	___Selfish	___Cluttered
30.	___Confrontational	___Naïve	___Flippant	___Sarcastic
31.	___Self-critical	___Impulsive	___Silently Stubborn	___Merciless
32.	___Easily Offended	___Withdrawn	___"In your face"	___Too Talkative
33.	___Disorganized	___Domineering	___Timid	___Fatalistic
34.	___Guilt-ridden	___Inconsistent	___Apathetic	___Intimidating
35.	___Easily Bored	___Crafty	___Unforgiving	___Passive
36.	___Aggressive	___Noncommittal	___Show-off	___Skeptical
37.	___Dictatorial	___Rule-driven	___Lazy	___Rule bending
38.	___Forgetful	___Short-tempered	___Suspicious	___Gullible
39.	___Exacting	___Rash	___Reticent	___Restless
40.	___Abdicating	___Unreliable	___Manipulative	___Alienated

SECTION 2
ATTITUDES AND BEHAVIOR

Please complete the sentences below by selecting the answer that is the most accurate. If none are accurate, pick the one that is the closest to being accurate and circle the answer. When you complete this section, record your answers to Sections 1 and 2 on the page following the end of this Section and tally how many answers you have in each column. The column with the highest number of answers is your personality group or DNA color. Those columns with the second and third highest scores are also important for reasons discussed in this book.

41. If a co-worker has said something that has offended me or if a conflict has arisen between a co-worker and me:

    (a) I try to stay away from the person hoping that time will ultimately cause the conflict or hurt to go away by itself.

    (b) I spend a lot of time thinking and worrying about the situation, re-analyzing what was said and rehearsing repeatedly how I will deal with this person in the future.

    (c) I tell the person directly what is wrong and how to make it right.

    (d) I confront the person by using humor to lighten up the situation before discussing the issue.

42. If I am called on at work to respond quickly and comprehensively to an unanticipated event, problem or crisis:

    (a) I generally respond effectively and perform at my best because such situations get me focused and I like the challenge.

    (b) I withdraw, get stressed and find ways to reduce the pressure such situations bring by asking others to take on a greater share of the burden such a response will require.

    (c) I feel anxious, frustrated and overloaded because I don't like unplanned surprises, but I still do what I'm told.

    (d) I make a game of it and or find a way to persuade others to help me fulfill my duty to respond.

43. As a parent, I'd motivate my son to do household chores by:

    (a) telling him the fun things we can do after the chores are done and maybe even joking around with him while he is doing the work.

    (b) explaining to him the need for every member of the family to contribute and the sacrifices I make on his behalf.

    (c) kindly requesting that he do the chores and hoping that he will do so without my having to get angry or do the work myself.

    (d) telling him what needs to be done and what will happen if he does not do it.

44. At a work-related party or get-together:

    (a) I look for people I know and engage in conversations with them and those to whom they introduce me.

    (b) I observe others and listen to various conversations without trying to be the center of attention.

    (c) I go there to have fun and freely talk with all those who I meet there.

    (d) I go there to network and establish or strengthen relationships with those who I seek to influence including customers, client and management.

45. When working on a project with an assigned team with co-workers:

    (a) I like to be in charge and direct the co-workers' performance.

    (b) I strive to ensure that the team first plans how it will complete the assigned project and that each team member contributes his or her share.

    (c) I prefer to listen more than talk during team meetings and like to work independently on completing my assigned portion of the project.

    (d) I try to avoid doing any boring assignments and like to liven up team meetings with humor and enthusiasm.

46. When I first wake up in the morning:

    (a) I feel happy and eager to start the day.

    (b) I focus on all the things I intend to accomplish that day and get started so as not to waste time.

    (c) I often feel overwhelmed with all the things I should do that day.

    (d) I prefer to relax by reading interesting literature, surfing the Web, watching TV or doing some other activity to pass the time.

47. If I were given a day off from work to spend however I choose, I would:

    (a) go through and tackle some of the things on my "to do" list that I had not had time to complete.

    (b) get out of the house and do something challenging or thrilling.

    (c) call up some friends and get something going.

    (d) relax and take it easy at home, preferably alone.

48. When I fail to achieve a goal I have set:

    (a) I am not too hard on myself but I am not inclined to set another goal in its place.

    (b) I take it hard but move on by setting a new goal that I will achieve instead.

    (c) I feel guilty and blame myself for not having done all that I could have to have achieved it.

    (d) I am disappointed but I don't worry about it; instead I enjoy what life brings to me anyway.

49. In a successful relationship, communication generally should be:

    (a) stimulating, constant and lively.

    (b) kind and tolerant of one another's differences.

    (c) sincere, open and deep; communication should be used to share feelings, not just facts or information.

    (d) clear, accurate and to the point.

50. When I am angry:

    (a) I often let it simmer inside without letting anyone know how angry I am.

    (b) I take action and even use the anger to motivate others to do what needs to be done.

    (c) I express it and get over it in a matter of minutes.

    (d) I brood and often use sarcasm to express it but I don't let go of it that easily.

51. If I were unhappy and dissatisfied with my job, I would be most inclined to:

    (a) stick with it because it pays the bill and because trying to find another job is pretty stressful.

    (b) move on because I don't want to be working at a job where it isn't fun or stimulating.

    (c) find another job that is more challenging and that has better opportunities for advancement and compensation.

    (d) stick with it and endure the frustrations because they need me and every job has its negative aspects.

52. If I want to correct the performance of someone who I oversee at work, I most likely:

   (a) suggest sensitively and perhaps indirectly how their behavior needs to change after complimenting her or him for what (s)he has done well.

   (b) tell him or her directly and succinctly what is wrong and what the consequences will be if the behavior does not change.

   (c) send an e-mail telling him or her kindly what area of performance needs to be improved and try to soft pedal it as much as possible so the person does not get angry or emotionally upset.

   (d) let the person know what area of performance is lacking and encourage him or her to make the change while remaining upbeat and positive about his or her being able to do so.

53. When I get a new electronic gadget that comes with a detailed set of instructions:

   (a) I review only that part of the instructions that I need to know to do what I want the product at that time to do.

   (b) I ignore the instructions and try to figure out myself from the pictures how to get the product to do what I want.

   (c) I find someone who knows the gadget or who has the necessary expertise to show me only what I want to know how to do.

   (d) I take the time to read through all of the instructions to assure I fully understand how to perform all of the functions of that gadget.

54. If I am suffering from the flu, a sore throat or a bad cold, I tend to:

   (a) let others know that I am sick and hope they feel some sympathy for my condition.

   (b) suck it up and keep going without letting anyone know I am weakened at all by my condition.

   (c) look on the bright side believing I will get over it quickly or use it as a way for others to pay more attention to me.

   (d) use it as an opportunity to slow down and get some rest.

55. Goals:

   (a) are great as long as they don't interfere with living life fully in the present moment.

   (b) tend to be overrated; goals often produce more stress than satisfaction.

   (c) are necessary to overcome one's weaknesses and become better in all facets of one's life.

   (d) are critical to being successful; I set and achieve goals regularly.

56. As a child in elementary school, I:

   (a) competed hard to get the highest grades in the class and took a lead role in group projects.

   (b) did all of my homework, behaved well in class and tried to get on the teacher's good side.

   (c) kept quiet most of the time, did my work and tried not to get the teacher mad at me or the class.

   (d) was popular and often kept the teacher and students entertained by my antics.

57. If my parents seemingly caught me doing something wrong as a child, I would:

    (a) become quiet and hope that my parents would not be too hard on me.

    (b) come up with a creative story to explain why I really was not to blame for my wrongdoing.

    (c) change the subject and point out something they or a sibling did wrong so they would lose focus on my wrongdoing.

    (d) admit I was guilty and plead for mercy promising I would not do it again.

58. When faced with a difficult decision as a child, I most likely would:

    (a) decide quickly and act on it.

    (b) spend a lot of time thinking about how I should decide and worrying about what might happen if I make the wrong decision.

    (c) either make the decision quickly hoping for the best or put it off and devote my attention to more enjoyable things.

    (d) avoid it as long as possible and hope that it goes away or that someone else can make the decision for me.

59. When preparing for a big test or final exam during my school days:

    (a) I prepared a schedule far in advance and stuck to it so I could fully cover all of the course materials before the test.

    (b) I crammed for the test because that is how I memorized the course materials the quickest and the best.

    (c) I studied when I could but would get easily distracted if there was something more enjoyable to do.

    (d) I studied as time allowed throughout the period I had to prepare but did it a little more intensely as the test date drew near.

60. My most rewarding times as a child were when:

   (a) I was fully occupied with a favorite game, sport or hobby.

   (b) I received a trophy, medal plaque or form of recognition for winning some competition or some other achievement.

   (c) sharing time listening to and talking with a best friend.

   (d) having fun doing crazy things with some friends.

TORQUE DNA TORQUE™ PERSONALITY SCORING SHEET

Look to your answers in Section 1 and place a check next to the trait that you selected from each of the forty rows. Then add up your check marks on each of the four columns and put the total at the bottom of each column. The four column totals should equal 40.

(Score Sheet on next page)

SECTION 1 NATURAL TRAITS

	RED DNA	AQUA DNA	YELLOW DNA	BLUE DNA
1.	Outspoken	Pleasant	Animated	Sensitive
2.	Competitive	Easy-going	Playful	Disciplined
3.	Strong-willed	Mediator	Sociable	Well-mannered
4.	Tenacious	Patient	Persuasive	Considerate
5.	Resourceful	Even tempered	Refreshing	Respectful
6.	Confident	Dry Humor	Charismatic	Analytical
7.	Focused	Self-governing	Funny	Nurturing
8.	Decisive	Adaptable	Spontaneous	Scheduled
9.	Assertive	Kind	Optimistic	Deliberate
10	Self-starter	Satisfied	Promoter	Planner
11.	Self-reliant	Diplomatic	Forgiving	Sympathetic
12.	Risk-taker	Open-minded	Cheerful	Detail-oriented
13.	Independent	Contemplative	Inspiring	Intuitive
14.	Positive	Consistent	Demonstrative	Committed
15.	Productive	Inventive	Innovative	Creative
16.	Future-focused	Tolerant	Conversationalist	Faithful
17.	Leader	Listener	Energetic	Loyal
18.	Mover	Steady	Engaging	Orderly
19.	Daring	Informal	Resilient	Self-sacrificing
20.	Powerful	Gentle	Storyteller	Precise
21.	Bossy	Ambivalent	Rebellious	Overly Cautious
22.	Abrasive	Distant	Obnoxious	Moody
23.	Impatient	Reluctant	Undependable	Resentful
24.	Blunt	Fearful	Distracted	Fussy
25.	Head Strong	Absent-minded	Haphazard	Insecure
26.	Insensitive	Indecisive	Unpredictable	Worrier
27.	Argumentative	Quiet	Interrupter	Hard-to-please
28.	Arrogant	Indifferent	Permissive	Pessimistic
29.	Selfish	Aimless	Cluttered	Inflexible
30.	Confrontational	Naïve	Flippant	Sarcastic
31.	Merciless	Silently Stubborn	Impulsive	Self-critical
32.	"In your face"	Withdrawn	Too talkative	Easily offended
33.	Domineering	Timid	Disorganized	Fatalistic
34.	Intimidating	Apathetic	Inconsistent	Guilt-ridden
35.	Crafty	Passive	Easily Bored	Unforgiving
36.	Aggressive	Noncommittal	Show-off	Skeptical
37.	Dictatorial	Lazy	Rule bending	Rule-driven
38.	Short tempered	Gullible	Forgetful	Suspicious
39.	Rash	Reticent	Restless	Exacting
40.	Manipulative	Abdicating	Unreliable	Alienated

TOTAL _____   _____   _____   _____

Red   *Aqua*   *Yellow*   *Blue*

(The total of the four columns should equal 40)

SECTION 2
ATTITUDES AND BEHAVIOR

Look at your answers to Section 2 and place a check next to the answer you circled; total up the check marks for each of the columns. Then take your score totals from Section 1 under each of the four DNA colors to come up with a Grand Total for each of the four columns.

	Red	Aqua	Yellow	Blue
41.	(c) ____	(a) ____	(d) ____	(b) ____
42.	(a) ____	(b) ____	(d) ____	(c) ____
43.	(d) ____	(c) ____	(a) ____	(b) ____
44.	(d) ____	(b) ____	(c) ____	(a) ____
45.	(a) ____	(c) ____	(d) ____	(b) ____
46.	(b) ____	(d) ____	(a) ____	(c) ____
47.	(b) ____	(d) ____	(c) ____	(a) ____
48.	(b) ____	(a) ____	(d) ____	(c) ____
49.	(d) ____	(b) ____	(a) ____	(c) ____
50.	(b) ____	(a) ____	(c) ____	(d) ____
51.	(c) ____	(a) ____	(b) ____	(d) ____
52.	(b) ____	(c) ____	(d) ____	(a) ____
53.	(a) ____	(c) ____	(b) ____	(d) ____
54.	(b) ____	(d) ____	(c) ____	(a) ____
55.	(d) ____	(b) ____	(a) ____	(c) ____
56.	(a) ____	(c) ____	(d) ____	(b) ____
57.	(c) ____	(a) ____	(b) ____	(d) ____
58.	(a) ____	(d) ____	(c) ____	(b) ____
59.	(b) ____	(d) ____	(c) ____	(a) ____
60.	(b) ____	(a) ____	(d) ____	(c) ____
Totals	____	____	____	____
Section 1	____	____	____	____
Grand Totals	____	____	____	____
	Red	**Aqua**	**Yellow**	**Blue**

(Adding the "Grand Totals" from each of the four columns should equal 60)

CHAPTER 3

"What lies behind us and what lies before us are small matters compared to what lies within us."
— *Oliver Wendell Holmes*

The Meaning of the Results

Now that we have the results, look to the column with the highest total. That is your primary "DNA" color or personality group. Then look to see which column has the second highest total. That is your secondary DNA color or personality group. Do all of us match perfectly with all the traits and behavior of our primary DNA color? Rarely. But you should match up **mostly** with the personality of your primary DNA color based on the responses you gave in the profile. If the two highest scores are very close, then check out the chapters on those two DNA colors you scored highest on to determine which better describes who you are.

Remember, no DNA color ranks above the rest. Each DNA color has natural aptitudes that effective leaders exemplify and each has weaknesses that undermine strong leadership. No personality group is better than the others just as no single color is more valuable than the rest. They simply are what they are.

Remember also that everyone is born into and leaves this earth with their same basic drives and needs. You can't drop, switch or pick up a new "DNA" along the way. That doesn't mean that you're stuck in a personality pigeonhole from which you can never escape. It does mean that your innate drives and needs have influenced and will continue to influence your way of looking at and responding to the world.

What you can change is how you choose to respond to their influence. You can embrace all the positive aspects of having the same DNA color you've had from the beginning and learn strengths from other personality groups that tend to erase or make irrelevant your biggest natural weaknesses. The following is a brief synopsis of each of the four colors, which will be followed in the next section by a much deeper, more detailed explanation.

Reds

Reds are defined by action. Their drives are to get results and have power; so I refer to this temperament as the "Powerful Red."

What does the term "powerful" mean to you? Some people react negatively to being "powerful" while others prize such a trait. "Powerful" denotes one who is able to make things happen or who has control or influence over people, organizations, companies or even money. Powerful Reds feel the need to make things happen, to take charge, to be in control, to move things ahead, to achieve goals or a certain status, to be at the top and/or to lead others to accomplish what the Reds are focused on achieving.

Powerful Reds often find themselves in leadership positions because that's where they desire to be. Their urge to make their goals a reality pushes them to be future oriented—always looking ahead to the next goal or challenge. They're drawn to careers and jobs that allow them to exercise power in accomplishing their targeted objectives. The great gifts that Powerful Reds generally bring to the table are focus and determination to do what it takes to get to the desired result.

Aquas

Aquas desire peace and tranquility so one adjective that aptly characterizes Aquas is "Peaceful". Peaceful Aquas are more low key. Aqua—that blue-green color you see looking out onto a calm tropical sea—is chosen for this personality group because it soothes and calms you when you gaze at it. "Aqua" comes from the Latin root for water and Peaceful Aquas are much like "water" because they tend to go with the flow.

Peaceful Aquas are **not** grounded in strong opinions about how the world and others ought to be but share a common philosophy that everyone should get along with one another. They're more interested not in **making** but in **letting** things happen; Aquas respect and champion everyone's right to choose their own path without being forced to go to the same destination at the same pace.

Peaceful Aquas reflect logically on deeper matters; they approach life from the perspective of a detached observer. Peaceful Aquas are usually well balanced and can see and understand the merits of differing positions or opinions because they're not tied to a particular viewpoint.

Yellows

Yellows tend to see life as a glass half full rather than half empty. (Some Yellows, however, may look first in the glass and see what's in it before they decide.) One of the adjectives that best describe them is "optimistic." Optimistic Yellows live in the present moment and generally enjoy what life offers. Optimistic Yellows are driven to have fun and to feel happy. People in this personality group don't like to focus on the past. Nor do Yellows like outlining long term plans for their future because too much scheduling takes away from the spontaneity and surprises of life. Optimistic Yellows love conjuring up visionary ideas of what the future could be; they just don't want to devote too much time and energy trying to bring that vision into crystal clear focus.

Optimistic Yellows are people oriented and interact well with most anyone. They love to talk with new people anytime, anywhere and tend to draw others to them because their energy is high; these people are not as intense as Powerful Reds in making things happen but intensely pursue stimulation, excitement and making the most of each day.

The color chosen for this group of people is Yellow, reflecting sunshine and a bright outlook on life. Optimistic Yellows see life through "amber colored lenses"; their enthusiasm is often contagious. What they bring to the table in a business setting is out of the box thinking, creativity, and fun.

Blues

Blues, akin to Yellows, are people oriented, but in a deeper and more complex way. Because Blues yearn to connect with people and champion the concept of team; a good adjective that describes them is "Personable." Personable Blues also seek perfection in their own character and in their environment. They often look to the past for guidance as to how to improve from their mistakes.

Personable Blues love order, justice, fairness and security. They avoid risk taking. The color Blue has been selected for this group because Personable Blues are genuine or "true blue" in their nature and tend to experience mood swings that may leave them feeling the "blues", when they think back on how things should have been or on how they or other people should have acted.

The Personable Blues' gifts to the business world are quality, order, detail and discipline. They're excellent in building and strengthening teams. They also are sensitive to others. People with this temperament are more people than thing oriented but tend to be much deeper, and therefore, more easily offended in their emotional attachments than Optimistic Yellows. Blues give much and expect much in return from their close relationships.

Blends

Can you be a blend of two or more of these DNA colors? Absolutely. But your primary DNA color will more strongly influence how you think, speak and act than the secondary or tertiary color and will generally govern your communication style. Within the scope of all who identify themselves inside your personality group are a variety of personalities depending on the blend and the other factors that have influenced such people over time including family, parents, sex, culture, socioeconomic background and experience.

Knowing a person's DNA, however, is like being given a giant key that you can use to enter into and explore the inner workings of someone else's mind. You understand the specific filters through which that person interprets and experiences life. Knowing the person's DNA leads to a series of "ahas" when the behavior coincides with how they see life (instead of "What's wrong with her?" or "It ticks me off the way he acts!").

When we begin to explore, observe and understand where others are coming from and discover in a sense their "operating systems", then we go a long way towards effectively leading them towards a mutually desired objective. In short, by understanding what makes you and others tick, you can then begin to avoid "ticking off" others and make great strides to influence them for the better. You will separate yourself from the pack of leaders who never try to understand, let alone value, how others have different aptitudes and ways of communicating than these leaders do.

"In the world to come, I shall not be asked, 'Why were you not Moses?' I shall be asked, 'Why were you not Zusya?'"

— Rabbi Zusya

DNA Color Comparisons

	Drives	**N**eeds	**A**ptitudes
Reds	Results/ Power	To Be Right, To Be In Charge	Boldness, Tenacity, Determination
Aquas	Peace/ Balance	To Be Respected, To Be Accepted	Kindness, Patience, Diplomacy
Yellows	Happiness/ Fun	To Be Praised, Freedom	Optimism, Creativity, Charisma
Blues	Connection/ Perfection	To Embody Quality, To Be Understood	Planning, Analysis, Loyalty

SECTION II.

You

C H A P T E R   4

"Far better to dare mighty things, to win glorious triumphs, even though checkered by failure, than to take rank with those poor spirits who neither enjoy much nor suffer much... in the gray twilight that knows neither victory nor defeat."

— Theodore Roosevelt

The Powerful Red

Red DNA at a Glance

DRIVES: Power and Results.

NEEDS: To be right, to be in charge, to be strong, to achieve, to get credit for achievements, to be competent, to be efficient.

APTITUDES: Boldness, action orientation, initiative, willingness to take risks, determination, resourcefulness, confidence, tenacity, clarity and decisiveness.

COMMUNICATION STYLE

Clear, concise, and efficient; high energy and confident; commands and orders;

Reds often say "I need... " or "Get me..."

The Powerful Reds' Drives

The Powerful Reds' drives are **power** (to be in control of their environment) and **results** (to achieve desired outcomes within that environment). These innate urges go hand in hand. Both direct them to focus on what is outside of themselves. Reds see setbacks as mere obstacles to leap over or drive through. Reds often see people as a resource to help them get the results and power they desire rather than as an end in themselves.

Powerful Reds are attracted to people who are competent and confident. Such people help them to achieve their goals; they also inspire Reds to do their best.

Feelings tend to be ignored or disregarded with Powerful Reds because they prefer to be grounded in logic. "Bonds" to a Powerful Red are not what you build in a relationship but rather something you buy and sell in the market place. Reds respect and value those who know how to get things done.

Reds are very direct people. They don't "beat around the bush." Reds get to the point. The quickest and shortest distance between two points is a straight line. The shortest way between where a Red is and where he wants to be is a straight line, even if there may be obstacles in the form of other people in the way. Powerful Reds have little patience for those who cannot communicate succinctly and directly what is on their minds because such people impede Reds from getting more quickly to where they want to be—the opposite point on that straight line.

Powerful Reds strongly prefer communication in small chunks such as memos that are punctuated with bullet points. Reds want to understand quickly what the gist of the communication is. When asked to make a decision, they prefer only a few alternatives with a short cost/benefit analysis of each so a decision can be made quickly and action taken. In fact, making a decision quickly is more compelling to a Red than making sure all relevant information has been considered. Powerful Reds would rather risk not having all of the facts than taking too much time to turn over every stone to find all the relevant information before deciding.

"A less than perfect decision, made in a timely manner, and vigorously executed, is better than the best decision made too late."
— *General George S. Patton*

Joe Friday's "Just the facts Ma'm" of *Dragnet* fame typifies the approach Powerful Reds take to life. Powerful Reds prize their logic as the ultimate tool to decipher and evaluate what they observe and take in. Feelings and emotions muddle what Reds believe is critical to the decision (facts); therefore, feelings should be ignored.

Powerful Reds tend to see things as black and white. They have little tolerance for ambiguity or for those who are wishy-washy in their opinions. Clarity and brevity show competence and Powerful Reds prefer to work with those who are competent.

The Powerful Reds' Needs

Reds have distinct needs, some of which have already been alluded to above. Reds need to be strong because they value themselves based on their ability to overcome all things and to make correct decisions. Their makeup does not allow them to feel vulnerable or weak. Feeling strong helps propel them to action.

Reds need to be in charge. Their drive for power—being in control of their external environment—pushes them to assume positions of power in any organization. Being in power also helps them fulfill their drive to get results. Time is viewed as a precious commodity from which results must be manifested so they want to be in control of how time is used and allocated. Getting to the top of corporate or organizational ladders where they can assume more power over their environment and achieve greater results is more important than enjoying the journey.

Reds need to get credit and recognition for achievements. You'll often find Reds tooting their own horn if they don't hear others proclaiming the Reds' accomplishments. However, Reds really don't need general adoration from the masses, just recognition and respect from those they respect.

Reds need to be competent in their own eyes and in the eyes of those they respect. Competence goes hand-in-hand with self-worth. If Reds don't see themselves as competent in an area, then they may turn to anger, manipulation and intimidation to assert power over those who may be more competent in that area. The usurpation of power reinforces their sense of self worth.

Reds need to be efficient. Reds pride themselves in the ability to do multi-tasking. According to Reds, those who cannot do two or more things at once are lazy or incompetent. Reds ignore or challenge those who try to direct them to do things in an inefficient way. Reds value themselves by how many things they can achieve each day.

Reds need emotional detachment. Reds tend to derive their power and energy from within and not from others. They're self-driven. Although Reds need recognition from others, such need does not extend below the surface. The need is geared to a reaction of another towards their actions rather than a longing for a deep connection to and acceptance from another.

Reds need to be right. Admitting a mistake or the merits of an opposing view is very difficult because it flies in the face of their need to be right. Getting a Red to apologize can be tough because Reds see it as a weakness and admitting weakness is tantamount to attacking their value as a human being.

Reds do not desire to understand others or have others truly understand them. They rarely try to understand why they do what they do. To Reds, their behavior is obviously the best and most practical way to do things and to live life. Reds connect more with their work and with the tasks and challenges at hand than they do with other human beings.

The Powerful Reds' Aptitudes (Strengths)

Reds have numerous aptitudes, most of which are listed in the beginning of this chapter. Reds are self starters. When confronted with roadblocks, they quickly find a way around them. When one door closes, they look for another door to open. Reds can create a laser like focus on what they want to achieve and that enables them not to get overly frustrated if something unexpected happens.

Reds have great tenacity when pursuing a goal or carrying out a project. They never give up easily because that is a sign of weakness. Powerful Reds despise weakness in themselves and others unless "others" means the enemy or the competition. Reds have little problem with someone else being weak if it can be exploited to get the Reds what they want. This allows them to be proactive and to switch to contingency plans on a moment's notice.

Reds are decisive. What makes it easy for Powerful Reds to decide is that decisions move them forward. Vacillation is against their nature. Reds have the confidence in themselves to adjust to any consequences their decisions bring. Reds do not stop to ponder all the possible scenarios where things won't work out. They view it instead as "where there is a will, there is a way." They focus on finding the "way" and don't want to waste any time deliberating the pros and cons of a host of alternatives.

Reds are efficient. They're always thinking of ways to do things faster. That motivates Reds to multi-task. They hate spinning their wheels for the sake of learning some lesson or waiting for something to happen. Reds don't wait to let things happen in their own time. They prefer always to make things happen.

Reds are determined. Once they decide what they want, they go after it. It goes back to the laser-like focus Reds were blessed with as part of their DNA.

Reds are future focused. Reds base their value on what they accomplish. To a Red, you're only as good as your last win. This makes Reds look ahead to the next milestone. They don't like to rest on past laurels, which quickly lose value in their own eyes.

Reds are action-oriented. Powerful Reds love leadership roles. They have the strength of visualizing what they want to accomplish and driving themselves and those on their team to achieve it. Reds can make the seemingly impossible happen within tight deadlines.

Reds are clear. Reds hate ambivalence and wishy-washy opinions. Reds let you know where they stand and tenaciously stand up for their positions.

The Powerful Reds' Weaknesses

Powerful Reds also have weaknesses, although they're very reluctant to discuss them. Weaknesses to a Powerful Red are viewed as the soft underbelly that leaves them vulnerable to attack. The Reds prefer not to let anyone know their weaknesses because doing so doesn't get the Reds where they want to be.

Aluminum foil has a shiny side and a dull side; so does each personality group. The Reds have as their shiny side determination and tenacity but their dull side includes over-aggressiveness, impatience and intolerance for those who might seek to point out the faults or weaknesses in their positions.

Powerful Reds can be dictatorial because they're so clear on where they should be headed; anyone who argues otherwise is wrong. Debating the issue is a waste of time and energy because Reds know they're right.

Reds don't seek input once they fall in love with their own ideas, opinions and strategies. This weakness often proves to be their Achilles' heel.

Powerful Reds hate to admit they're wrong because being wrong lowers their value as a human being. Remember, Reds value themselves based on results—what they accomplish. A direct path to their goal is essential and they have natural confidence that whatever they choose to believe or decide is right. Those who would challenge them are viewed not as potential teachers but as obstacles to go over or push aside. Other points of view seem designed to challenge or change a Red's decision or beliefs. Consideration of competing views may make things muddled and cause Reds to vacillate in indecision, which Reds hate. Clarity, simplicity and a single "right" point of view is a Red's number one protocol.

Reds are critical and can be abrasive and rude when others don't meet their expectations. Their blunt criticism of those who don't meet their expectations can alienate those whose help they need.

The Powerful Reds' Communication Style

Perhaps the most telling feature of a person's temperament is the way in which he or she communicates, verbally and non-verbally. People who score highest with Powerful Red may have one or more of their needs and behaviors from a secondary DNA color but their communication style almost always is Red (assuming they're psychologically healthy).

Reds are probably the easiest temperament to identify by their communication style. They're high energy, direct, clear, succinct and rarely say "I feel..", " I believe..." or "It seems to me...". Such phrases are weak, tentative, and ambiguous.

Reds get to the point. In fact, many Reds often point their finger as they communicate to reinforce their message. When others are communicating slowly or seem to be meandering without purpose, Reds often interrupt by saying, "What's your point?" or "Get to the point!" or "And your point is..?"

Reds have little patience for those who lack clarity or direction in their communication. Communication must be purposeful—a tool to achieve results. Those who talk in a stream of consciousness mode without any purpose or direction are quickly dismissed as a waste of time. When someone isn't "cutting to the chase" quickly enough, Reds will tend to cut them off in mid sentence. They may even finish the speakers' sentences for them.

Reds exude confidence. It is in their voice and their gestures. Their whole body resonates with the drive to move ahead and achieve their goals.

How The Powerful Reds Control

Reds are the most obvious in their desires to control or influence others. Reds don't waste time. If they want you to do something for them, they'll tell you. Their sentences tend to be brief and explicit. Often, they'll say "I need ...." Or "Get me ...." Reds value clarity and their focus is on the task at hand so expressing their demands clearly and concisely is a natural for them. The challenge becomes motivating those who are not either positively or negatively inclined to obey their directions or commands.

Powerful Reds will often resort to the compulsion or control approach when they sense a need for immediate action and they're certain that more gentle tactics just won't get them what they want when they want it. Often Reds won't even consider any alternative that requires patience. The Reds' other drive for results leads them to use the force of their will and intimidation to get what they want or need. Reds are so confident and forceful in their demands that people respond with the demanded behavior, particularly if disobedience carries with it a threat of punishment.

Reds often don't have to threaten a negative consequence. Their very personality compels people to act because they fear facing the brunt of the Powerful Reds' anger and displeasure. The problem comes when fear no longer works as a motivator. How long will an employee stay with a company led by a Red who compels compliance and performance through intimidation and force of will? The influence will last only as long as that person sees no more desirable alternatives or no longer buys into the fear. In fact, people will often perform at a level high enough to keep their job without giving their all for the benefit of their Red leader. Attrition will grow worse. No power generated through force of will or intimidation can be maintained in the long run to achieve enduring success.

The Powerful Reds' Potential Pitfalls

Powerful Reds often see themselves as masters in whatever career they choose. This mindset, of course, causes arrogance, pride and stubbornness. In fact, the quality that is most difficult for Powerful Reds to develop is humility.

As I mentioned earlier, Reds hate feeling vulnerable; humility makes them feel vulnerable. Humility is an acknowledgement that Reds don't have all the answers and that they may not be in total control of their chosen pathway to success.

A friend shared a story about her life that aptly illustrates this point. Her two daughters were taking piano lessons from a Powerful Red teacher who considered herself a maestro—unequaled in her knowledge of music and her ability to make her students excel above and beyond other teachers' students. This teacher unquestionably knew her craft very well but her dictatorial and critical style often was grating.

Both of my friend's two children performed well enough to qualify them to perform at the statewide teachers association's annual music convention. All that was necessary was to fill out and submit an application to the association. However, the association was very strict in how the form needed to be filled out including identifying the piece, the composer, and the time it took to perform the piece. That is what the music teacher agreed to do for her two students.

The master teacher filled out one application correctly and it was accepted; however, the teacher inadvertently left out some essential information from the other application. The association denied that application. My friend's daughter felt devastated; my friend was not only saddened by the news, but also was amazed by how the master teacher reacted. This "maestro" expressed anger at the association for **its** incompetence despite the fact it was **her** mistake in filling out the application that led to the rejection.

The master teacher called up the person in charge of accepting applications for the association, a fellow music teacher, and berated her for not having returned the faulty application earlier so the teacher could correct it. The master teacher didn't apologize to the association or to my friend for her error; instead, she made the association's representative the villain.

When my friend tried to discuss with the teacher how to get her daughter what she had earned—the right to perform at the state music convention—the teacher didn't accept responsibility for her mistake. Instead, she boasted of her talent as a master teacher and angrily attacked the association for its incompetence. The teacher explained how underlings at the association simply don't know how to treat someone at her level.

Instead of letting the teacher continue her verbal jousting with the association to get it to allow the student to perform at the convention, this friend asked her husband to call the association; the husband did and apologized to the representative for the teacher's error. He then asked if there was any way his daughter could qualify to perform at the convention. The association said there was and asked him to send in the application again with all the right information. He did.

When the association agreed to accept the new application, the master teacher took credit for the result, and indicated that the association finally did what they were supposed to do. Not surprisingly, my friend found another piano teacher for her two daughters a few months later.

This piano teacher undoubtedly was qualified to help her students develop their musical talents but her arrogance and dictatorial style often overshadowed her strengths. This teacher ended up losing many wonderful students who otherwise could have benefited greatly from her talents.

The natural aptitudes of the Powerful Reds, if not balanced by the complimentary strengths of the other DNA colors, can ultimately sabotage success. The indisputably valuable strengths of being focused, decisive and determined, if not tempered with people skills that include humility and openness to influence, can turn into manipulation, arrogance, tactlessness and over-aggressiveness. The key for Powerful Reds is to balance their natural strengths with developed strengths in other temperaments that make the Reds' natural weaknesses irrelevant. Alternatively, a Red can choose others to work with whose natural strengths offset where they're weak.

Another example of a strength turning into a fatal flaw, if left unbalanced, is the Powerful Reds' drive to achieve. The drive can bring about many great results but it also can lead to self destruction. A Powerful Red who focuses exclusively on career or business to the exclusion of all else ultimately sacrifices key relationships and perspective that can generate sustained success. Sacrificing everything for the sake of achievement of money, prestige, status, or power prove to be hollow victories. Don't be surprised the next time you hear a Red tell you how great everything in her life is going except for her relationships.

Powerful Reds in the Workplace

Where do you find the Powerful Reds in a company? Reds are everywhere, but they long to be at the top. In the companies I have trained, Reds make up thirty to forty percent of the employees and often constituted a majority of the executive team.

Powerful Reds love positions that allow them some leadership responsibilities and some autonomy to do things the way they want. The world of business is the world of Red because it is focused on results—the production of goods and services and making profits.

Reds thrive in this environment. Reds similarly do well in the military where clear battle lines are drawn and there are winners and losers.

Reds love the competition that the workplace fosters, not only with other businesses but also with co-workers. Reds like to be top producers, whether it be in sales, marketing, manufacturing or finance. They tend to do well in any position that allows success to be rewarded either through commissions, bonuses, perks or promotions.

Reds delegate responsibilities and they enjoy new challenges. The standard incentives of money and promotions tend to work well with Powerful Reds. They enjoy the recognition that comes from winning an internal competition, getting the management position, and moving into the corner office.

Danger may arise when a Red is overlooked for promotion in favor of someone the Red believes isn't as competent or deserving of his or her respect. Reds may then seek to undermine the leadership of the appointed leader by open criticism and balking at directives. Political battles are common under such circumstances and the leader must have the skill to give the Powerful Red some responsibilities that will allow him or her to exercise leadership skills without undermining company morale.

Reds are very comfortable with win/lose scenarios. Most Reds have little problem in generating situations where they win at the expense of a colleague, co-worker, competitor, vendor, or even boss.

The key for those working with Reds is to make clear to the Reds that win/lose won't work if the Red wins while one or more team members and/or the team itself lose. Give Reds the alternatives of win/win or lose/lose and encourage them to choose the former. For example, if a Powerful Red seeks to undermine the leadership of his boss by open criticism and doing things contrary to that directed by the leader, a one-on-one meeting is important. At that meeting, the boss presents a positive alternative that allows the Red to shine, progress and be recognized for his strengths and a negative alternative for continuing not to be a team player—discipline, demotion and/or firing. Simply playing hard ball may lead to the Red leaving and such a departure means throwing away all the talents, natural strengths and experience that the Red can bring to the company.

A Harvard Business School study concluded that **the cost of replacing an executive in a business exceeds or is equal to his or her total annual compensation**. Losing a Red leader because you decided to "fight fire with fire" or go "mano a mano" can prove to be very costly to the company. So the goal is to bring out the Reds' strengths by meeting their needs rather than simply offering them one of two clear alternatives: "My way or the highway!"

Powerful Reds are more comfortable with competition than collaboration unless there are clearly defined roles within which each is allowed to exercise initiative and control and Reds see the benefits that collaboration brings them. I observed great success through the collaboration of two Reds in one client company. One Red was CEO and the other was COO and they achieved enormous success because there were clear lines of demarcation drawn between them; each played to his natural talents—the CEO was a great marketer and sales person and the COO was very talented with logistics—effective delivery of the goods and services sold. When two Reds can collaborate like that, they're a formidable team.

Powerful Red Personalities

Reds are found in all industries and most homes, businesses and occupations. The majority of CEOs in America have Powerful Red temperaments.

Reds tend to gravitate to the top of the corporate ladders because they love to lead; they're willing to take the risks of leadership and they're adept at politics—**the allocation and distribution of power.**

Jack Welch of General Electric fame exemplifies a Powerful Red. Welch led General Electric to perennial double digit growth and profitability. He had a longstanding policy of open debate and no holds barred challenges to existing or proposed strategies; this was the hallmark of his leadership because it brought out the best ideas and strategies to move ahead. Welch's openness to all ideas and opinions turned a potential blind spot into a strength and helped make him a business icon.

Bad examples of a Powerful Red leader are Al Dunlap of Sunbeam notoriety and Dennis Kozlowski of Tyco fame. Dunlap's initial reputation came from being hired to turn around companies but his approach ultimately lead to self destruction. How did he gain profitability? He immediately fired most, if not all, of the management team and thousands of employees to cut costs to the core so he could report a profitable quarter on paper. By doing so, he destroyed the trust level with the survivors and pushed them into a survival mentality instead of a thriving passion for growth. The Red weaknesses of pushing his own agenda to look good and to disregard and trash the most valuable assets that had been developed—the human work force—ultimately undermined the continued viability of the companies he was hired to turn around.

The fatal flaw of former Tyco CEO, Dennis Kozlowski, was to believe that Tyco existed to satisfy his every need. Those working at the company were there to serve him instead of he serving them and the shareholders. The distorted Red selfishness and lust for power ultimately led to his fall from grace.

Donald Trump is a very successful Red. His demeanor exudes confidence about who he is and what he wants. He has no problem firing people when it is time to do so. He doesn't concern himself with what will happen to the outcast but instead focuses on the more important task—picking the right individual to lead one of his companies.

Trump is a man of action and no wasted words. Words are tools to get results and he enjoys the recognition and status that comes from high achievement. He loves to arrive in his helicopter or jet to show how powerful he is. Trump also has learned to listen to various viewpoints. He doesn't need to go along with another viewpoint but it is far better than being ignorant of some idea or opinion that can help create his desired outcome.

In the political world, Reds find themselves on both sides of the aisle. Jesse Jackson, Rush Limbaugh, Al Gore, Hillary Clinton, John F. Kerry, Rudy Giuliani, John McCain, and Dick Chaney are all Powerful Reds. George W. Bush also is Red, although he has strong secondary and tertiary DNA colors. George W. Bush's communication style is Red. All of Bush's speeches tend to have short and direct sentences and he continually emphasizes results over good intentions.

However, President Bush, unlike some Red leaders, developed an ability to connect with people at an emotional level with much of the populace. In his speech at the National Cathedral a few days after the 911 tragedy, Bush exuded emotion akin to a Blue. Blue may be President Bush's secondary color or he could have learned it from his very Blue mother, Barbara. Another Blue trait of George W. Bush that conflicts with a Red DNA is that his rise to the presidency seemed to many Americans to be driven more by a desire to serve America (a Blue motive) than to amass and exercise power. Others, however, see George Bush as a power monger who acts like an Old West sheriff that thinks he's in charge of the rest of the world; so they see no positive Blue, only negative Red motives.

George W. Bush acts like a Red in most ways. He tends to have little patience with those who do not perform or aren't competent. Bush values efficient and effective use of time. Meetings start and end on time. People dress formally in the White House. Bush seems to hold strongly to his positions particularly when it comes to foreign policy. Bush operates confidently in the Red world of politics and pushes his agenda forward.

General George Patton was a Powerful Red. He used his natural strengths to lead his army to do things no other armies could do. During the Battle of the Bulge when allied troops were bunkered down in northern France and about to be annihilated by German forces, Patton volunteered to have his troops march nonstop from the south of France over a 48 hour period and engage the enemy to save allied troops that were surrounded. His feat was astonishing but also characteristic of a strong Red leader. On the other hand, his bluntness and "in your face" approach sabotaged his effectiveness. He offended allies and enemies alike.

Patton had no tolerance for those who were weak or suffered from battle fatigue or psychological trauma. He loved war because to him things were clear in that arena—good/evil, win/lose, friend/enemy. War played to his strengths. Patton dismissed those who believed differently or wanted to chart a "safer" course. They were just wrong and trying to convince them of their error was a waste of time.

Margaret Thatcher is a Powerful Red. Her no-nonsense approach to the challenges she confronted earned her the title of "The Iron

Lady." She too had little tolerance for those who vacillated or stood fearful of possible failure. She had principles she believed in. They gave her the clarity she needed to act and move forward despite those who opposed her. Tony Blair similarly is Red—driven by results and power—but also appears to have the Blue strength to connect with others deeply and to be loyal to his friends even if the cost of doing so is high.

Simon Cowell of *American Idol* fame is a Red. His criticism of aspiring singers seems blunt to many, but clear and concise to just as many. Martha Stewart has overcome a criminal conviction and imprisonment to make her brand even more valuable using her Red strengths. David Letterman also has used his Red strengths to rise to the top of the late night talk shows.

> *"When I dare to be powerful, to use my strength in the service of my vision, then it becomes less and less important whether I am afraid."*
>
> *— Audre Lorde*

CHAPTER 5

"I went to the woods because I wanted to live deliberately, to front only the essential facts of life and to see if I could not learn what it had to teach, and not when I came to die, discover that I had not lived."

— Henry David Thoreau

The Peaceful Aqua

Aqua DNA at a Glance

DRIVES: Peace and Balance.

NEEDS: Space to reflect and contemplate, to be respected, to be accepted, to please others and self, harmony in relationships and freedom from confrontation.

APTITUDES: Kindness, diplomacy, adaptability, patience, calmness under pressure, steadiness, even temper, independence, tolerance of differences, open mindedness, humility, and gets along easily with others.

COMMUNICATION STYLE

Relaxed body language; soft spoken; not opinionated or dogmatic; calming, low key presence.

The Peaceful Aquas' Drives

Peaceful Aquas have two natural urges that influence their thoughts, words and actions: peace and balance. A small percentage of Peaceful Aquas are driven only by peace but the vast majority have some blend of the two. These drives work hand in hand. "Still waters" not only run deep but also are peaceful and balanced.

The peace Aquas seek is freedom from opposition, contention, confrontation and disruption. Change in work, family, relationships, residence or even lifestyle can be a major disruption to settled patterns so Aquas generally resist it. This drive for peace often stops Aquas from taking risks, trying new things, sharing their opinions or ideas, and/or voicing their needs. Yet these drives help Aquas to mediate disputes, to consider and weigh objectively the merits of competing alternatives and to resolve crises inside a business.

The natural urge for balance makes Aquas less inclined to go overboard with anything in their lives including being a workaholic or fixating on a certain outcome. Aquas are willing to explore all of the alternatives and to adapt to negative outcomes by being willing to try another approach.

These drives for peace and balance underlie all of the Aquas' needs and strongly influence their behaviors. Aquas are willing to give up attractive and rewarding career or business opportunities if they demand that the Aquas be consumed in their work or face constant challenges and/or opposition.

The Aquas' mantras are: "Can't we all get along?" and "Take it easy." Aquas see little value in conflict and contention and prefer to take it easy themselves.

Aquas are not ego driven beings. They're not dogmatic. They're like water—flowing down the path of least resistance. Being opinionated and demanding isn't the path of least resistance because it invites conflict and debate.

Aquas easily see the merits in opinions expressed by others. Aquas listen more openly and don't resist being influenced by others unless they feel pushed or unless going along with what another wants puts them in an unknown and undesired situation. The Aquas' openness to influence is a great gift, if it is properly exercised. Taken too far, Aquas become wishy-washy and immobilized by indecision.

The biggest challenge for Aquas is fear. Fear of conflict or contention often leaves them as a bystander in life. Goals are often resisted because they require a change in the status quo. Goals may require Aquas to face roadblocks and challenges—resistance. Avoiding the stress that comes with resistance often leads Aquas to giving up on the great results that they would otherwise accomplish.

Fear inhibits Aquas from contributing ideas in a team setting. Fear stops them from challenging a leader even though that leader may be acting contrary to what the Aqua knows to be the correct course. Fear often keeps them from seeking leadership positions even though their natural objectivity and humility are valuable strengths for leaders. Fear can keep Aquas on the sidelines of life when they could be out there on the playing field sharing their innate strengths and talents.

Peaceful Aquas in some ways are quite different from the Powerful Reds in their behavior. Reds are high energy. Aquas tend to be lower energy. Reds seem driven to control circumstances and others around them. Aquas seek not to control directly but even more not to be controlled by others. Reds have definite opinions that they're not inclined to change. Aquas hold few opinions strongly and are open to be convinced of the merits of another view. Reds are geared to making things happen. Aquas prefer to go with the flow and let things happen.

Reds love action and welcome the challenges and resistance they face when pursuing their objectives. Aquas love tranquility and prefer to contemplate the deeper things and mysteries of life. Reds love leadership. Aquas will accept leadership roles, but they do not hunger to be in control over others.

Reds are political; Aquas are often apolitical because politics invites conflict, confrontation and exposes them to open criticism. Reds love goals. Aquas often don't like goals if going after them causes friction and resistance. Reds can easily become workaholics. Aquas want balance more than status so they rarely get consumed by their careers.

Reds and Aquas, however, also have many things in common. They both are more comfortable in focusing on things rather than people. Reds and Aquas most often rely on their logic and intellect in living their lives. Reds and Aquas both tend to be independent and prefer to march to their own drumbeat. Reds and Aquas share the need to please themselves. Reds and Aquas don't want deep emotional connections with others; neither are comfortable expressing emotions (other than enthusiasm or anger for the Red).

The Peaceful Aquas' Needs

Peaceful Aquas are the only temperament that share at least one or two of their core needs with each of the other three temperaments. This helps Aquas to better adapt to and understand people with all types of DNA.

Aquas, akin to Reds, need to please themselves; however, Aquas are more sensitive to the needs of others than Reds. Similar to Reds, Aquas also need to be respected, but what they need to be respected for differs. Reds need to be respected for their competence and accomplishments. Aquas seek respect for who they are.

An Aqua feels the need to please others, which is akin to a Blue need. Unlike the Blue, however, an Aqua will often tend to their own needs at the same time, especially when it involves the basics. For example, an Aqua parent will come down and prepare herself breakfast at the same time she is preparing breakfast for the children. In fact, she may even get her own breakfast first.

The Blues, on the other hand, generally attends first to others' needs and then might feel angry if such efforts prevent them from attending to their own needs. Blues may feel frustrated that others aren't as inclined to address their needs as the Blues are inclined to address others' needs.

Aquas sense a strong need to have space and time to reflect and contemplate what is happening in their lives and not to be so structured in all that they do. They often retreat from what is going on around them and immerse themselves into their own thoughts. They're deep thinkers. This need is akin to the Yellows' need for freedom from structure, deadlines and heavy obligations. However, the Yellows' need for freedom is a whole body experience, not an escape into one's own thoughts.

Aquas, however, have their own distinct needs. Aquas need tranquility, but they often don't share that or any of their other needs openly. To an Aqua, sharing a need can be counterproductive if it causes anger, contention, hostility or rejection. So the Aquas often prefer to stay quiet about their needs until the stored frustration becomes too large to suppress any further. At that point, the Aquas blow off steam disproportionate to whatever caused the reaction. (So watch out when an Aqua is ready to erupt!)

The Aqua drive for peace creates corollary needs such as the need for acceptance. When they're accepted by others, Aquas feel peace. Aquas often perform at very high levels not because they're driven to succeed and stand above the crowd, but because of the need for acceptance and respect by those they hold in high regard.

Aquas need harmony in relationships. Aquas expect other personalities to act with the same kindness that they routinely show. When another person is unkind or rude to them, Aquas often resent it. Aquas will also resent those who are rude or unkind to anyone else. The big problem is that the Aquas don't speak up so others are often ignorant of the fact that they're offending the Aquas.

Aquas need to move at their own pace and they willingly allow others to move at theirs. They march to the beat of their own drum. More often than not, the pace is slower and less directed and purposeful than that of the Reds and Blues and seemingly less stimulating than that of the Yellows. The Aquas' desire to go at a slower pace is often viewed by others as being lazy. But Aquas don't need or desire to devote high amounts of directed energy to life and so they often choose to keep it in reserve. Unfortunately, that reserve tank may never be used to make their own and others' lives happier.

The Peaceful Aquas' Aptitudes (Strengths)

Aquas have many aptitudes that can help businesses to succeed. Aquas are balanced. They tend not to overdo anything. They're calm and easy going. Because of their desire not to make waves, they get along with most everybody.

When attacked, Aquas seem not to take it personally most of the time and so they can seemingly handle business and personal crises without overreacting (unless the latest crisis is the proverbial "straw that breaks the camel's back"). Aquas also tend to be far more objective in assessing the merits of ideas, opinions and alternatives and to see value in others' opinions that others, who are too grounded in their own belief system, aren't able to see. When parties can't get along, you can recruit an Aqua to help each side see where the other side is coming from so that differences can be resolved.

Aquas are adept at detaching themselves from heated arguments among other team members; Aquas then can help the team to get back on track by defusing the negative energy. Aquas are not inclined to promote their own agendas. Aquas are driven both to please others and themselves so they can take a pretty objective and balanced approach to difficult situations and resolve them.

Other temperaments often love having an Aqua around when they're having emotional swings because the Aquas can calm them down without lecturing them. Observing an Aqua is akin to watching a duck floating in a lake. On the surface everything is serene, but underneath the duck is paddling like crazy. Aquas often are doing a lot of inner "paddling" that isn't revealed by their facial expressions.

Aquas are also adept at shutting out distractions and sticking to what they're doing. This can be both a strength and a weakness. If they're focused on solving a problem and working out a solution to something in their head, then they have a tough time keeping up with a conversation. But the Aquas' ability to focus on their project when distractions are all around them can be a major asset to completing the project on time.

Most of us have experienced (and some of us have demonstrated) "the Aqua stare." The Aqua stare is the blank look that suggests "the lights may be on but nobody's home." What non-Aquas don't understand is that during these moments, the Aquas are in fact totally alert but they're thinking about something other than what is being said in the conversation. Instead of cutting the speaker off because they aren't interested in what he or she has to say, Aquas prefer just to tune out the speaker. Thus, the mind is going full steam ahead while the face is in the shut off mode. The Aquas have separated their consciousness from anything going on outside their own thoughts.

A common misunderstanding among other personalities is that people with Aqua temperaments are not strong. To the contrary, Aquas can be quite strong and competitive. For example, Aquas have risen to the top of the sports world—Tiger Woods (golf), Pete Sampras (tennis) and Vladimir Guerrero (baseball). Aquas have also risen to become great leaders who change the course of human history—Mahatma Gandhi.

Once Aquas are able to overcome their fears, they can be tremendous leaders because their disposition allows them most easily to learn and develop complimentary strengths. Their kindness and openness draws others to them and their quiet strength in standing for principles they believe in can inspire all around them to follow their leadership.

Aquas are not controlling types so any demands will be in the form of requests and often use the words "Please" or "Is it possible…?" Their lack of ego makes it easy for them to give credit to others for all contributions that are made. Aquas feel no need to spin or bolster their image to look good.

The Peaceful Aquas' Weaknesses

There are shiny and dull sides to the Aqua aluminum foil as there are with the other DNA colors. Their need for peace can make them great mediators and diplomats but it also can mean not asserting their rights or opinions when they matter because they prefer peace more than the growth that comes from the interchange of ideas. The Aqua's skill at going with the flow can also mean resistance to change even if going with the flow isn't in his best interest.

Aquas tend to be lower energy so that often leads to laziness, procrastination and/or indifference. Taking a stand or achieving a goal often seems to an Aqua as demanding too much out of them. Better to wait or forget about it. The Aquas tend to give up on their dreams too easily while continuing to support others in their dreams.

> *"If you don't invest very much, then defeat doesn't hurt very much and winning is not very exciting."*
>
> *— Dick Vermeil, NFL Coach*

Because they're not strongly grounded in their belief and value system, Aquas often have a difficult time making decisions. Decisions have consequences and Aquas would prefer not to face them. When a decision becomes necessary, they will often defer to another or to group pressure.

Aquas can also be more stubborn than any other personality group in resisting the influence of others. They enjoy solitude and don't mind being ignored, so the harder others try to get them to interact, the more they resist; however, the resistance is passive. They don't tell you directly to your face to stop. They may even promise to do what you ask, but simply not do it. Aquas don't return your phone calls. They don't respond to your e-mails. Aquas simply choose not to communicate and can stick to their guns far longer than the other personality groups can endure.

Aquas don't want to resolve problems that may involve strong conflict with those displeased by their decisions or actions. Their first tendency, therefore, is to try to put off such decisions or hope the issues get resolved on their own. Unless Aquas recognize things will be in greater turmoil and unrest if they fail to act, progress toward objectives may be stymied.

Aquas feel no need to generate team camaraderie or team spirit. They often don't like to socialize with co-workers. Without the need for social acceptance and interaction, an Aqua may be a strength in times of crisis but also can be a poor fit during times where a leader needs to build rapport and instill trust with his or her followers. This represents the shiny and dull side of the Aqua's aluminum foil. Aquas have the mistaken notion that as long as they're not unkind, there will be no problems with their relationships. Aquas aren't needy so they expect their co-workers not to assert their needs. Aquas forget the needs of the other DNA colors (Blue and Yellow especially) to communicate. So their level headedness and kindness may calm the tempest but their detachment and disregard for those who need to interact can create its own crisis.

Aquas derive their energy most often from solitude, not from other people. They love to reflect and ponder ideas and principles. A weekend or day alone can totally recharge Aquas, particularly out in nature. So when human engagement is necessary to move things ahead, an Aqua may be off on a walk, reading a book or on some other solitary activity.

Punishing an Aqua child by sending him to his room isn't a punishment. It's a blessing. He will find something to do and there will be no one there to bother him while he is doing it.

Aquas can spend a month or two alone and not feel lonely particularly if they have a computer, Internet access, TV, books, gardening or other hobbies to entertain them. They simply don't need to communicate with others. Thus, Aquas often miss out on the growth and blessings that come from deep emotional commitment and communication.

Aquas aren't inclined to participate in team meetings. However, if quietly and patiently encouraged to come out of their shells, they can become very strong, promote unity and resolve dissension.

Aquas feel no need to entertain or to be entertained by others. So they probably won't distract the other workers from performing their duties. On the other hand, they can easily tune others out when they need to be focused and attentive. As leaders, Aquas may forget the need for social events and for taking the time to have fun so the work environment could become pretty boring and routine.

Aquas fall into routines fairly easily. Getting them out of the routines sometimes can require a lot of prodding because where there is comfort for Aquas, there is peace. Such routines may drive Reds and Yellows crazy but for Aquas, traveling outside the box can be a very scary venture.

The Peaceful Aquas' Communication Style

The Peaceful Aqua is generally soft spoken, speaking only when it seems necessary. Aquas are more comfortable with their own thoughts than human interaction. When problems arise in relationships, Aquas aren't inclined to share issues they have with friends, afraid it might cause contention or other undesirable results. They hesitate to speak in groups unless they feel completely comfortable.

In education seminars, Aquas will sit back without asking questions in front of the group. They feel more comfortable going up to the speakers or presenters afterwards and dealing with them one on one. Even then, they may walk away if they feel such questions may be burdensome or if others are in front of them monopolizing the speaker's time.

Aquas are kind and humane people. They hate harsh words being spoken and are offended and hurt by those who ridicule others. They rarely express their disgust openly but they'll remember those who have acted unkindly toward them or others.

Peaceful Aquas are totally comfortable hanging around with others without having to communicate. Aquas will build strong bonds with people who are as comfortable being in silence with Aquas as Aquas are when they're alone.

Aquas tend to store their memories of perceived wrongs against them without open confrontation or complaint. Over time, these stored wrongs fill up their internal garbage can to the top. Once the garbage can is full, one more offensive act may lead to the Aqua responding in a fit of anger, only to return to a quiet state a short time afterward. The garbage can needs to be emptied and once emptied, things are back to normal.

A former colleague of mine who performs marriage counseling shared an experience where he counseled a Red husband and an Aqua wife. The husband didn't want to be there but once he was, he dominated the counseling sessions with his repeated criticism of his wife's shortcomings.

On one occasion, when the Red husband's last barb had filled up the garbage can, the Aqua wife stood up, stuck her face inches away from his and proceeded to shout out all the wrongs her husband had committed against her. Her husband retorted that some of the complaints dealt with things done years earlier but his wife responded that he had done them nevertheless and she had had enough of his criticism given all of his past mistakes. Her outburst completely changed the dynamics. This was the Aqua wife's way of emptying the garbage can.

Aquas often share pieces of information that are incomplete, not realizing or recognizing that the listener isn't up to speed on the complete thought processes surrounding the bit of information shared. Aquas tend not to raise difficult issues until absolutely necessary. Finally, when they do, the others are confused as to the delay or the abbreviated information that they receive, not knowing how it fits into the equation.

Aquas often have dry wits. They can come up with the one liners that leave others cracking up because they deliver it so deadpan. They see humor in things that others miss.

Despite the phenomena of the "Aqua Stare," Peaceful Aquas usually develop great listening skills. Because they tend not to be dogmatic and prefer to avoid arguments, they will listen to your point of view and be open to being influenced by it. They will also listen to people who voice complaints, criticism and frustration.

People feel like they're being heard because the Aquas are not as intent on presenting their own point of view as understanding what the speaker's opinion is. Such conversations are generally monopolized by the other personality groups with the Aqua providing occasional comments, but Aquas seldom try to change that person's views.

Aquas are informal in their communication. They aren't loud people. Aquas' nonverbal communication is relaxed and non-assertive. They don't need to look you in the eye and may even be less than comfortable when you look them in the eye. They don't try to intimidate and hate being intimidated. Aquas will share their views if they feel comfortable with those hearing them.

How Peaceful Aquas Control (or Avoid Being Controlled)

Aquas aren't seen as controlling people. It is because they prefer to go with the flow. Aquas resist force, and therefore, are sensitive about "forcing" others to do what they want. So Aquas devote most of their energy to avoid being controlled by others. Other personalities may take advantage of Aquas' reticence to "force" others to obey and think that because they aren't being confronted or challenged directly by the Aqua, they shouldn't be concerned. Aquas find a way to challenge but it is generally passive-aggressive.

Peaceful Aquas may agree to do what is asked but never plan on getting around to it. They may resist by consciously or unconsciously creating obstacles to being pushed in a direction that they don't want to go. Or they may sandbag you by not responding to your attempts to assess the status of a project all the while looking like they're busy working on it. All of these techniques are designed to control the outcome by not letting the other person get his or her way.

Aquas are quietly stubborn and not inclined to take risks. Routines are comfortable. If another personality seems to try to push them out of their comfort zone, they may agree to go but they will find ways to delay or disrupt movement towards the desired goal until the other person becomes so frustrated with the lack of progress that they give up. The Aqua controls essentially by keeping the status quo, not by pushing others to change the status quo.

Aquas use silence as a tool to control. They can outwait any efforts by others to get them to talk or respond. The silent treatment can drive Blues and Yellows crazy to the point that they will almost do anything to get the Aquas to speak up. Blues and Yellows, more than Reds, need human interaction and feedback. Aquas think they're not being cruel by clamming up because they're not screaming, attacking or criticizing, but Blues and Yellows may be just as offended by the silent treatment as by verbal lashings.

As mentioned earlier, anytime a person seeks to control, he or she is working through the negative side of their temperament. The person is using one or more of their natural weaknesses to force another to behave or act in a certain way. The effort may work in the short term but the price is high because it undermines the trust in the relationship. The person being manipulated will resent it and resist future efforts to be influenced, even if it is through the passive/aggressive behavior that Aquas often use to get their needs met.

The Peaceful Aquas' Potential Pitfalls

Aquas are open to entertaining others' views as long as they're not presented aggressively. This openness, however, can turn into gullibility if Aquas aren't conscious of such a pitfall. Aquas turn off to loud mouths, regardless of the merits of the views expressed. But Aquas may give undue credence to crazy opinions and wild schemes if presented in a kind, entertaining and apparently innocent way. They're more inclined to trust someone right off the bat while ignoring the red flags that accompany their experience with the person they're trusting.

In that regard, Aquas tend to be naive about the motives behind actions of those who might be described as "wolves in sheep's clothing." Aquas often aren't tuned into a gut instinct that separates the sincere from the phony and so easily become victims to fraud and manipulation, particularly if they believe that the proposal or offer will bring them peace or freedom from anxiety or contention. Aquas are more gullible than Reds or Blues.

Early in my career, I had a prospective client I will call Ken from Australia, who called me up after having been sued. When we first met in person, Ken told me how he was associated with one of the world's richest people who was ready, willing and able to pay all of our fees after his fortune found its way into America; although Ken didn't have any money, Ken would be working with that rich man and receive millions of dollars annually in compensation. Ken even got me the large retainer that I demanded up front. (I now wonder who he tricked into sending us the retainer check and how he did it.) Not surprising to my wife, the retainer check was the only payment we ever got.

Once Ken fell behind on paying our bills, every telephone conversation and face to face meeting included some credible explanation for the delay; yet, when you took a hard look at what he said, the numbers didn't add up. After explaining the situation to my Blue wife shortly after we agreed to represent this man in the lawsuit, she immediately sensed he was not for real and told me that I shouldn't trust him. I was surprised that she could say that without even having met Ken. I thought I knew better, so I marched forward with our representation fully expecting to vindicate him in the lawsuit and to be paid fully for our services.

Neither happened. Ken opted to move to Las Vegas and failed to show up at his deposition. Ken stopped returning calls after his move and our firm was left with a huge unpaid bill before we formally withdrew as Ken's counsel.

Ken was so smooth and polished in his presentation. He was a con man, but I trusted his supposedly sincere pleas for help; I didn't begin to question whether all of his explanations added up until it was too late.

Ken took advantage of my natural inclination not to leave someone stranded in defending themselves against a stronger opponent. My gullibility is an Aqua trait—Aquas are open to taking others at face value and not suspecting the motives of those who interact with us kindly. My Blue wife, on the other hand, easily could see through Ken's façade and false sincerity.

Aquas are vulnerable to becoming immobilized by fear. They may hesitate to take action in their lives leaving themselves to be tossed to and fro by the actions of those around them. Powerful Reds are proactive but Peaceful Aquas living through their natural weaknesses are often inactive when action is critical. They prefer to put their heads in the sand and hope the problems either go away on their own accord or that others come to their rescue. In the business world, this can be disastrous for an Aqua leader because change in the marketplace is a constant and hoping that problems arising from such change will go away if they're ignored will often lead to the death of the business.

In one company I worked with, the Aqua leader recognized that changes in the marketplace were turning the company's services into a commodity and thereby increasing the competition and lowering the profit margins to unacceptable levels. Other challenges arose when former employees started up competing enterprises and offered lower prices for their services to the company's actual and prospective clients.

That was not all. Rifts and unrest were appearing in the sales force because of the perceived lack of response to the new pressures. Some questioned the leadership and competence of their sales manager. For many who desired quick action, the Aqua leader seemed oblivious and unresponsive, preferring to let the sales team and other departments work out their own solutions.

The Aqua leader's laissez faire approach caused the morale of those who came to the Aqua president for direction and solutions to drop precipitously. Whether it was fear of what such intervention and action might create or a general belief that his underlings should work out their own problems, the president didn't seem eager to take decisive action to cure the ills befalling the company.

In that regard, Aquas in leadership may inadvertently create power vacuums by holding tight to the status quo. Those managers who report to them may be given enormous latitude in running their departments. The problem arises when the leadership in each department runs things the way they want without aligning their team to the overall mission and purpose of the company.

Peaceful Aquas in the Workplace

Aquas are not a majority in corporate America. Companies that have an Aqua culture are fairly rare because those Aqua leaders who head companies either allow the culture to be developed by others or consciously incorporate the best of the other DNA colors into the culture. Aquas are often found in greater quantities in the information technology, research and engineering departments of companies. Aquas often become dentists, forest rangers or psychologists, preferring not to build big businesses.

Aquas enjoy the opportunity to be somewhat independent and working with tangible things such as software, computer systems, and product development laboratories of larger companies. Aquas often enjoy working with their hands and not having to interact constantly with other people. Aquas also are hired in other departments. Aquas can be good at sales especially if they have a drive to succeed. Aquas don't use high pressure tactics. Aquas instead use their listening skills to build rapport and trust.

Aquas will tend to go along with changes without openly complaining to management or often not even to co-workers. Aquas often conclude it isn't worth the energy to object or challenge actions that negatively impact their jobs because they don't want confrontation or contention. If they do complain, it may likely be in writing because they're more comfortable doing it indirectly. If their complaint is ignored or disregarded, they may let it go. Again fear often plays a big role. When combined with their natural tendency to be low key even about their own agendas, the drive to challenge or object is generally lacking.

Peaceful Aqua Personalities

As mentioned earlier, Aquas have risen to be great leaders. This includes the Presidency of the United States; Ronald Reagan, Gerald Ford, Dwight Eisenhower and George H.W. Bush are Aquas.

President Reagan had Red, Blue and Yellow strengths that masked his Aqua core. President Reagan was an avid reader and loved to write— Aqua strengths. Although President Reagan had no problem confronting the Soviets, he was very reluctant to confront anyone on his staff who needed to be fired. He asked others to do it—an Aqua weakness. President Reagan would go to parties and talk with the butler or maid instead of the celebrities in attendance, which also reflects an Aqua desire not to be the center of attention and not to think he is above anyone. President Reagan championed the principles he espoused instead of himself. When asked how he felt when others called him "The Great Communicator," President Reagan responded that he didn't think he was great. President Reagan stated that the ideas and principles that he communicated were great, but they originated long before he was born. I originally thought Ronald Reagan was a Yellow based on his humor, his love of people and his communication skills. But his core was driven by peace; he was determined to do what he could to achieve it, even if it meant making others angry.

President George H. W. Bush, the father of George W. Bush, showed his Aqua core in the Gulf War. After the Iraqis had been driven from Kuwait and coalition forces had driven deeply into Iraq, the first President Bush had a choice to make. He could allow his generals to continue and thereby destroy Saddam Hussein's regime or stop at the request of the United Nations and retreat back into Kuwait. He opted for the latter. His mission to push back an army who had wrongfully invaded its neighbor had succeeded and there was no need for further conflict.

I first concluded that former President Jimmy Carter is an Aqua. Carter's leadership style in the Presidency and his quiet service to others with Habitat for Humanity during the first decade after he left the Presidency seemed consistent with that of an Aqua. Furthermore, Carter's diplomatic efforts in the Middle East displayed an Aqua's strengths. However, Carter's behavior over the last four years conflicts with an Aqua DNA. Carter has become very vocal in criticizing President George W. Bush both here and abroad. Unlike George H.W. Bush and Ronald Reagan after they left the Presidency, Carter seems to enjoy center stage and the power and publicity it brings. Carter wanted to be the one officially representing the United States at Pope John Paul II's funeral. Carter's strident criticism fuels controversy, which isn't what an Aqua likes. The jury is out whether Carter is an Aqua acting Red, a Red, who led the United States like an Aqua, or an Aqua whose garbage can is full in tolerating what he believes is bad foreign policy.

George Harrison was an Aqua. In fact, what is so incredible about *The Beatles* is that each one in the group had a different temperament. John was a Red; Paul is a Blue; Ringo is a Yellow. John and Paul competed with each other to be the driving force in the band. Both were prolific song writers and sang well. George was a songwriter who sung well and played the guitar better than the other two. If George had competed with John and Paul to be the leader of the group, the Beatles may never have survived as long as they did. Instead, George avoided the limelight. George played what John and Paul wanted him to play and it was George's attitude and personality that helped create an environment where *The Beatles* could shine. Perhaps what made *The Beatles* so successful is that they created music that resonated with all of the personality groups.

George led the group to Indian maharajahs and meditation. Everyone seemed to like George because he didn't invite controversy and he didn't try to draw attention to himself. He just wrote and performed many memorable songs.

Enya's ethereal music style is Aqua. Simon & Garfunkel sang many Aqua songs including, *The Sounds of Silence*.

In the movie, *The Sixth Sense*, Bruce Willis played a child psychologist to Haley Joel Osmond, a child troubled by apparent contacts with spirits who suffered violent deaths. Their spirits returned to him and he ultimately learned it was because they thought he could be of help. The boy could not deal with the terror of seeing such spirits, but the psychologist helped him by taking the time to listen to him and help him discover what was behind their appearances. Both were Aquas.

It didn't dawn on the Aqua psychologist for a long time that his wife wasn't talking back to him because he already had died and she couldn't see or hear him. The psychologist didn't need daily (or even weekly or monthly) conversation with his wife. The troubled boy also kept his thoughts and fears to himself. The psychologist only got the boy to divulge his secret (that the boy saw dead people who talked to him) after they had spent a lot of quiet time together. *The Sixth Sense* highlights the strengths and the weaknesses of the Peaceful Aqua.

"Nothing is so strong as gentleness. Nothing is so gentle as real strength."

— Frances De Sales

CHAPTER   6

Carpe Diem! — Seize the Day.

The Optimistic Yellow

Yellow DNA at a Glance

DRIVES: Have Fun and Be Happy.

NEEDS: To be praised, stimulating environment, freedom, play time, social adoration, flexibility and minimal structure.

APTITUDES: Optimism, embraces change, warmth, high energy, charisma, enthusiasm, creativity, communicative, resilience, story teller, forgiveness, fun and persuasiveness.

COMMUNICATION STYLE

Engaging, high energy, loud, laughs easily, loves to talk, loves to share stories about life's little adventures.

The Optimistic Yellows' Drives

Optimistic Yellows have the natural urge for excitement and stimulation, which many might refer to as fun. They also are driven to feel happy. In that sense, emotion plays a larger role in their lives than the lives of Reds or Aquas. Both drives lead Yellows to focus on living in the present moment.

Yellows don't like dwelling on the past because it is over and such mental exercises really aren't that thrilling. Optimistic Yellows certainly can get excited about the future when they conjure up the possibilities, but they're not driven to make detailed plans about making their dreams a reality. That too can lead to burdensome and boring tasks such as writing down short and mid- term goals, identifying milestones and making lists of things to do—things they'd rather avoid.

Optimistic Yellows enjoy life. The Yellows' motto is the Latin adage:" Carpe Diem," which means "Seize the day!" Optimistic Yellows place a high priority on being alive and fully engaged in the present moment. Often this drive will lead Optimistic Yellows to engage in stimulating activity and social interaction. On other occasions, however, having fun can be a more solitary experience. Regardless, this drive leads Optimistic Yellows to brighten up their own and others' lives with animation and interaction.

Unlike Reds, Yellows' high energy isn't focused on achieving a particular objective but on experiencing life itself. Unlike Aquas, Yellows don't enjoy spending time being in their head reflecting on deep truths or working out problems or formulas; nor do they mind confrontation or opposition to their opinions or ideas. They banter and debate others easily, stimulated by the interaction and sparks they create. In fact, Yellows learn more from human interaction than from studying books.

Yellows don't like to dwell on the negative because it goes against their natural urge to be happy. Yes, Yellows have down time but they cannot stand for it to last too long.

The Optimistic Yellows' Needs

Optimistic Yellows need a stimulating environment. They hate to be bored. Years ago, my Aqua daughter, Marisa, was taking cello lessons at a home several miles away. My wife Laura had to take Marisa's two younger sisters with her to these lessons; my Red daughter Savannah was a baby at the time but Emily, my Optimistic Yellow, was a first grader. Emily hated being bored. Because the cello teacher lived so far from home, Laura would generally wait outside in the car during the one hour lesson. Emily couldn't just sit there, color, read or play with toys. Unless they drove a short distance away to a park or engaged in some other fun activity, Emily would sleep. Sleep helped Emily deal with the unbearable boredom of waiting for her sister to finish. Suffice it to say, Yellows need stimulation.

Yellows rarely enjoy being in a social setting where there is silence. They will break the silence with a monologue or dialogue because too much silence drives them crazy.

Yellows derive their energy from interacting with others; without interaction, they'll be frustrated. That frustration may be expressed by bugging others until they get them to react or even pouting. The Yellows' reactions to perceived boredom fulfill their needs for attention and excitement.

Yellows need freedom. Unlike Personable Blues, Yellows don't find security in structure and routine. Yellows relish the idea of escaping from the constraints of rules, duties, obligations, schedules and deadlines, so they can enjoy the moment. Developing the discipline to create and stick to schedules is a challenge. Yellows prefer an environment that gives them the freedom to do what they want to do when they want to do it.

Yellows avoid careers where there's a highly regimented and structured environment. It cuts them off from their drive to enjoy life. Freedom allows spontaneity. Freedom gives Optimistic Yellows the stimulation to stay in the present moment. As you might guess, Yellows don't thrive in the military.

In fact, in one of my training seminars, I asked the audience if there were any Yellows present who served in the military. A gentleman raised his hand and affirmed he had served in the Army. I was surprised and asked him how he dealt with a regimented military culture that tolerated little freedom and expression. He indicated that he carried around a clipboard all the time and tried to look busy. The audience and I broke out in laughter—a Yellow trying to pretend he was all business. By the way, this attendee was wearing glasses with what color tint to the lenses? You got it—**Yellow**! Before putting them on, I asked him how strong the correction was. He told me the lenses had no correction. **This Army veteran enjoyed looking at life through yellow tinted lenses**.

Another Yellow I know is a screenwriter and author, who I will call Charlie. Charlie told me one day that he had registered with the draft back in the Vietnam era. There was a lottery conducted annually. In the batch were balls representing each day of the year. The government would then randomly pick out the balls one by one and assigned them a number in order of selection—from 1 to 365. If a low number (0 to 100) was selected for the birth date of an individual of draft age (19), then the Selective Service would likely draft him into the military and send him to Vietnam. Charlie was of draft age and his birthday was selected among the first 100 numbers.

Charlie believed his only way to escape from Vietnam other than being a draft dodger was to join the reserves. Charlie reluctantly went down to the office of the Army Reserves; but when he arrived at the door, he couldn't get up the nerve to open the door and enter the office; instead Charlie walked away risking being drafted into the Army. Charlie's need for freedom "out-trumped" the imminent risk of being drafted. Charlie would rather have faced the great, but uncertain, risk of being drafted and sent to Vietnam than lose the certain freedom that came from enlisting in the Reserves.

Yellows need to be liked. With that comes the drive to entertain others and to get their attention and esteem. This often leads Yellows to test the limits of etiquette. One man shared with me that he had an Yellow son who took second place in a track and field event competition. At the end of his event, the first three to place were invited to stand on a platform to receive their medals. This man's son grabbed a "Cat in the Hat" type hat and loved the attention he got from boisterous observers, despite how embarrassing it was to his image conscious and very serious Red father.

Life is Beautiful is a wonderful movie about what an Optimistic Yellow can do for his son. Rather than tell his son the harsh truth of their being Jewish prisoners who might be executed by their German captors, the father created a fanciful tale that led his son to believe that it was all a game and that if they won, the son would get to ride on a big army tank. Remarkably, after his father was killed, the Allies freed the camp and let his son ride on a tank.

The father's optimism and indefatigable spirit was the light that saved his son's and wife's lives while sacrificing his own. The father's heroism was a product of his Yellow zest for life and optimism. Even when the father was completely exhausted by the hard work and brutal treatment, he would return to the barracks filled with high spirits and exciting tales about what he did that day. The Yellow father created freedom and hope in the midst of a prison that offered virtually no hope.

The Optimistic Yellows' Aptitudes (Strengths)

The primary gifts that Optimistic Yellows bring to the table are optimism and resiliency. The resilience to setbacks, trials, hardships and disappointments comes from the drive not to dwell on the past but to seek happiness and enjoyment in the present. Optimistic Yellows see the glass as half full, not half empty. To Optimistic Yellows, focusing on the future, as Powerful Reds do, carries a price—missing out on life in the present moment. So Optimistic Yellows are not motivated to focus too much on the future or to dwell on past mistakes or offenses against them.

Yellows love people and social interaction. Emotion generally has a stronger influence over their behavior than logic. Seeking happiness and fun isn't an analytical enterprise; it is one filled with emotion.

Yellows love to learn new things from a variety of areas. Why? It's fun to learn new things in response to their own curiosity but it also helps them to converse with others on a variety of subjects. Yellows prefer superficially understanding many different subjects over depth in any particular subject.

Yellows often are kinesthetic; they love to touch and be touched. Hugs are natural expressions of their feelings because Optimistic Yellows are naturally warm in social interactions. Yellows do have their tough times but their zest for life re-emerges because it is the most powerful influence on their behavior.

I have an Optimistic Yellow friend. Rarely do we have a conversation where he isn't smiling and sharing a story about some recent entertaining adventure or funny experience. Rarely do I see him down and never do I hear him expressing pessimism about the future. He often advised me on the stock market and even in the midst of the bear market, he remained cheerfully confident about brighter days ahead.

Optimistic Yellows often are great story tellers. They have a knack for good timing so that the stories entertain and lighten the atmosphere. When other temperaments try to tell the same stories, even if they relay the same facts, they mostly fall flat because they lack the nonverbal expressions, the vocal variety and the timing that make all the difference.

Yellows have a natural advantage over the other DNA colors when it comes to keeping others entertained. Many laugh at their own humor in such a way that even if the story wasn't funny, their reaction makes it funny.

An Optimistic Yellow once told me that the first thing he does in the morning is look in the Obituary section of the newspaper and if he does not see his photo, he knows he is going to have a good day. Another Yellow that I trained reaffirmed what I said about the Yellows' motto when he pulled out of his wallet a card that said "Seize the Day."

Yellows bask in environments where there is little structure but a lot of interaction. Unlike Personable Blues, Optimistic Yellows do not feel secure in a highly structured environment. They see a prison, stifling their free spirit.

Optimistic Yellows are naturally filled with self-esteem. They like who they are. For example, a friend of mine is dating a Yellow that spends a lot of time in front of the mirror. Each time my friend asks why, her response is always the same: "I love myself." Unlike Personable Blues, Optimistic Yellows do not feel the need to be good by erasing all of their imperfections. Unlike Powerful Reds, Yellows do not define their value based on their achievements. They value themselves for who they are without the heavy weight of self-criticism pulling them down.

Unlike Peaceful Aquas, Yellows are not worried about how others will react to their antics. Nor are they fearful of initiating conversations with strangers. In fact, they almost feel compelled to strike up a conversation because they want the attention that it brings.

Yellows innately love and accept who they are without taking any time to examine or analyze why they feel that way. Life isn't to be examined but to be experienced. In the short-lived television series, *The Dinosaurs*, there was a "toddler" dinosaur that always was happy and eager to cause mischief. Each time the parents were about to scold the "toddler" because of his latest prank, he would respond "Gotta love me! Gotta love me!"

That kind of self adoration typifies how Optimistic Yellows feel unless their natural self-esteem is squelched or destroyed by parents who do not recognize or value the gifts the Yellow brings to the table. A psychologically healthy Yellow is naturally optimistic because happiness and fun come from looking at the brighter and lighter side of life. And their drive is to be happy and have fun.

Optimistic Yellows are animated and enthusiastic. They're high energy people who enjoy interacting with others. Yellows seem to have a knack for breaking through the ice and getting to know other people. Warmth is expressed naturally and others respond to their open and friendly nature.

Yellows are strong communicators. They may even enjoy the banter of debating, but they do not take themselves too seriously. Yellows can walk away from heated verbal jousts and not hold any anger or animosity for those who attacked their opinions.

Yellows also have a knack for staying in the present moment and enjoying what life brings them. Yellows will often wake up each morning happy and eager to meet the day even when there may be a host of reasons to be grumpy or despondent. They get over the hard times because Yellows do not focus on the past.

I once worked with a great Yellow, who I'll call Melinda. With her bleach blonde hair, petite frame, freckle filled face and funny remarks, I always felt a little lighter and more carefree whenever I was around her. Her conversations were spiced with humor; she rarely, if ever, took herself too seriously. Even her criticism of others came in the form of playful jabs followed by a grin or chuckle. With her Yellow DNA, Melinda successfully landed many clients even over the phone because her voice exuded natural enthusiasm that got the prospects interested in what she wanted to say.

Melinda came into my office one day telling me about her recent breakup with her boyfriend using what I had taught her about the personality groups. This wasn't a solemn or sad occasion; the way she explained it just made me laugh (which is what she wanted). What she said and how she said it was so reflective of her Yellow DNA core that I asked her to put it in writing, which she did with the same humor as she told it to me the first time. Here it is— unedited:

Here I am - a happy go lucky yellow- aqua person. I moved up here to be closer to my unhealthy blue over-analytical boyfriend because we were doing GREAT for the last 6 months and we talked about possible marriage. I move up there & he starts picking fights- every week (very annoying). With each argument- I pull away more & more & start to do more things with my friends & driving down to OC where I am happy & having a great time with my circle of supportive & fun friends. By giving me a reason to pull away (who wants to be around a moody depressed critical angry blue when you are fun yellow who hates to over-analyze stuff)- he is eliminating the very thing he is asking me for- tenderness & nurturing (Does a real man actually ASK for this??? I think I am dating a WOMAN! Little joke there ... aha) Now me being yellow- I am not sympathetic to his requests because I am still hurt from his ridiculous and irrational arguments and have already pulled away emotionally for self preservation and I have lost respect for him since he is not appearing to be very strong (This is why I like red men- they seem to have it all together & I really like having a ROCK as my support- I think my dad is a red-so for future dating I think I will look for this trait) SO to make a long story short- we broke up and knowing how he reacted last time (he blamed me for "breaking his heart" when the reality is he pushed me away) and last time I shared all the great funny stories of how lame his arguments are...It's apparent how a yellow pulls off a painful situation- she makes them funny stories that she can share with others for a laugh while the blue laments and goes to therapy and over-analyzes every little thing and is wounded forever...(He still talks about how rotten his childhood was & how poorly his parents, ex girlfriends, ex wife etc treated him...bla bla bla ....LET IT GO SAYS THE YELLOW. LIVE FOR THE PRESENT BABY!!!!

As you can see, Yellows lighten up their own follies, knowing they can be the source of wonderful stories to tell down the road.

Yellows are quick to forgive others and their light heartedness makes it easier for others to forgive them. It is often quite difficult to stay angry at a Yellow because of their enthusiasm and zest for life. Yellows make friends easily because they don't worry about whether others will like them. Yellows naturally assume all will like them because they're loveable. They easily see the good in others and that warmth opens up others to seeing the good in them.

Yellows are the most inclined of all four personality groups to like themselves without question. They like themselves for who they are without having to measure their worth according to their achievements or social status.

Yellows are spontaneous. They don't like schedules. They embrace change because with it comes stimulation and new adventures. This helps Yellows to better adapt to the rapidly changing marketplace in which their businesses compete. Because Yellows are so naturally warm and fun to be around, they generally become fairly popular and win elections and other popularity based contests more easily than others.

Yellows can become very charismatic leaders. The key for Yellows is to have the focus and tenacity to push ahead towards their objectives no matter how hard or how long it may take to achieve them.

Yellows are the most likely of all the personality groups to be misdiagnosed as having ADD (Attention Deficit Disorder). Yellows often engage in antics in school or at work to get others to focus their attention on them. The lively, disruptive behavior is easy to misinterpret as a chemical imbalance requiring medication.

The Optimistic Yellows' Weaknesses

Optimistic Yellows have their fair share of weaknesses, too. Depending on their secondary temperament, Yellows are usually not organized and disciplined. I know one Yellow business leader whose car is filled with note-filled pads that he never organizes, so he can't find his notes when he needs them. If he does happen to find them, he often can't read his own handwriting.

This Yellow business leader loves the thrill of creating deals, ventures, alliances and strategies but does not enjoy spending the necessary time and energy to follow through with the projects he envisions. He jumps from one project to the next quickly because of the stimulation each new project provides. This executive told me once that he never worried about a potential deal falling through because his business life was like a bus station. If he didn't hop on the bus of one deal, he need only wait fifteen minutes for the next deal to arrive. **That is Yellow.**

Yellows tend to trust others too easily even when others haven't earned that trust. This leads them to become easy victims to scams. On the other hand, Yellows are such good communicators that they can successfully promote the very scams to which others fall victim. Others tend to believe and trust them because of their natural warmth. Deceitful Yellows will take advantage of this skill.

Yellows often can be show-offs. They'll walk into a party and try to be the center of attention. When others turn their attention elsewhere, Yellows may do outrageous things to grab it back again. If positive attention isn't given, then Yellows will draw negative attention because it's better than nothing.

Optimistic Yellows can be flaky. The life of the Yellow is the life of the better offer. Yellows will make a commitment to attend a meeting or event or to complete an assignment and will fully intend to follow through with their commitment unless or until a better offer comes along. For example, if one of their friends asks them to go skiing on the day they're supposed to help you on a school or business project, they might not show up but may offer some pretty creative excuses for not being there.

Optimistic Yellows generally aren't time driven people. Bill Clinton, a Yellow President, was known for being late to most meetings or events. Yellows often arrive late because they let the time get away from them while they're having fun or engaged in a conversation with someone interesting. A Yellow friend may ask you to wait for him for a few minutes while he gets something inside a store. The Yellow comes out of the store an hour later while you sit there ready to erupt. The Yellow has no trouble apologizing, but wonders why you just can't let it go and move on. After all, the waiting is over.

Another Optimistic Yellow I know is consistently late on meetings, phone calls, etc. His assistant will often call to excuse the tardiness and ask if he can call back in a minute; "a minute" may end up being a half hour, an hour, half a day or even a week. But when he does call, he listens well and you feel easily inclined to forgive him for his lack of punctuality.

Another weakness is that Yellows often forget to call you back if something distracts them. They aren't inclined to keep clear schedules and make out "To Do" lists. Yellows not only get distracted but also distract others from getting their work done.

Yellows aren't known for being quiet, contemplative and deliberate people. So Yellows will often fill in any silence in a meeting or conversation with their own voice. Sometimes they don't know when to back off so that others may contribute but they're so entertaining that the Peaceful Aquas or Personable Blues may just let them run on and on until the Powerful Reds tell them to shut up.

Yellows have a difficult time focusing on a single project particularly if involves painstaking attention to "boring" details. Life is to be lived, not analyzed, and such work plays not to their strengths but to their weaknesses. The lack of focus can lead to many projects beginning but few ending as planned.

During her college days, a Yellow friend of mine probably changed her major three or four times. Once she elected a major, she grew tired of it after a few quarters and wanted to switch. Suffice it to say, she had a longer college experience than most, but she also had a lot more fun.

I met a business woman a year or two ago who I will call Sally who had just taken over a frozen yogurt business near my home. Prior to meeting her, I stopped by to grab a yogurt only about once every few months because it was out of the way; but I saw a change in the store's outer appearance, so I decided to go in to see what was going on. The store had changed dramatically and it looked very inviting. In my first visit, Sally gave me a larger sized smoothie than I had ordered and only charged me for the lesser amount. Sally's generosity and enthusiasm struck a sharp contrast with the prior owners. I felt eager to return often.

In the first few visits, Sally seemed so enthusiastic about the business. She had brought in so many fun gifts and toys and really brightened up the place. Sally was handing out coupons and generously apportioning larger shares of yogurt and smoothies than what people ordered.

Three months later, Sally told me she was closing the doors the following day. The sellers had lied to her about the revenues the business was supposed to generate. The sellers indicated that the business was generating a net profit of over $100,000 a year, when she later learned it probably was generating far less than half of that figure.

Sally thought she was protecting herself by agreeing to pay only half of the sellers' asking price to test out the store for the first three months; if she didn't like the business, Sally could walk away without paying the rest. But the owners would get to keep half of the sales price and still own the business.

Sally trusted the sellers' representations without verifying any of their numbers. She didn't check with the neighboring businesses to see how busy the store had been with the sellers running it. They could have told her that the foot traffic was minimal as they later did. The sellers took advantage of Sally's gullibility.

Before buying the yogurt store, Sally had just extricated herself from a retail toy business she had owned in downtown Los Angeles. What was troubling to hear was that she bought that business from another seller who also lied to her about its financial condition. Sally hadn't learned her lesson, so she was bound to repeat her mistakes.

Sally told me she was a happy person and that she would rather give up and move onto another business than fight the sellers in court. A lawsuit wouldn't make her happy and she wasn't the vengeful type. Sally was feeling miserable hanging around the business now that she understood what she had really bought. Rather than dwell on all the money she lost, Sally told me her investment was gone and there was nothing she could do about it. She wanted to move on just as she did when she was swindled with the toy business.

Sally shared with me how upset her family was with her buying these businesses and how "stupid" they thought she had been. In reality she wasn't stupid, just naive. Sally needed to join forces with someone who was strong where she was weak. Sally is a Yellow that naturally trusts others and sees the best in people. Sally's willingness to trust wasn't balanced with the Blues' cautionary approach to make sure things are what they're represented to be. A positive Personable Blue business partner would have been a great advantage to compliment Sally's natural strengths in marketing, sales and people skills.

I asked Sally if she lived nearby and she told me that she lived eighty miles away. I asked her why she would buy a business so far away from where she lived. Sally said she liked the type of business it was. Sally's purchase of the yogurt business made little business sense; Sally responded to her emotional impulse to buy a business that she could give to her son.

Sally was so warm and engaging. I instantly liked her, but I could see how the weaknesses of her Yellow core had contributed to her business losses. Nevertheless, in the game of bringing warmth and laughter to others, Sally remains a strong winner.

Some weeks after our last conversation, Sally turned the business back over to the owners after having forfeited her initial payment. Sally got what she bargained for—a trial period—but the price was far too great. Sally, nevertheless, moved on with her life, showing remarkable resilience to the failures and frustrations she had experienced.

Sally's experience illustrates the shiny and dull side of the aluminum foil for Yellows—their natural strengths (warmth, openness, trusting) can become their weaknesses (naivete and gullibility) if they aren't careful. But their yearning to be happy and let go of the past allows Yellows to overcome the trials caused by those who exploit the Yellows' trusting nature.

The Optimistic Yellows' Communication Style

Optimistic Yellows love social interaction. They generally come across as warm and happy. This makes it easy for others to get to know them. Optimistic Yellows care about others but it usually isn't at the same deep level as the Personable Blues. Yellows also enjoy talking. In fact, it is common for Yellows to walk into a room talking.

Yellows develop rapport with other personalities fairly quickly. This motivates other personalities to trust Yellows just as Yellows trust them. Yellows use humor to engage others; they rarely take themselves too seriously and so it's easy to feel good being around them.

Yellows enjoy variety in conversation and in entertainment. Having conversations with some Yellows is like channel surfing, except that you have no control over the remote. You may start on one topic but the conversation can easily swerve off in another direction and yet another until you really have no idea how the conversation strayed so far and what the topic was you introduced.

Yellows often interrupt the conversation of others or even what you're saying because they're eager to share what they're thinking or react to what others are saying. Yellows can be a disruptive force in the classroom, but it is only because they seek stimulation. If the teacher becomes boring, it's hard for the Yellow to just sit patiently and quietly until class is over. Yellows may interrupt, make off-the-wall statements or ask bizarre questions to stoke the fire and provoke some reactions.

Yellows usually aren't as good at listening as talking. Listening requires patience and they're too antsy so they either blurt out what they want to say or to move onto a more lively conversation or activity.

Yellows' conversation tends to be light, humorous and friendly. Rarely does social interaction with a Yellow feel heavy and negative.

Yellows are good storytellers; Yellows engage the attention they desire through their stories. Yellows rarely sound pessimistic or depressed. If they do, wait a while and they'll likely bounce right bck to their normal jovial selves.

Yellows tend to speak more loudly and enthusiastically than Blues and Aquas. It is because they're high energy people driven by a zest for life. Such zest leads to lively and stimulating conversation.

How Optimistic Yellows Control (and Avoid Being Controlled)

Optimistic Yellows can be as controlling as the other personality groups when they want their needs met. Yellows may not be as overt as a Red, who tells others clearly what she needs or wants them to do, but the motivation of Yellows to control others is often just as strong.

In their youth, Yellows will often use pouting to get control. Yellows may ask for something or for permission to go to some party and the parent says no. The Yellows refuse to take no for an answer. She may use charm and humor if she knows it has worked in the past or she may pout or bug the parent until she prevails. The Yellow may even pit one parent against the other. Yellows may resort to acting so miserable that the parents go along with their request just to get them "out of their hair." If the parent doesn't give in, then the Yellow may walk away but not quietly. She wants to make sure the parent knows how miserable or frustrated she is.

Yellows generally control by grabbing attention from others— negative or positive. This is different from the Aquas, who use silence and passive resistance as a way of getting their needs met. The Aquas will promise to do their homework but fail to turn it in if they don't want to do it, thereby showing indirectly who is in charge. The Yellows will come up with a grandiose story of how the hamster ate their homework while being trained to do gymnastics on the wheel. Yellows hope the entertainment will more than offset the credibility gaps that pervade their outlandish tales.

Yellows are adept at drawing on a variety of tactics to get their way. They may be direct as a Red or silent as an Aqua. They will see where the apparent chink is in the other person's armor and then exploit it. It may even be so entertaining for the person being controlled that she gives in to the Yellows' wishes.

Yellows aren't driven by order or structure, so they'll generally look to bend the rules if rules start to get in the way. Yellows are masters at pushing the envelope. Rules restrict freedom so the Yellow will look for an escape clause unless or until they see the benefit of obedience.

Optimistic Yellows' Potential Pitfalls

One of the biggest challenges for Yellows is to stay focused and disciplined to achieve what they have committed to achieve. As mentioned earlier, Yellows may commit to a meeting or to completing a project of task over a period of time, but if a better offer comes along in the meantime, they may be quick to jettison the prior commitment. Long term commitments to projects are tough because they're perceived as interfering with the spontaneous enjoyment of life and as living "inside the box." Yellows prefer new adventures and experiences.

Many Yellows end up with a life of unfinished projects and a business that tends to oscillate instead of grow. The need for stimulation takes priority over patient and steady progress towards a few clear objectives for the business. The price the Yellow entrepreneur ends up paying is finding herself stretched too thin because she takes on new commitments without fully considering whether she has the time to complete even the pre-existing commitments. She gets frustrated because her business isn't moving ahead. Business partners of the Yellow become frustrated because their mutual commitment seems to lose steam until it ultimately comes to a halt.

Another pitfall is organization. Yellows generally don't want to take the time to be organized unless it can be done in a fun or entertaining way . Getting organized can seem like pure drudgery. This lack of discipline, when it comes to taking care of the details on a project and being organized, often leads Yellows to break commitments they make, miss meetings or arrive late to important events.

Yellows aren't time driven people; time tends to get away from them because Yellows tend to totally immerse themselves in an activity or conversation. Unless they acquire the discipline to stick to schedules, Yellows may sacrifice key relationships that will help them and their businesses grow.

Optimistic Yellows often are forgetful. Because they're so easily immersed in the present, Yellows lose focus of what's happened in the past or of commitments they make. Yellows who recognize their propensity to forget can succeed or fail depending on how they make up for it by using discipline to make entries into their personal digital assistants, date books or electronic calendars. Yellows can also retain assistants who are strong planners and who will keep the Yellows on task and on schedule.

Optimistic Yellows in the Workplace

Optimistic Yellows have led many successful companies. Richard Branson, the head of the Virgin empire, is a great example. Another company that stood out over the last twenty years for having a Yellow culture is Southwest Airlines. Herb Kelleher, the former CEO, instilled the Yellow strengths into the company. They hired those who knew how to have fun and they trained them to embody the Yellow attitude.

Flight attendants would dress more casually, tell more jokes, take more time to talk with the passengers and turn what would otherwise be a drab flight into an experience worth remembering. That attitude lifted Southwest to the top of its industry in the eighties and the nineties while its competitors were suffering enormous losses, cutting routes and flights and trying to survive.

"If people come to a place that they regard as fun, entertaining, and stimulating, their minds are turned on. They're looking for solutions and they'll find them."

— Herb Kelleher

Great leadership and some discipline to follow through with its low cost strategies are certainly a major factor in Southwest's success. But they achieved it with a distinctly Yellow approach to competing, as reflected by the above quote. Kelleher proved to the world that you can succeed and have fun at the same time.

Yellows often gravitate to the sales and marketing departments of a company. They love the interaction with prospective and actual clients and customers and they're skilled in influencing others to buy. The challenge of taking someone from the cold contact list to being a customer or client is exciting and the constant interaction with new people attracts the Yellow. Unlike the accounting department, Yellows do not need to focus all their attention on details and numbers. Unlike the Information Technology or Research and Development Departments where employees tend to work with machines or objects, Yellows can devote their attention to talking with, getting to know and influencing people.

In the companies I have trained, there are far more Yellows in sales than in any other department. I have worked with Yellow companies and the number and dispersion of Yellows in all departments is greater there than in all other companies, but still more

Yellows are found in the sales departments because that is where their natural strengths are best deployed.

Yellows tend to do well in places where they have the greatest freedom while still maintaining minimal structure. Yellows do not like punching time clocks. Yellows have no problems pulling "all-nighters" on stimulating assignments or projects, but they love working with teams that respond to their playful and fun nature.

Yellows are great at generating camaraderie among team members. If leaders can allow Yellows on their team to use their creativity to make the project fun and exciting, then all members on the team will benefit and the projects will be more successful in what they achieve and how fast they achieve it. People having fun while they're working are far more efficient and productive than those feeling stressed and overburdened.

Optimistic Yellow Personalities

Robin Williams typifies a positive Yellow. So do Magic Johnson and Shaquille O'Neal. Yellows have led this country as Presidents; John F. Kennedy and Bill Clinton are Yellows who occupied the Oval Office.

The Yellow strengths were the source of Bill Clinton's popularity, but the Yellow weaknesses were the source of his troubles. Staff members working with President Clinton and members of the press recall how often meetings didn't start on time. However, his Yellow nature made it so easy and fun for others to connect with him that they forgave his chronic tardiness. Camaraderie and informality among his staff were more important to him than formal structure. Moreover, President Clinton's charisma opened up doors with other world leaders and with the people of other countries. Both Kennedy and Clinton remain very popular to this day in Europe and other areas of the world because of their Yellow charisma.

Bill Clinton's resiliency was also a Yellow strength. Despite the frequent predictions of his ultimate demise from many political battles, Clinton often came away from them without a scratch. This led many to call him the "Teflon President." He used his Yellow strengths to regain popularity.

Clinton is an articulate speaker that can speak extemporaneously on most any subject. He is sharp intellectually and quick to grasp new information and ideas. On the other hand, Clinton often seemed to get distracted and lose focus, perhaps because he often lost interest and switched his attention to some new and more stimulating issue or concern.

"Whoever is happy will make others happy, too."
— Mark Twain

CHAPTER 7

"It is enough to be friendly to one's friends. But to befriend the one who regards himself as your enemy is the quintessence of true religion. The other is mere business."

— *Mahatma Gandhi*

The Personable Blue

Blue DNA at a Glance

DRIVES: Perfection and Connection.

NEEDS: To embody quality, to plan for the future, to be understood, to be genuine, to please others, to be appreciated, to feel secure, to be treated fairly, structure and order.

APTITUDES: Planning, details, analysis, team building, loyalty, sincerity, supportive, organization, helpfulness, self-sacrificing, sensitivity to others' needs and feelings, and fairness.

COMMUNICATION STYLE

Sincere, looks for nuances in content, shares insecurities and mistakes openly, loves to connect from the heart, thinks before speaking, sensitive and indirect in conveying criticism.

The Personable Blues' Drives

According to research, more people are Personable Blues in the corporate world than any of the other three DNA colors. In the businesses I train, the Personable Blue averages anywhere between 35% to 45% of their workforce. Studies by a former colleague of mine in the elementary schools also reveals the Personable Blues are the most common of the four personality groups.

Personable Blues have a blend of two drives: (1) perfection (which includes structure and order) and (2) emotional connection.

The Blue drive for perfection primarily may seem logic based but has an emotional underpinning—the desire to be a quality human being doing quality work. The companion drive for human connection is emotion based. A very small percentage of Blues are steeped heavily in the regimented life where all things are planned and nothing is left to chance without any apparent urge for deeply connecting with others. Another very small percentage are driven solely by deep connections to people and have no core desire to have order and structure in their lives, but the vast majority of Blues have some blend of the two.

Personable Blues' drive for perfection leads them to seek discipline, planning and organization and to abide strictly by the governing rules of the organizations where they work. Such Blues ensure that the details are taken care of in achieving the broad objectives of a business. Blues' don't need the limelight and are comfortable working and supporting others behind the scenes.

The companion natural urge for connection makes Blues adept at building and strengthening teams. Their framework for looking at the world is centered on "we" rather than "I". Teams, therefore, provide the framework where Blues can shine.

Personable Blues are the only DNA color with two drives that don't seem at first blush to go hand in hand. Blues, however, are grouped together under one DNA group for two reasons.

First, almost every Blue seems to have a blend of both drives even though one may seem dominant in a particular setting. An analytical Blue driven by perfection at work generally wants deeply to connect with others in the family, social or religious settings.

Second, even those Blues that seem to have only one drive or the other still share four fundamental core values. One is to be good and genuine. Another is a deep conviction that justice be served and that everyone play by the rules. Personable Blues probably originated the adage: "It isn't important whether you win or lose; it is how you play the game." (Grantland Rice) A third core value is to do their best in whatever they do. Finally, Blues feel comfortable inside structured environments. Thus, there is a strong and unified value system among Personable Blues that emanates from these dual drives.

Often, the secondary DNA color either shapes or determines which of the two drives is more controlling in the lives of Personable Blues. Personable Blues with an Optimistic Yellow secondary DNA color tend to be far more influenced by connecting with others emotionally while Personable Blues with a Powerful Red or Peaceful Aqua secondary DNA color tend to be driven more by perfection, structure and order.

Creating structure and order appears at first glance to be the more valuable drive in the business setting, but the team spirit that Personable Blues generate because of their desire to connect with others is often just as crucial to business success. Optimistic Yellows are more emotion driven and Powerful Reds are more logic driven than Personable Blues.

Personable Blues generally have more energy than Peaceful Aquas but less than Powerful Reds or Optimistic Yellows. But when a Blue becomes committed to some cause outside themselves, few can match the energy that the Blues will devote in fighting for that cause. Blues work from the heart in doing what's "right" and a devoted heart will outlast a practical head almost every time.

In cultures such as ours where it isn't viewed as appropriate for men to be caring and compassionate in the business world, Blue men's behavior, particularly in the workplace, will reflect the perfection drive more often than the connection drive. Even though men in business may have a strong emotional desire to connect with friends and associates, that desire will be subverted and directed towards organizing, planning, discipline and performance.

As stated earlier, Personable Blues <u>love</u> order and structure. It gives them a sense of security and Personable Blues are security-seeking people. Expectations of how things are supposed to be regularly impact the range of emotions they go through in a given day. Surprises are not welcomed if they seem to interfere with pre-set plans. Risks are not embraced. In fact, Personable Blues plan out the future to avoid surprises and unreasonable risks.

This all comes back to structure. When their order and structures are shaken, Personable Blues are shaken. And those structures are filled with expectations not only about how people are supposed to behave in general, but particular expectations with individuals based on pre-existing patterns developed either with the person or with previous similar relationships. Logic and emotion are both entwined in these structures.

The Personable Blues' Needs

Personable Blues' needs naturally flow from the dual core drives of perfection and connection. As to the former, Blues need to embody quality in whatever they're involved in. Quality is more important than efficiency to Blues so they are willing to take more time than expected if it achieves the quality they need.

Personable Blues need structure in their lives. Having chaos around them with no sense of where they are or where they are going is a living nightmare that often leads to chronic depression. Structure brings order and order gives them security because they know and can rely on things being the way they expect them to be.

Blues thrive in work environments where there are policies and rules for everything. In businesses where there are few rules and no consistent approach to what actions are acceptable and what aren't, Blues will become very frustrated and complain vocally or brood silently about the "unfairness" of it all.

The need for structure and order also fosters the need for consistency. Blues are happy about having employee manuals. They want rule breaking behavior to result in the same punishment every time for all employees.

Blues need feedback. Because their focus is on others, others' opinions are very important to Blues. If they perform work, they need feedback to let them know if they're producing a quality product, project or service.

Personable Blues will ask more questions than any other personality group in seminars and classes because they want to make sure they understand what is being taught and they seek the approval of and attention from those whom they respect and admire. It goes back to their desire for perfection.

Because perfection often cannot be achieved in this life, Blues tend to be hard on their imperfections. The feedback from others is critical to Blues validating their own worth and gauging whether they're going forward or backward on the path to perfection.

Justice is a value that Personable Blues highly prize. "It's not fair," is a common statement uttered by Personable Blues. Because life is messy and things cannot be completely "fair" at all times, Blues often may stew for months or even years on perceived injustices or unfair treatment. Blues often misread into words and statements things that show unfair and inconsistent treatment.

Of all the temperaments, Personable Blues need closure the most. If something is wrong, they need to discuss and resolve it. This draws from their need for structure and order. If they sense a lack of closure, then the box isn't closed. If the box isn't closed, then the structure around their lives isn't stable and strong.

Personable Blues' energy may be completely sapped by the absence of closure. In relationships, if there is an argument, Personable Blues are not inclined to forget about it and move on. They prefer to confront and resolve the conflict; otherwise, there is no order. Resolution of tension is critical to restoring order and structure to their lives. If someone has committed a wrong, they must apologize and order won't be restored until they do. Insincere apologies don't suffice. They must come from the heart so that the Blue really senses the sincerity. For those other temperaments who choose not to apologize, they may bear the brunt of a grudge that will remain indefinitely.

The Blue drive to connect with others carries with it the need to be understood and appreciated. Blues are driven to make deep connections in those relationships where others take the time to listen to Blues and understand their deepest feelings. When they sense such understanding, Personable Blues will give their all to that relationship. Their loyalty to friends is unsurpassed by any of the other temperaments.

On the other hand, if someone chooses not to understand or appreciate them, the Personable Blues will remember and the offending party will have to work hard to get back into their good graces. Personable Blues give so much and they do it in such a quality way that any lack of or insincere reciprocation may likely cause deep pain to the Blue.

Blues need to feel comfortable. This often comes from meeting the needs for structure and order (perfection drive) as well as those for understanding and appreciation (connection drive). Personable Blues are very comfortable inside the box if there are others around to value their contribution fully and to relate to them deeply.

Personable Blues feel the need strongly to keep their commitments because they need to be good and have integrity; breaking a promise to someone they love is very bad to the Blue. It reveals a flaw in their character. Even when the other person forgives them, Blues often may not forgive themselves. When Blues feel they have wronged another, they need full hearted and sincere expressions of forgiveness from that person.

The Personable Blues' Aptitudes (Strengths)

Personable Blues bring great gifts to the table in both the business and personal arenas. Because of their need for structure, they're great at planning and taking care of the details to insure that an objective is reached. They readily sacrifice their time and energy on projects in order to increase the quality of the result or outcome. Their discipline and willingness to give it their all make them a great asset in any company.

Personable Blues are very sincere and genuine people when they're psychologically healthy. Blues need to be good inside and out and so Blues are inclined to work on improving their strengths and ridding themselves of their weaknesses. Their determination to grow leads them to be the most likely among all the personality groups to buy self help books and attend self improvement seminars. Personable Blues are more inclined to take and fully participate in personal workshops and training classes so that they can become better people.

Personable Blues don't try to put up a false front about who they are and they turn off to those who do. Personable Blues have almost an inner sense of what is genuine and what is phony and those who act phony will be placed on their blacklist.

Personable Blues tend to be meticulous planners because they take the time to think of all possible scenarios where something could go wrong and plan ahead on how to deal with it. Because Blues hate surprises, especially nasty ones, they will prepare better for the unexpected than the other DNA colors. If companies set long term objectives for growth and success, assign Blues to keep the team on task and to monitor progress toward the desired objectives. Healthy Blues will rarely let you down, because that is how they naturally measure their value to others and their own progress towards perfection.

Personable Blues detest disorganization and chaos (unless they have a secondary Yellow temperament). Blues will find some way to get things back in order if they find such disorganization.

My mother is a Personable Blue and things were always put in their place when I was growing up. The joke around the house was that you could take off your coat and prepare to drop it on the floor and it would miraculously be picked off in mid air and hung up. My mother made sure everything was put in its place even when she was exhausted late at night, because she hated to find things out of order when she woke up the next morning. We, as her children, were blessed because of it.

Blues are very sensitive to others' feelings. Unless they have a Red secondary, Blues are inclined to soft pedal any criticism they have of others so that the person receiving it often isn't sure if he or she just got criticized. Blues will sandwich the criticism between laudatory comments about things that the person did well. But Blues will be openly critical of others outside their presence.

When teams are working on projects, the Blues most commonly look to see that everyone is comfortable and has an opportunity to contribute. A Personable Blue will most often be the one to seek the feedback of a quiet Aqua or to go up after the meeting to a team member if he or she feels that person had his or her feelings hurt by a critical comment from another member.

The connecting Blues are governed more by the heart and use that strength to discern the emotional needs that others on the team may have. Connecting Blues are naturally nurturing and supportive because that is what they want from others. Because they're more centered on the other person, they'll take the time to talk with those who may seem ostracized or alone in the team. Their sensitivity can be the means of keeping some team members committed to the team despite the perceived attacks by others against them.

Blues are incredibly loyal to their friends and family. They really care about relationships and feel the need from the heart to stay true to the relationships where they feel deeply connected. Blues are also loyal to their companies. They may complain about a company and its leaders consistently but it is hard for them to leave even when things are going bad. This reticence isn't only because of their feelings of loyalty to the business but also because they don't like change; changing jobs is very traumatic for Blues.

Blues strive to be just and even handed. They'll be the ones who make sure no one breaks the rules and gets away with it. They'll strive for true consistency in all that they do, but they expect the same commitment from those with whom they work or live. They want you to be consistent and they're quick to measure things in terms of fairness and to feel negative about perceived unfairness regardless of whether fairness can really be achieved.

The Personable Blues' Weaknesses

Blues have the shiny and dull sides of the aluminum foil to their nature. In other words, their natural strengths can become their Achilles' heel in different settings. The Blues' natural aptitude for discipline, structure, and having everything in order can become a weakness when the marketplace requires their businesses to change and adapt or die. Change disrupts not only the structures Blues have built but also their set ways of doing things. Blues have a tough time dealing with such changes.

I have a Blue friend who I'll call Paul. Paul worked as an independent contractor with a training company and was licensed to train companies using their curriculum and materials. Paul was very upset with the training company because they never called him to check up on how he was doing. When Paul called them, he got little or no attention; they didn't want to spend any time listening to his concerns. Paul became increasingly disillusioned not only with the company but also with its president; Paul had had a close personal relationship with the president for many years. Paul, however, saw that the president no longer seemed to be interested in talking to Paul.

What did Paul do? He didn't leave as others might have done. Paul shared with me repeatedly for almost a year how horrible and inattentive the president was being to him, but Paul didn't decide to break off the relationship permanently until the company demanded that Paul attend a recertification class in order to keep his license. Paul told the company that his wife was in poor health and that he didn't want to leave her alone in her condition to travel out of state to attend; the company told Paul he would lose his license if he didn't attend. The president didn't respond to Paul's plea to reconsider their decision. To Paul, it seemed like they didn't have a heart.

Paul's loyalty to his wife and his sensitivity to her condition outweighed his reluctance to break off the relationship with the president. Paul sent the president an e-mail indicating he couldn't come, and therefore, was resigning as a trainer. Paul later lamented about the lack of appreciation they showed for his major contributions to the company's success. Paul had made a deeper, heart felt commitment to the president and the company that he wasn't willing to let go of easily, despite how he was being treated; yet, the company and its president were ready to move on without skipping a beat. Many Blues have had similar experiences in their jobs or careers.

The Blues' wonderful ability to forge deep relationships and strong loyalties (the shiny side) limits them when others betray the trust that the Blues extend. Blues have a very tough time letting go of the pain and rejection from such a betrayal (the dull side) because they have given so much of their heart to these relationships.

The Personable Blues' natural strengths are phenomenal; but instead of focusing on and magnifying those strengths, Personable Blues tend to focus on their weaknesses and chide themselves for not being stronger, better, more effective, and more caring than they are. They'll let others know about their weaknesses and imperfections lest they be misjudged for being a phony. If they have had a troubled past or childhood, you will soon know about it if you become a Blue's friend. Some Blues even lead out a new conversation by telling the other person their deeply personal tragedies. Personable Blues take on the badge of "victim" willingly and wear it with honor. They often relish the pity that comes from wearing that badge.

Personable Blues often don't take compliments well. When told how well they did on a particular assignment or project, they'll respond by telling you how many mistakes they made or by telling the person that the compliment isn't deserved. Blues have a hard time simply saying, "Thank you," to others who give them compliments because they focus on the areas where they need to improve.

Personable Blues generally don't delegate well. Blues think that the person who has been delegated an assignment can't really do it as well as the Blues, so they often end up taking over the assignment and assuming responsibility for its completion simply so they can assure themselves it'll be done the way it should be done.

In fact, "shoulds" occupy major real estate in Personable Blues' collective consciousness, because the desire for order generates expectations and definitions of how things need to be. These expectations then become the bar so that all activities and conduct that fall short of the bar are unacceptable. Blues will be as or even more critical of their own behavior and efforts as that of others, because it's part of their nature to want to be good and their worth is reflected in the quality of their work.

Blues often are guilt ridden because they focus on the past. When a mistake or wrong is committed, Blues will be the first to feel guilty and the last to let go of the guilt. It is as if they get stuck on how things should have been or how they should have acted. Guilt works on their psyches long after it ceases to serve any purpose.

Guilt is also used by Blues as an attempt to control the behavior of others. Blues will rely on the "guilt trip" to motivate others to change their ways. The guilt trip usually involves the Blue telling the person all the sacrifices that the Blue has gone through for that person and how that person gives nothing in return and the Blue is "sick and tired of it." Well the guilt trip may work fine with other Blues but most non-Blues get turned off by it fairly quickly.

Personable Blues are hard to please generally because the quality they give is the same as the quality they expect others to give.

Blues find it hard to forgive because it is in their nature to want the same depth of contriteness for offenses against them as they would feel in that situation; if that doesn't occur, then they'll be reluctant to let go of the pain and anger even when they're hurt more by this inflexibility than by the original offense.

Personable Blues tend to worry about the future as well as feel guilty about the past. Blues look at how things could go wrong rather than focus on creating the right result. They see risks in taking action and may tend even to exaggerate the parade of horribles in their own mind. Even though the chances of negative consequences may be small, Blues tend to see them as just as real a possibility as the desired result. Taking risks for Blues is delving into the unknown and the unknown cannot be controlled as tightly as Blues want. Their natural impulse then is to do everything possible to eliminate risk and their overly cautious approach may turn into complete paralysis.

Another weakness that Blues have is that they tend to be overly suspicious. In one business I worked for, we had an auditor who often suspected that fraud was being committed by employees of our clients. Fellow auditors took his suspicions with a grain of salt, but it was because he suspected the worst in one audit that he uncovered millions of dollars being embezzled by an employee. This Blue auditor's drive to dig deeply and not accept explanations at face value proved to be very valuable to his employer and the client.

Being suspicious can sabotage key relationships when it becomes uncontrollable jealousy. Blues are inclined to question the motives of those who have violated or not yet earned their trust. Blues naturally question their honesty and loyalty until trust has been earned through consistent and ethical behavior.

Those who betray the trust of a Blue will find it very hard to regain it. Because trust runs very deep with them, Blues cannot easily open up to re-building what was lost or destroyed. It may take months, years and perhaps decades to restore that trust, if it can be restored.

As alluded to above, Personable Blues are just as unforgiving with themselves as they are with others. When they make mistakes, fail an exam (which may be getting anything less than an "A") or break a promise, Blues feel horrible. The other person affected may be quick to forgive them, but Blues will hold onto the guilt. Mistakes may be carried in their psyche for years.

Personable Blues plan their lives based on experience. Experience in essence creates the box within which they choose to operate; that box can become their safety box from all outside threats, thereby stifling the growth that comes from doing things differently. The key to helping Blues expand their horizons is to give them the support and encouragement so that they feel there is a net beneath them if they choose to "go outside the box."

The Personable Blues' Communication Style

Personable Blues enjoy communicating. One of their primary needs is to be understood and appreciated and those needs cannot be satisfied without communication. If Blues are offended, they may choose to withdraw and not talk, but that is when they need communication even more. They may say there is nothing to talk about or that they don't want to talk in such circumstances, but patience will open them up to sharing and getting their needs met.

Blues often ramble when asking a question, giving an explanation or relating an experience. It's not as important to Blues to get to the point as it is to relay the whole picture in all of its complexities.

Personable Blues not only listen to the words you say but also take in all aspects of the communication. Blues listen to the tone of voice and observe the nonverbal communication and are quick to notice if there's incongruity between what you say and how you express it. This is their skill. Blues naturally discern when one is sincere or just putting on an act. Because Blues detest spin and phonies, the person communicating with Blues better be genuine and honest or she will lose the Blues' trust.

Blues love to share their own experiences and to hear the experiences of others. Unlike Reds who want just the highlights, Blues want to know the whole story. They're just as interested in the context as the text. Blues are inclined to even question the real meaning behind what was said rather than take the text at face value. Communication is a multi-level experience for Personable Blues and other personalities may find they have inadvertently offended Blues not because of the words spoken but because of what seemingly was implied by how they spoke the words. A message that may seem clear to Reds or Yellows at face value is far less clear to Blues who sense the nuances behind each word.

Blues communicate sincerely and honestly from the heart. A deceitful Blue is a very sick Blue indeed because he is going against his core need—to be genuine and have things in perfect order.

Personable Blues often expect communication from the other personality groups to be at the same level as they communicate—deep and meaningful. The Blues' feeling of being understood is far more than understanding the text of what Blues say; they need to sense that you really understand the emotional context that accompanies the actual words. That's why it's critical for other personalities not to be flippant in communicating with Blues.

In talking with Personable Blues, you may find them asking: "What did you mean when you said _____"? If you respond: "Just what I said," it's not likely to go over well. Rephrasing what you mean using different words will result in a better outcome. Remember, they're relating to what you say in a multi-sensory level, rather than taking the words at face value.

Personable Blues are analytical and they often use that skill to break down any communication they receive. This helps them to truly understand what the other person is communicating. Communication for a Blue isn't the mere sharing of information as Reds view it. There is emotional content that goes along with the words and it must lead to a deeper connection or to closure. That makes many see Blues as more complex and more difficult to please.

Personable Blues care and their emotions are strongly tied to their beliefs and values. They take things seriously. Being "light-hearted" doesn't come naturally to Blues unless their secondary DNA color is Yellow.

Personable Blues are generally very open to feedback. They care about others' opinions and ideas and so they'll often ask questions at seminars, meetings and other arenas of public discussion so they feel they fully understand what is being taught. Blues love to learn and yearn to constantly improve as human beings because of their innate desire to be good and their candid appraisal of their own weaknesses, mistakes and imperfections.

Personable Blues tend to be realists rather than optimists. Blues will tell you dozens of ways a project, objective or personal dream won't work out and they're often too quick to become fatalistic if obstacles show up on their path to their dream. On the other hand, they will stay true to the end when they believe in you or a cause and never give up on something that they see as important as or more important than themselves.

Personable Blues also use sarcasm, but it is rarely light and humorous. The heaviness of guilt or anger is thinly veiled by the sarcasm; that is why when a Blue uses sarcasm to be funny, it rarely is. If an Optimistic Yellow uses sarcasm, he or she generally gets away with it because it does not seem to be too biting; however, when a Blue does it, it carries a sting, as if you just got pricked by a sharp knife. There is too much truth and negative emotion beneath the surface of the sarcastic remark.

Blues are great supporters and they will often ask you if and how they can help. Blues are more inclined to sacrifice their own dreams than let others fail in their pursuit of their dreams. They really believe in people and they can make the difference for other personalities between success and failure. Blues will support others when they need it most and even when the price of support is high. Blues are so willing to give their all when they see that is what is required. **A close friend who is a healthy Blue can be one of life's greatest gifts.**

How Personable Blues Control

Personable Blues control, but do it using the same techniques that work with them. Blues are prone to feel guilt about mistakes and heed to duty to avoid those feelings of guilt. That is how others can control them. If someone claims they have suffered and will suffer more if Blues continue some behavior, Blues will stop the behavior because they don't want anyone to suffer because of their conduct. Blues also don't want to feel that others have contributed more than the Blues have. That's unfair. Therefore, any indications by a Blue parent to a Blue child about how much he has sacrificed for the child will probably work in getting the Blue child to contribute more.

The guilt trip is designed to push people into doing something they were not inclined or desirous to do to avoid the guilt that comes with inaction. In that respect, the technique may get the short term results at the expense of the long term relationship.

Personable Blues are adept at the guilt trip because they use it on themselves and it works wonderfully, even over long periods, The guilt trip tactic plays to Blues' inclination that they aren't as good as they should be.

Personable Blues control by trying to impress on others how they should act—what is the fair or proper or considerate thing to do. If that does not get the result, Personable Blues will point out how many things they did for you and how you are on the negative side of the ledger when it comes to reciprocation. Or Blues may threaten how they won't talk to you again if they're really desperate for you to give in. All are designed to control but not with the same direct force that the Reds use.

Beware, however, of the consequences of resisting the Blues' efforts to change your behavior because they really may feel betrayed if you ignore their suggestions. Best to point out where you're coming from and how doing what they suggest may not be desirable for anyone.

The Personable Blues' Potential Pitfalls

One of the biggest traps for a Personable Blue is to care so much about something that they totally lose sight of the big picture. Blues tend to get so wrapped up in a relationship, job, career, company or cause that they cannot let go even when it is in their best interest for their own or another's health, happiness and well being to do so. Blues may stay locked in a dead end job for years or for a lifetime thinking all along that they can't leave because their boss or the company needs them. They may hold tight to a relationship that the other party has long since abandoned emotionally because they made the commitment when they said, "I do," to make the relationship work.

Another potential pitfall of Blues is to become immobilized in fear about what may go wrong with any alternative they choose. Blues often devote so much energy to pondering all the potential pitfalls of moving ahead that they ignore the biggest truth—staying stagnant may be the worst outcome of all. It, therefore, is important for Blues to learn how to take action even in the midst of uncertain outcomes.

Guilt and an unforgiving attitude are potentially major pitfalls for Blues. Blues wallow in their past mistakes and in past wrongs committed against them. The former produces guilt and the latter produces anger, hostility and vengeance. All of these emotions are poison to their success because none leads to growth, prosperity and healthy relationships with others and more particularly with themselves.

Personable Blues can be their own worst enemies because they set the bar regarding their behavior higher than what is realistically achievable and then become hard on themselves for not meeting their own expectations. If others wrong them, then Blues often set the conditions for forgiving the wrongdoer so high, that are not likely to be met and the person who suffers most ends up being the Blue because he or she gets stuck in the past instead of living in the present.

Guilt comes from bringing up the past to consume the present moment. If one feels sorrow for having offended or hurt another, such sorrow is healthy if it leads to seeking forgiveness, righting the wrong and not doing it again. In other words, Blues should learn from past mistakes, and not punish themselves continuously for not having acted correctly. Blues, however, often get stuck wallowing in their guilt or self pity.

Personable Blues in the Workplace

Personable Blues are very comfortable in the business world because their strengths are highly valued there. The planning, discipline, organization, and detail orientation are what businesses need internally to survive and grow. The honesty, sincerity, sensitivity, compassion and loyalty are necessary to build great teams and business relationships.

Personable Blues are generally head of the human resource departments of companies. They care about others, know how to communicate, know how to create rules and structures necessary to govern the workforce and know how to address the personal issues that might arise in the course of performing in the business.

Personable Blues are common in the accounting and disbursement departments and even in the administration departments. Again, they play to their strengths when placed in positions requiring human interaction, accurate reporting, steady and consistent completion of job responsibilities and being a support for those in the field.

Blues can make great leaders because of their people skills and their talent to organize and execute. They generally aren't as visionary as the Powerful Reds or the Optimistic Yellows but they do know how to interact with the members of the team and inspire them to perform their roles.

Personable Blues may struggle with taking decisive action in the wake of many unknown risks and a rapidly changing marketplace. They may need to have a Powerful Red spark them to act while minimizing the risk to the extent possible

Personable Blues are committed and care not only about reaching the desired business objectives but also that everyone gets fair compensation for their contribution. That strength instills employees with the desire to contribute to the "cause".

When Personable Blues are assigned a project and asked to report the result in writing, they generally will ensure that all the facts they think are relevant are included in the report. This may turn into a very lengthy report but Blues would rather include too much than too little.

For the Red who is receiving the report, it can be frustrating. She would prefer the key points summarized up front, preferably in one or two paragraphs or better yet, in bullet point format; all the backup can be reviewed if necessary, but the Blue is as interested in letting you know how they got there as in the results. Brevity and efficiency aren't as highly valued as thoroughness and quality.

Personable Blues are attuned to deadlines and will plan ahead to assure completion within the deadline. Unlike Reds, who seem to thrive when the pressure to meet the deadline is highest, Blues prefer to do everything possible to avoid such pressure. Blues don't function as well with surprise deadlines that require intense and quick action, but they thrive in situations where they have the opportunity to fully plan out, perform and report on projects to which they're assigned.

When a Personable Blue is assigned to be the administrative assistant to a Yellow who hates to plan and who changes his schedule on the spur of the moment, the Blue can be driven crazy. I saw that happen with one client company. The Blue tried to have everything in order and the Yellow continually turned order into disorder because it was natural for him not to be tied down to schedules. The Blue repeatedly had to contact those who had appointments with the Yellow leader to reschedule or to tell them he was delayed. This Blue, however, had developed flexibility as a strength. Her natural organizational skills, combined with some flexibility with altering the schedule, made her the perfect fit for her boss' personality.

Personable Blue Personalities

One of the most well known Blues in the entertainment industry who has become a powerful voice in the business world is Oprah Winfrey. Oprah has made it to the top by embracing her natural blue strengths of being sensitive to and having compassion for other people. When the first issue of her new magazine was launched, Oprah wrote an article about what led her to the point of producing the magazine and within it she revealed a variety of struggles she had faced and overcome. Oprah was letting the world know she isn't perfect and has her struggles just like we do. That approach endeared her even more to her fans.

Paula Abdul of *American Idol* is Blue. She hates to hear Simon openly and bluntly criticize a singer for his or her performance. She is naturally supportive of the singers' efforts and sensitive to their feelings, so she often tries to protect them from Simon's ridicule.

Tom Cruise is a Personable Blue with a strong drive for structure and order. In the movie *Mission Impossible*, Tom insisted he do all the stunts and made sure things were done right. Tom Hanks is also a Personable Blue. He is well liked by fans and peers because of his sincerity and compassion. His connection with his emotions and those of the characters he portrays reflects his Personable Blue nature.

President Abraham Lincoln was a Blue. He struggled with depression and mood swings and continually strived to improve as a person. He battled his way up from humble beginnings, but never lost his natural humility and never tried to be someone he wasn't. He connected with people and his sincerity and diligence made him one of our most popular presidents.

Friends was one of the most popular television comedy series of our time. What made it work was three of the characters were Blue and three were Yellow. All connect emotionally with each other and with the audience. Ross is the serious "anal" Blue who seeks a deep relationship and keeps striking out. He dwells on his failures, mistakes and imperfections and has that "woe is me" attitude.

Chandler and Monica are the other two Blues. Monica is a perfectionist always trying to ensure things are in order. Both are emotional and find a deep connection with each other. Joey, Phoebe and Rachel are the Yellows. The combination of different shades of Blue and Yellow is a hit with the audience.

In the movie *Meet the Parents*, Greg, the wannabe son-in-law, is Blue. He is a nurse, a profession to which Blues are drawn. He worries a lot and takes things seriously. He is stressed and anxious about meeting his fiance's parents. Jack, played by Robert DeNiro, is the strong Red who sees weakness and vulnerability in his daughter's boyfriend and who is very protective of his daughter. The Red/Blue struggle is played out and the results are hilarious.

In real life, Blue/Red struggles are common with the Red trying to control with his or her logic and the Blue trying to control with emotion. The Red is practical and the Blue is committed with his head and his heart. They may often see the other as totally out of touch. In the case of *Meet the Parents*, the father finally acceded to the desires of his daughter to marry Greg.

Paul McCartney is a Blue. His songs reflect Blue values. For example, in the song *Yesterday*, Paul writes:

Yesterday…all my troubles seemed so far away; now it looks as though they're here to stay. Oh I believe in yesterday. Suddenly, I'm not half the man I used to be. There's a shadow hanging over me. Oh yesterday came suddenly. Why she had to go I don't know, she refused to say. I said, "Something's wrong," now I long for yesterday…yesterday.

That is where a Blue goes when a relationship fails—back to the past where things were right - trying in some way to understand it and find closure.

Carole King's *You've Got a Friend* is another Blue song. Blues will stick with their friends through thick and thin. They will be there when you need them because relationships are highest priority with the Personable Blue.

Charlie Brown is a Personable Blue. He wants to be good and do the right thing. He meets failure time and again but urges his team to keep on trying. Charlie Brown sometimes gets down on himself and seeks some psychological analysis from Lucy—the Red. What a mistake.

Lucy reaffirms Charlie Brown's imperfections and weaknesses but Charlie Brown keeps coming back for more. Charlie Brown keeps trying to fly his kite, knowing that it will end up tangled in a tree. Despite his premonition that disaster looms, Charlie Brown goes out anyway and ends up with the kite and even himself tied up in the tree. Yet people love Charlie Brown because he connects with their hearts, especially the hearts of fellow Blues.

In *Peanuts*, you find all four personalities. Charlie Brown is the Blue. Snoopy and Peppermint Patty are the Yellows. Lucy and Sally are the Reds. Linus is the contemplative Aqua. Schroeder is the creative Aqua who sees no need to relate to anything other than his music.

> *"To put the world right in order, we must first put the nation in order; to put the nation in order, we must first put the family in order; to put the family in order, we must first cultivate our personal life; we must first set our hearts right."*
>
> *— Confucius*

C H A P T E R   8

"First say to yourself what you would be; and then do what you have to do."

— *Epictetus*

DNA Pointers

Now that you've discovered your DNA color, what do you do with it? Well, it depends on what color your DNA is. One principle holds true for all. Get your needs met by working through your natural aptitudes or strengths rather than your weaknesses.

Here's an example. If I'm an Aqua, I need peace. If my Red boss initially refuses my written request to change my office setup so that I can feel more peace, I can use my natural kindness and diplomacy to meet with her face to face and work out a solution that will meet both of our needs. I'm using my strength—diplomacy—to get my need for peace met and my relationship with my boss probably grows. Alternatively, I can give up or withdraw because "it's not worth it" and feel resentful that she so rudely denied my (non-confrontational) written request. So when my boss asks me next time to help her on an urgent matter, I'll say I can, but then do less and take longer than she needs. I'm sure I can come up with a few great excuses for my sub-par performance. When it's over, I successfully stopped my boss from getting her need met; **but I'm still not getting my need for**

peace met. My relationship with my boss gets worse. I've created either a lose/win or lose/lose outcome and I'm the loser both ways.

Working through your weaknesses may get you a desired result quicker, but it'll carry with it a heavy cost. For example, if you're a Yellow and flake out on a commitment to complete a project because someone offered you an exciting activity to do instead, you may get the instant satisfaction of your drive for fun, but the person you disappointed won't be as trusting or accommodating when you need him to help you. The price you ultimately pay could be a lost opportunity for a promotion that offers more freedom and stimulation or it could even cost you your job. Working through your strengths, on the other hand, may seem tougher and you may not always get you the instant results, but when the results come, they'll be more rewarding and enduring.

The key for you, whatever your DNA color, is to be conscious of how you're getting your needs met and if you aren't getting your needs met, of how it is affecting you and those around you. If you're a Blue who lets others victimize you for their benefit because you feel the need to please others, you'll likely build up anger, resentment and self doubt inside; it'll fester and poison other relationships and your approach to life. If you're an Aqua, you may tend to withdraw even more from others to protect yourself from further pain; you may also let the anger build up inside, which will explode when you've had your fill of these kinds of outcomes. (Pity the fool who is nearby when you explode.)

Reds are quite good at looking out for themselves. They avoid assuming the "victim" role; they prefer the "villain" role instead. Their challenge is that the short term win/lose outcomes they try to produce will ultimately lead to lost relationships and barriers to prolonged or sustained success down the road. Reds will have burned too many bridges by using their weaknesses (manipulation, force, intimidation) to meet their needs.

If you're Yellow, you too may end up burning too many bridges. People may enjoy your energy and enthusiasm but when they get used by you once too often, they'll conclude it isn't worth keeping up the relationship no matter how entertaining or fun it might be at times. Your natural charm will wear off on those who you love or seek to influence.

Read only what applies to you for now. If you prefer, go to Appendix 2 to see pointers for your primary DNA color in bullet point format. If you want more depth, however, read what applies to you in this chapter and then go to Appendix 2 when you need to be reminded.

You'll learn in the next section about how to deal with other colors. If you do want to read all of this chapter, don't let suggestions to others diffuse the power of those pointers directed specifically to you.

You may even want to read your section in small bits and chunks—like daily quotes or doses to think about and work on one at a time. I strongly encourage that approach. Otherwise, you may gloss over it and miss all the ways that these suggestions can increase your natural power to influence others. Let's get started.

Powerful Reds

By focusing on your own agenda, you often ignore what the other person wants from the relationship, transaction or alliance. Just because you value your own opinions and ideas does not mean others are inclined to want to hear your opinions if you do not listen to theirs. Encourage others to give their opinions or ideas and restate them in your own words to ensure that you've heard what they intended to say and that they know you're listening. You don't always have the best idea and they may have information that you've not considered that would affect your opinion or conclusion. Jack Welch of General Electric fame became a successful Red leader because he encouraged and listened to varying positions before making a decision.

Even if you think the idea or opinion is useless, let them know that you understand what they're saying before discounting or rejecting it. Let them know why you think it won't work and thank them for contributing it anyway.

Learn to compromise and cooperate with others. If you treat your group project as if it were a one person show, then you will end up as a one person show. You won't have anyone to help you meet your goal.

Recognize that others have needs that differ from your own so don't expect everybody to want the same result for the same reasons you do. Open yourself up to the idea that alternatives can be pursued because they satisfy not only your objectives but also objectives of different personalities with different needs.

Learn to relax. Step back a second and recognize that things are often not as urgent as you make them. If you act with the same or similar urgency in all matters, your influence will suffer when time really is of the essence. Slow down on things that don't matter as much, particularly if the other person does not sense any urgency.

Learn to apologize. Apologizing is generally hard for you because you think you're right and apologizing may seem to you as weak and silly. Recognize that we all make mistakes and that you may be right on a particular point but your dogged determination to prevail on that point has its price; that price may be the destruction of your ability to influence this person down the road. Learn to apologize not only for any mistakes you make but also for any callousness or arrogance you may display when others commit errors.

Lead, don't push. Remember the fable about the wind trying to blow off the man's coat without success and how quickly and easily the coat came off when the sun warmed up the man. Pushing others to get the results you want may work in the short term, but it depletes the trust level and undermines your effectiveness to have sustained influence with those that you lead. They may respond with just enough effort not to get fired, but they won't give their best effort, even though you may demand it.

Lighten up! Don't make being around you so intense. Let things happen without you having to be in control or in charge. Take the time to laugh at your own follies and stupid mistakes.

Use "please" and "thank you." Send thank you notes and cards to those who do things on your behalf. Yes, that may be part of their job responsibilities but if you show appreciation, you may likely get more sustained effort the next time.

Don't expect everyone to want to do it your way. You may be convinced that the right way to do something is your way. Others often have alternatives that they think are even better. If you always choose your way, then people will stop contributing.

Don't assume everyone comes to you seeking your advice. Sometimes people share difficulties they're having, but they aren't interested in your providing the solutions. They only want to be heard and understood. Don't jump to the conclusion that each time someone shares problems he or she is having, they want you to solve their problems. So ask them if they want your advice before giving it.

Don't expect everyone to have the same intensity and focus that you have naturally. They may not produce at the same level as you, but they can bring assets to the table that you don't have. Adjust your expectations and focus on how their talents and skills are complimentary to yours and can bring value to the project that you would have a tough time bringing.

Finally, be careful not to embarrass individuals when others are present. Taking the time to critique performance one-on-one along with recognizing what was done well will motivate others to respond to the criticism by correcting the mistake and performing at a higher level. Remember that the ultimate objective is to hone the skills and talents of other members of your team and build in them a passion to perform their best for the good of the team or the business.

Peaceful Aquas

Now it's your turn, Aquas. Your challenge is to be a player in the game of life, not a spectator. It's easy for you to detach and let others contribute, but you lose out on the growth and benefits that come from contribution and they miss out on your good ideas and your natural strengths.

Raise your hand literally and figuratively in the game of life. Don't worry if someone shoots you down. That is part of the process and it doesn't take away from your value.

When you have an opportunity to present or speak, give your opinion and don't give up on the merits of what you've offered at the first critique or contrary opinion. As an Aqua, it's easy for you to let others' opinions carry the day, but your ideas can make a positive difference. Consider the criticism or suggestion, weigh it against the advantages your opinion brings, and see if it still merits your and their support. If it does, then stand up for and defend your opinion.

Resolve to contribute your talents and volunteer for assignments. Don't let others assume roles that you can perform simply because you didn't volunteer. Put yourself out there. The more you put yourself on the line, the more confident you will become and the more you and others will see the value you can bring to any team.

Listen with interest to what others are saying. It's easy for you to block out what others are saying to you. I know from experience. But take in what they say and respond in a way that lets them know you're listening. Look them in the eye. It's easy for you to stare blankly, close your eyes or even turn your eyes away from others as they talk but engaging eye contact affirms that you're interested in what they have to say. That makes them want to hear what you have to say. Remember, the most interesting people are those who are the most interested in others.

Learn to speak a little louder when introduced and asked how you are. Let others know who you are. Don't just passively listen all the time; interact with those who talk to you.

Focus more on your strengths than your weaknesses. Your tendency is to do the opposite and use it as an excuse for not participating. Take the chance. Don't let fear stop you from growth and fulfillment. Freedom from confrontation, opposition or challenge isn't an abiding peace if it means giving up on your needs and desires. Don't go to the grave with your song still inside.

I don't want you to be something you're not. If there's something you don't like doing at all, then don't do it. But if you're going after something that's important to you and if you encounter opposition or resistance, stand up for yourself. Don't give up on your priorities to avoid dealing with resistance or challenges.

Set goals and then set milestones along the way to achieve those goals. It's easy for you to dismiss the goal setting process as a waste of time, preferring to "go with the flow," but the flow you're going with isn't yours; it is someone else's. You need to forge your own path.

Find what you're passionate about and pursue it. Start to notice what gets you excited and what lifts your energy level. Look at career opportunities in those areas or at least ways to develop your talents, skills, knowledge or competence in that area. When you have passion for what you do, your creativity flows. You can create the job that taps into that passion, but it takes courage and stepping out into the unknown. Remember the adage: "Go out on a limb. That's where the fruit is."

When something is bothering you, don't hold it in. Share it in a kind way and it won't build up and burst under pressure down the road. Stand up for yourself each time someone may try to take advantage of you and you'll earn the respect of others as you do. Don't try to appease others to maintain peace if that peace is nothing more than a surrender of your own needs and values. That false peace doesn't lead anywhere worthwhile, only to future capitulation and declining self esteem.

Don't get locked into routines. They can be the biggest impediment to growth even though they seem "safe." They generate a false sense of security and squelch your innate creativity. Try doing things differently or in a different order. Try new things. Take chances and your God given creativity will start to emerge and your confidence will grow.

Don't be a wet blanket on the dreams of others because it may introduce change into your relationship. Change can be great because it forces you to reexamine where you are and make new choices that can lead you to a better place or help you grow in your character. When others share an idea to try something new, hold off from rejecting it. Ask for some time to think about it and then get back to them. Often, if you give yourself a chance to reflect on the idea, you will see its merits much clearer than you initially thought.

Don't sacrifice your own dreams for the sake of avoiding conflict. If you do, you're trying to get your need for peace satisfied through your weaknesses, not your strengths. The risks of failure, challenge, objection, confrontation and resistance are often present as you pursue your dreams. Overcoming these challenges gets you through to the success you deserve and lays the foundation for future dreams to become reality.

Don't sell yourself short. Too often, you have the inclination to give up on your ideas or dreams to get along with others or to let them use you for their ambitions. You rationalize this by saying your dreams aren't as important or that you can wait until later. When you sell yourself short like this, you build up a pattern that leads to more failures and shattered dreams. Recognize that you bring great gifts to the table and that you deserve to achieve what you've dreamed, particularly when it is something that ignites your passion.

Finally, don't procrastinate and let others do your work. It is easy to assume a helpless status and let others watch out for you. Others often cover for you thinking you somehow need to be protected. Let go of that urge and pull your own weight on a project.

Optimistic Yellows

I tell the Reds to lighten up, but that's easy for you; your challenge is to take all of your commitments more seriously. Keep your promises, even if doing so may not be as much fun as you'd like. Take that as your challenge.

You have no problem participating on teams unless you feel rejected. You have no problem telling others what you think. Listen to what others say instead of thinking about what you're going to say next. Help them to feel that they are a valued part of the team by the attention you give them rather than by the attention they give you.

Learn to listen so well that you can repeat in your own words what you heard the other persons say and let them affirm whether you understood them. You may be prone to interrupt someone when some thought jumps into your mind. Hold back. Don't speak before you think; nurture the habit of thinking about what you're going to say first and how it might impact the listener.

If you've been interrupted telling a story, pause to consider whether you should jump back into the story or whether the interruption is intended to get you off a tangent so others can move forward with the subject at hand. You could even ask them if they want you to continue.

Sometimes you may need to tone down the volume or energy depending on the situation. Your energy and enthusiasm is a great asset most of the time, but be sensitive to times where it may impede rather than advance the communication. Sometimes, people might prefer you to speak less and listen more.

Draw others into the conversation. If you find that your entertaining communication style tends to dominate a conversation in a group, draw others into the conversation with questions about them. The most "interesting" people to talk to are the people who are most interested in others.

When someone shares a story, your tendency is to "one-up" that story with a better, more exciting or more outrageous one of your own. Resist the temptation. Examine why you want to "one up" what others share with you. Your motive probably isn't to affirm the value of the other person.

Get a personal calendar to keep yourself organized. If you have a hard time, let software such as Microsoft Outlook keep you on task and on schedule. Recognize that others' time is very valuable and being delinquent for your appointments has a ripple effect; it even interferes with the schedules of those who end up waiting for those who had to wait for you.

Find someone who loves you but who will hold you accountable. Set up regular meetings with them to ensure that you're moving ahead with your plans.

Find someone who will help you manage the details whether it's at work or at home. You probably don't have that talent naturally because immersion in the minutiae isn't fun.

Be more patient. Your tendency to react quickly and to make impulsive decisions without learning all the important facts can undermine your success.

Wait patiently for what you need. Very few things are truly that urgent. Waiting for others who go at a slower pace will be tough. See what you can learn from slowing down to their pace. Step back from the urge to move, leave or walk ahead and examine whether you will be benefited in the long run from acting on that urge.

Take time to learn how to be comfortable in silence. Insights can come quickly in still, silent moments. Learn stillness in the form of meditation or Tai Chi as a way of slowing down to take things in and ruminate. The word "ruminate" means to turn ideas over and over in your mind. It's the mental equivalent of a cow chewing its cud, but it's not as gross. Your patience will be rewarded when you ruminate about options, alternatives, ideas and differing opinions.

Don't be lax with others' schedules by having meetings last longer than scheduled. Time is precious to them. Show others you value their time by ending meetings on time. Don't be self absorbed. It is so easy to be locked into your own world and to be inclined to tell stories about yourself instead of listening to what others have to say. You lose a lot when you make the conversation solely about you.

Don't exaggerate. Repeated exaggeration of facts leads to loss of influence. If others sense you're prone to exaggerate the facts, then they'll place little weight on whatever you claim to be a fact. You're much more effective at influencing others when you understate rather than overstate the facts or your achievements.

Don't commit yourself to too many projects. You often are inclined to take on whatever projects interest you without considering whether you have enough time and resources to do it. Take the time to consider what time and effort will be required before making a decision to take on new projects or assignments.

Don't "jump ship" when things get rough. Stay the course even when it's not fun. More fun and stimulation will come your way because you'll have the respect and influence you need to get your needs met.

Personable Blues

OK, Blues, first of all, don't fret about all the areas where I suggest you improve. Work on a little at a time. Perfection is a long journey, not an event. Be grateful for how far you've come along the path. You tend to be too hard on yourself despite all the gifts you bring to the table. Focus on your strengths rather than dwell on past mistakes or weaknesses. Reflect on all the good you've done for others. Your tendency to devalue yourself is far greater than you letting your ego get too inflated, so don't worry about feeling good about what you've done for others.

Receive compliments graciously. When people say good things about your work or efforts, simply say "Thank you." Don't diminish it by saying what you did wrong or, "It was nothing," or "You did far more than me." You may think such responses show humility, but they don't. Someone is giving you the gift of gratitude and appreciation. Your unwillingness to receive it isn't humility. Receiving the gift graciously is true humility. That is how you can show your gratitude or appreciation for them.

Don't overwhelm others with details. Sometimes people want just an abridged version, not the whole encyclopedia. Take the time to ask what they want. You may want it detailed if you were in their position but that doesn't mean they would. Some just want you to get to the point and would welcome the details after the key points have been shared.

Look for and share positive observations about others. You tend to find fault with others as easily as you do with yourself. Resist that tendency and focus more on what you like about them.

Recognize that unrelenting "perfection" often is the enemy of good or great. Being so focused on making sure everything is perfect can sabotage the whole effort, particularly if there are time deadlines. Waiting to decide until everything is perfect often leads to lost opportunities, because perfect conditions for taking action or moving ahead are rare.

Your strength is seeking quality; it often needs to be balanced with competing priorities if achieving the highest quality consumes too much time, energy or resources among competing priorities. Take time to consider what priorities need to be balanced and optimized and adjust your efforts accordingly.

Be willing to delegate and let others be accountable for what you've assigned them. Don't look over their shoulder so much that they feel no freedom or independence to achieve what you've asked. You could undermine them from becoming responsible individuals if they know you'll always bail them out in the end.

Open yourself up to your natural God given creativity. Don't let your inner critic carry the day. Take the time to get out of rut thinking by exploring the problem or opportunity from different perspectives, including those of other DNA colors.

Let go of perceived offenses against you. This is much easier to say than to do because so much emotion is tied to the hurt you feel from the offense. If you've experienced the joy of being forgiven by someone you've offended, then share that gift to someone who has offended you, regardless of whether they're willing to accept the gift. This gift to them is also a gift to yourself because it frees you to be fully alive in the present moment and to love and be loved by those you care about most in this life. Open your eyes and heart to the many wonderful things others have done for you and recognize you can only be the best "you", you can be when you're not hanging onto past offenses, and when you're totally aware and open to the blessings each day can bring.

Surround yourself with upbeat people—people that see you for who you are and who accept you. Be around people who are grateful for the talents and gifts you share and who listen to you and understand you. You find those kinds of people by being that kind of person yourself. Light attracts light.

Fill your heart daily with gratitude for all the things you have. People are about as happy as they're grateful, so make gratitude—deep felt gratitude—a daily expression from within.

If your needs aren't being met, don't withdraw, be sarcastic or put guilt trips on others. Share what your needs are and ask others to help you meet them. Better yet, learn new ways to get those needs met.

Lighten up. Don't take things too seriously. Learn to laugh at yourself and others and you will find your load lightens with you.

Don't get immobilized by your own failures or mistakes. Laugh at them, learn from them and move on. Too often, such mistakes become giant roadblocks to your growth. Be willing to take the risk to go forward knowing that you may make even more mistakes. Success comes from getting up one more time than you're knocked down.

Don't expect everyone to be as organized as you are with the schedules and lists that structure your days. People may be late; it is ok to ask them to be on time. Don't dwell on it if such a pattern persists; be proactive by deciding whether this flaw can be tolerated because of the other benefits the relationship brings or if this is a red flag requiring action. If you aren't in a position to end the relationship because the person is a business colleague, co-worker or boss, then assert your needs in a positive way.

Don't let your schedule keep you from seeing or doing what is optimal at a given time. Schedules and lists are great tools to make us more efficient, but if they govern us instead of our governing them, valuable opportunities that arise in the spur of the moment will be squandered and progress will be limited. Be open to adjusting the schedule. Don't underestimate the power of flexibility and adaptability to your ultimate goals.

Don't take everything personally and over-read what others say to you. You understand nuance. You routinely read a lot into seemingly benign statements. Sometimes this is good because you're taking in the entire message and testing its consistency with what was actually stated, but other times it's a hindrance because you read too much into it and let it consume your life. If you aren't sure what was intended, then ask; don't assume and get offended by what you haven't confirmed with the person who made the statement.

If you're in a bad mood, don't make everyone play twenty questions to try to find out why. Be up front. If you need time to be alone, then let them know and tell them you can talk more about it later.

Finally, live fully in the here and now. Your inclination is to get stuck feeling guilty about the past or worrying about the future. Neither direction helps you. You're at your best in the present moment being fully immersed in sharing your gifts with others and being open to the daily joys that come your way.

"A 'No' uttered from deepest conviction is better and greater than a 'Yes' merely uttered to please, or what is worse, to avoid trouble."

— Mohandas K. Ghandi

SECTION III.

You
Influencing Them

C H A P T E R   9

What Color is Their Puddle?

Now that you have a good sense of who you are and your natural strengths, what can you do with that to influence people? Knowing who you are brings power. Now you need to channel that power of understanding your own DNA color into learning the DNA color of those with whom you interact and then treating them as they want to be treated—communicating to them in their own language. For those of you who decided to skip right from the chapter on your DNA color to this section, I suggest a little backtracking to get a better grounding on people you're dealing with from the other personality groups.

We start here with a simple principle—people naturally leak their DNA. Their DNA color oozes from their verbal and nonverbal communication. Your challenge is to observe which of the four DNA colors the behaviors reflect. So start looking at the imaginary puddle or puddles that start to form around them. Then ask yourself what color(s) are their puddles?

If you're trying to identify someone else's DNA color, observe the whole way he or she communicates—not just the words they use but the body language and voice inflections. People "leak" their DNA colors not only with what they say but how they say it. In face to face communication, over eighty percent of what we communicate is nonverbal—something other than the words we speak. For example, think about what you say when someone asks: How are you? You can say "fine" or "good" in a variety of ways, each of which communicates a different overall message of how you really are.

There is so much being communicated when people talk face to face. Often the words used are belied by what is communicated with the eye contact, the tone of voice, the facial gestures, the posture, and even the feet. We often sense some incongruity between the actual words and what is the real message being shared even though we may not be able to pinpoint why we don't trust or believe what the speaker is saying. (Haven't you ever thought shortly after meeting someone that there is something about him you don't trust, but you can't explain why?)

There are, however, a couple of complicating factors. First, people often try to be someone they're not because they believe that is how they're supposed to be. They have been conditioned to believe that modeling the behavior of another person is what they need to do to be accepted and/or successful. A person may model his behavior to create a image that people will like or that protects him from being hurt. So you'll probably encounter "puddles" of one DNA color at the feet of a person whose real DNA is another color.

Second, most of us are "blends"—a score of over 10 in any DNA color on the *DNA Torque Personality Profile* will likely have some influence over your behavior; you could naturally be leaking a smaller puddle of a color that isn't your primary DNA. Remember, however, that over time the primary DNA color of a person will have the most influence over what she says and does. So identify the color of the largest puddle—the color of what she mostly says and does—to determine what personality group she belongs to.

This takes some educated guessing at times. Don't let that stop you. If your colleague's behavior seems consistent with a Blue, then treat him as a Blue—speak to him and relate to him as if he were driven by perfection and/or connection and see how he responds. Is your behavior increasing your rapport with him or is it a nonstarter?

If it is a nonstarter, try the color of the second largest puddle. The more you do it, the more proficient you get. Rarely will it require more than two tries if you really take time to consider what you've observed.

There is an alternative. Have your colleague, friend, family member or acquaintance take the *DNA Torque Personality Profile* and find out for herself or himself. Sometimes that will be easier and sometimes it will seem impossible. You be the judge. The key to influencing people is to understand through which of the four types of DNA filters that person experiences life. Then adapt your message both verbally and non-verbally to the drives and needs of that color so that what you communicate gets understood as you intend it.

It isn't as hard as it sounds. The key is persistent effort to observe and listen to others and then a willingness to test your hypothesis to see if it's accurate. Test, test, test.

This book certainly is designed to increase your consciousness of your own DNA color. Successfully influencing others, however, means you have to be just as conscious about their DNA color. In fact, if you observe someone's behavior closely, often you will end up knowing what makes them tick better than they know themselves. Actually, it can be pretty fun if you approach it as a game instead of a duty.

DNA Detectors

Here are some ways to help you figure out who you're dealing with, particularly in a business setting. Again, others leak their DNA color when they interact with you, so be on the lookout. (A chart summarizing these detectors can be found at the end of the chapter.)

If you're trying to sell something to a prospect either in person or over the phone and don't know what DNA color you're dealing with, observe how the prospect approaches the decision. Reds will want to get quickly to the bottom line for benefits and costs. Aquas will seek additional time and space before they decide and will avoid sharing with you anything they don't like about the product. If it feels like you're pulling teeth to get any sense of where they're at, there is a good chance that your prospect is an Aqua.

Blues want to avoid all risks so they may ask you about what warranties or guarantees come with the product or service. They will also ask a lot of questions about the product or service you're selling. Blues don't want to make a mistake. Yellows want the product to be easy and fun to learn and use. They will have more emotion and vocal variety in their voices.

Reds and Yellows tend to decide pretty quickly while Blues and Aquas either are more deliberate or want to procrastinate making a decision. The good news about Blues and Aquas is that once they do decide to buy, they'll probably be your customer or client for a long time if you prove worthy of the trust they place in you. Blues stick with you because they want to be loyal to those they trust while Aquas want to avoid the anxiety of finding another supplier of the goods or services you sell.

How loud are they speaking? Reds and Yellows tend to be loud. Yellows are fairly expressive with their non-verbal gestures. Blues are not as loud and Aquas are generally soft spoken.

If you're meeting with them in person, what is their eye contact like? Reds are very direct in their eye contact. Yellows will engage you with eye contact, but it won't be as focused. Their eyes may dart around as they speak. Blues may not give you eye contact at first, until they feel comfortable with you; then they will give you the type of eye contact that tells you they're listening and care. Eye contact is not important to Aquas so you won't see it as much and even when it is there, it may be the "Aqua stare".

How are they communicating? Blues and Yellows tend to draw on more emotion than Reds and Aquas. Yellows will often have more vocal variety and nonverbal gestures. Aquas won't use a lot of gestures and show little vocal variety. Reds will be very direct and succinct. Blues will often begin their sentences with "I feel . . .", "I believe . . ." or "It seems to me . . ."

Once you determine what DNA someone seems to have, then you can follow some or all of the suggestions later on in this section about how to develop rapport and influence their behavior. Sustained influence, however, comes only from valuing them for what they are. Don't use the principles you learn here to manipulate others without them understanding what is going on. Manipulation will ultimately lead to your own undoing.

DNA Detectors in the Workplace

	POWERFUL RED	PEACEFUL AQUA	OPTIMISTIC YELLOW	PERSONABLE BLUE
DISPOSITION	STRONG WILLED / DECISIVE	EASY GOING / QUIET	HAPPY / OPTIMISTIC	APPROPRIATE / SINCERE
ASSIGNS TASKS	DELEGATES AND DEMANDS COMPETENCE	ASSIGNS "IF HAS TIME TO DO IT"	NOT AS STRONG AT DELEGATING OR HOLDING ACCOUNTABLE	TENDS TO TAKE OVER DO IT HIS OR HER WAY
INTERACTION WITH OTHERS	DOESN'T SEEK INPUT OR APPROVAL UNLESS REQUIRED	SEEKS APPROVAL AND INPUT OPEN TO DIRECTION	SEEKS INPUT FROM THOSE WITH WHOM THERE IS GOOD RAPPORT	SEEKS OTHERS' INPUT AND DIRECTION
DESKTOP	ORGANIZED BUT NOT NEAT	DEPENDS ON PERSONALITY BLEND	LESS ORGANIZED WITH NON-BUSINESS OBJECTS (CANDY, TOYS ETC.)	ORGANIZED AND POSSIBLY SPOTLESS
QUESTIONS AT MEETINGS	DIRECT QUESTIONS	FEW QUESTIONS	LOTS OF QUESTIONS IN STORY FORM	ANALYTICAL QUESTIONS

DNA Detectors in the Workplace

	POWERFUL RED	PEACEFUL AQUA	OPTIMISTIC YELLOW	PERSONABLE BLUE
YOUR PROGRESS REPORTS	WHAT'S THE BOTTOM LINE?	LITTLE FEEDBACK OR QUESTIONS	POSITIVE FEEDBACK AVOIDS NEGATIVE NOT WANTING DETAILS	WHAT'S THE CAUSE? WANTS THE DETAILS
FRIENDLINESS EXPRESSED	USED OFTEN TO ACHIEVE DESIRED AIM	KIND BUT NOT WARM	VERY FRIENDLY	UNLESS STRESSED OR CROSSED
ANGER EXPRESSED	LOUD AND DIRECT	OCCASIONALLY BIG OUTBURSTS BUT USUALLY HOLDS IT IN	JOKINGLY OR FLIPPANTLY; GETS OVER IT QUICKLY	INDIRECT AND INTENDED TO MAKE ONE FEEL GUILTY; BROODING
COMMUNICATION	LOGICAL FACT-BASED	LOGICAL AND INFREQUENT	FREQUENT FRIENDLY EYE CONTACT HIGH ENERGY	MORE LENGTHY DETAIL ORIENTED OFTEN INDIRECT
RESPONSIVENESS	QUICK	DELAYED	QUICK	DELAYED

C H A P T E R   1 0

"A musician must make music, an artist must paint, a poet must write, if he is to be ultimately at peace with himself. What a man can be, he must be."

— *Abraham Maslow*

Personalities in Context

In addition to blends, context is another factor to determining another person's DNA color. Context is a powerful influence on behavior. People often behave differently at work than they do at home or with their friends—so differently that some might believe a woman is Red if they're her co-workers but Blue if they're her husband and children. The arena in which you're operating (the context) may cause you to change your behavior to something other than what is natural for you normally. This phenomenon also applies to many with whom you work.

In the world of business, people exhibit more of the Red behaviors than they do in other arenas in life. Whether ingrained by society into believing that such behaviors are necessary for business success or learned first hand from Red leaders who want you to be like them, people sense that the confident, no-nonsense, "time is money" approach is the preferred way to do business.

Certainly such behavior will work for the Red who needs to gain more power, stature and recognition for their accomplishments. But how does it meet the needs of Blues for security, appreciation, understanding and stability? How does it meet the Aquas' needs for tranquility, independence, time for reflection, and balance? How does it meet the Yellows' needs for freedom, playtime, flexibility and spontaneity?

What happens for non-Reds is that if they use the Red weaknesses (e.g., intimidation, abrasiveness, impatience) to meet their needs and objectives at work, this increases their own stress, dissatisfaction and frustration. They aren't being who they are and the incongruity between what they do and how they want to be saps them emotionally and physically. What is more surprising to many non-Reds is that trying to succeed by acting Red while ignoring their own innate drives, needs and aptitudes (their "DNA") won't work.

I wholeheartedly concur that the other personality groups can develop some Red aptitudes and use them successfully in the business world. The phenomenon I am talking about, however, is when personalities don't embrace their own value and strengths and instead try to adopt what they think is necessary to thrive in a specific arena. They try to be "like Mike" (or like Jack Welch, Martha Stewart, Meg Whitman or Donald Trump). They may want to mimic some other successful role model they see in business publications, in a movie or on a TV series. Trying to be someone they aren't born to be is why so many feel burned out with their jobs or professions.

That is why I felt burnt out as a trial attorney. I was in the high pressure world of win/lose where verbal combat with opposing counsel was a daily occurrence. Yes, I acted Red and fought on my clients' behalf for their best outcome. But when I left the office, I couldn't leave it behind. Instead of meeting my needs for balance and peace, I was heading in the exact opposite direction because that was what I thought my profession demanded from me.

Adversaries, clients and judges saw strong Red behavior. But to those who observed me when the curtains went down, they saw Aqua—quiet, lost in my thoughts, overstressed and sometimes in somewhat of a trance. How many out there are adapting their behavior to the demands of their job and feeling miserable about where they are and what they're doing? They conclude they're "burned out" or not cut out for the job. If they're Blue or Aqua, they may be afraid of leaving their jobs or careers because of the insecurity of the unknown—wondering whether they can make a living doing something other than what they spent years of education and on the job training becoming.

Yellows may endure the constrictive environment of where they're working and turn off what makes them shine because that is what they feel they need to do to provide for themselves and their families.

How much of "you" are you sacrificing in order "to make a living"? And what are you going to do about it?

Personality tests may ask questions and classify contextual behavior under a certain personality type **when all that the test identifies is not necessarily who they are but who they are trying to be**. I took many other personality tests before developing my own profile and regularly came out as socially active and driven to succeed—a Yellow/Red blend. But that wasn't me and the results for many of you may similarly be skewed due to context — trying to be someone or something you aren't.

One Red business executive took the *DNA Torque Personality Profile* and lambasted it because it focused too much on how she behaved as a child. She cavalierly dismissed it as useless and irrelevant because the only thing that counted with her was how she and others behaved in the work place. She simply didn't get it. What good does it do to pigeonhole people based on their behavior in one arena? What good does it do to identify and classify people by contextual behavior if it doesn't pinpoint the individual needs that aren't being satisfied by that contextual behavior? You will often try to motivate them in ways that won't produce sustained results.

Yes, context can be a powerful influence on behavior. Yet, identifying contextual behavior as indicative of a personality type will often lead management and the individual into going down the wrong path. The individuals won't be identified, affirmed and valued for their own unique gifts. They'll be reinforced to be something they're not and performance will suffer because their actions run against the natural current that flows inside them.

The world of work values the Red strengths of confidence, brevity, clarity, boldness, action, results, calmness under pressure and performing well within tight deadlines. But you don't have to abandon who you are if you aren't a Red to succeed in that environment. You just need to recognize and value your own DNA and find the niche where your natural aptitudes can be deployed. When you do, you can always augment them with Red strengths while staying true to your DNA. You can draw on any natural or developed aptitudes without trying "to be like Mike". *Remember the key to successful and sustained influence as a leader is to be who you are. Everybody else is already taken.*

The personality tools that rely on how people are behaving at work to categorize personality types cannot work well in many situations because they won't help companies choose the right people for the positions they want to fill. For example, they may pick Blues or Aquas thinking they are Reds. Management will train them as if they're Red when they learn best through hands on interaction rather than lecture (as Yellows do); management will use Red tactics such as money and possible promotion to motivate these people to give their heads and their hearts to do the best job possible when what actually motivates them better will be appreciation, understanding or even independence. If they're Aquas, they may not want to be promoted, because that makes their job more stressful and confrontational. The personality tool must be able to identify the main current that has flowed through them since birth, not just how they've learned to behave in the workplace.

Since you've taken the *DNA Torque Personality Profile*, the possibility of misidentifying yourself is small *unless you were answering based on the way you think you should be or want to be instead of the way you really are and were born to be*. Just be conscious of how, when, where and why you change your approach to interacting with others. What assumptions do you implicitly make about how to act in certain arenas? Are those assumptions really meeting your needs? Becoming conscious of these patterns is the biggest step to getting rid of what doesn't work for you.

So blends and contextual behavior complicate how you determine the color of the puddle or puddles. You'll make mistakes in defining those with whom you interact. I too have made mistakes. But the mistakes decrease as the competence and observation skills improve. It isn't a matter of being right all the time. It's a matter of devoting the time and energy to understand how others view their world and incorporating your findings into how you relate to them.

The DNA Colors Under Stress

One context that evokes different "colored" behavior from most of us is stress. Life can be stressful at times, and each of the personality groups have their own way of dealing with the stress. Reds, for the most part, thrive in stressful situations, including the pressure of meeting deadlines, because it causes the adrenaline to flow and things to happen quicker. Reds are probably the best at cramming for exams. However, stress does make Reds even more impatient and dictatorial, and it can drive Reds crazy if what is causing their stress is outside their control.

Aquas often withdraw from the world under stress. They become immobilized and lost in their own thoughts. If the stress becomes too great, they'll just take off somewhere where it seems more peaceful and calm.

Yellows don't like the stress of deadlines and intense time constraints. Their reaction to such pressure may be to take off and/or flake out on the commitments they made.

Blues generally hate stress, especially when it comes from unexpected events interfering with their plans and structured lives. They can go into a panic mode and begin ranting and raving and/or become completely immobilized by stress, worrying about all of the potential "disasters" that loom before them.

Stress often causes those within all personality groups to act in ways that aren't consistent with their primary DNA color, which leads to even more confusion if we're trying to figure out what color their DNA is. For example, a calm and collected Aqua can suddenly become rude and abrasive under stress, dropping into the negative Red mode; in other words, the Aqua may surprisingly start to use negative Red traits to get his needs met. A Yellow may start putting guilt trips on others like a negative Blue because she is under too much stress. People will wonder what happened to her carefree nature. Intense stress can and often does draw out the worst in people, even negative behaviors from their secondary and tertiary DNA colors.

Take the time to notice what your behaviors are when under stress. Do you drop down into the weaknesses of your primary DNA color or to those of a secondary color? Part of your behavior pattern may have been learned from your parents. You may have adopted almost unconsciously their behaviors in dealing with stress rather than staying true to who you are.

One thing is clear. When we act outside of our primary DNA color under stress by using the weaknesses of other DNA colors to get our needs met, we don't succeed; and we sabotage the positive influence we can have on others. The effects of your behavior can hurt or even destroy all the trust you've built up to that point. So you need to understand the patterns you fall into under stress and consciously choose to act differently, knowing that doing it the same way as you have in the past won't satisfy your needs over the long term and will decrease your influence over others.

I haven't seen a consistent pattern that occurs when the different personality groups are under stress except that most drop down into their own or another group's weaknesses to get their needs met. Reds may be an exception at times, but even Reds may rely on their weaknesses to achieve the desired results when the stress is intense.

In summary, look for your stress adaptation pattern and that of those you lead; find ways to work your way back to meeting your needs under stress by using your natural strengths. If someone else is under stress, don't reach any decision as to their DNA color until after you observe them when they aren't under stress. Behavior under stress often sends the wrong signals about their true DNA. If you do know their DNA color, encourage them to see that their behavior doesn't really help them get what they need and show them a better way.

C H A P T E R   1 1

"And as we let our own light shine, we unconsciously give other people permission to do the same. As we are liberated from our fear, our presence automatically liberates others. "

— Marianne Williamson

Influencing Others in the Workplace

Now that you understand your DNA and how to optimize the natural aptitudes with which you've been blessed and are more consciously observing the color of others' puddles and the role of context, you have the foundation for influencing others by speaking to them in their language. The ability to influence often depends on what role you're in and what role the person you're trying to influence is in. When you don't have the ostensible authority to tell another person what he needs to do, you have to rely on your people skills to influence their behavior. In reality, those same skills should be applied even when you can order them to do something because you're their boss.

I once participated in an experiment involving more than eighty business professionals from a variety of companies. The experiment was conducted by John H. Zenger and Joseph Folkman, authors of *The Extraordinary Leader, Turning Good Managers Into Great Leaders*, a book I highly recommend.

We were divided into fourteen tables of six; seven of the tables received one list of seven traits and the other seven received a different list with the same number of traits. We were then asked on a scale of 1 to 10, 10 representing "complete trust", how much we would trust a leader that exhibited the traits on the list we received. Secondly, we were asked on a scale of 1 to 10, 10 being "completely willing", how willing we would be to follow a leader with those traits. Here are the traits on our list: **Intelligent, Skillful, Industrious, Cold, Determined, Practical and Cautious**. Our mean score on trust among the seven tables in our group was a little over 4 and the mean score on willingness was only slightly higher (but still less than 5).

We were aware that the other seven tables had a different list but we didn't know what was different. They too voted at their tables and then they came up with the mean score, which was between 7 and 8 on both questions. The leaders of the test then told us that the only difference between the two lists was one trait. *"Cold"* was replaced by *"Warm"*. **In other words, one trait among seven almost doubled (going from a little over 4 to almost 8) the "trust" and "willing-ness to follow" ratios.**

When our table discussed the traits initially, I immediately sensed from the comments how the *"Cold"* trait colored all of our impressions as to the quality of the leader. I remember asking myself and the rest at my table before the results were tallied if the other group had *"Warm"* on their list.

What that experiment validated is that having the "people" skill produces an exponential rather than an incremental difference in others' perception of your leadership. Being "warm" actually makes your other strengths look stronger. Conversely, being "cold" weakens your other strengths and probably accentuates your natural weaknesses. That is why knowing yourself and others and applying that knowledge in how you relate to them produces such enormous payoffs. **Others will "warm" up to you when you speak and listen to them in their language and when you value the gifts they bring to the table**.

With that in mind, let's take a look at each of the roles where you will find people with DNA colors other than your own. Remember, if you learn to speak their language, your other strengths will look stronger and your weaknesses will fade away from their sight. In a sense, it's a supercharger for motivating others to trust you and follow your influence.

Charts with suggestions on how to deal with other DNA colors in bullet point format are found at the end of the book. I suggest, however, you read this chapter first and use the charts as a "cheat sheet" to remind you about what you learned reading this chapter.

The Red Boss

How do you handle a Red boss? How do you relate and build a strong relationship with him or her? Very few of us will ever go through life without working for a Red boss in some capacity whether it is business, education associations (PTA), churches or non profit associations. That is because Reds naturally work their way up to the top of any organization and stay there.

If you're not Red, then you can succeed with a Red boss if you show two qualities—competence and confidence. Reds focus on those two qualities and they quickly assess new people (vendors, job applicants, etc.) on whether they meet the standards they consciously or unconsciously set in those two areas. If their first impression of you is one of self doubt, insecurities, weaknesses or passivity, then you'll likely be toast. It'll take a long time for you to overcome their first impression if given the chance.

Eye contact, energy, strong handshake, strong voice and articulate answers will go a long way towards building a solid foundation with that Red. Clear, concise and logical responses to their inquiries will make things even better. A can-do attitude with a penchant for taking action will also advance the relationship and gain their respect and trust.

Reds don't like excuses because they believe for every door that closes, another one opens. Those who come to them with excuses for missed results or incomplete projects without offering alternatives they've pursued to achieve the desired results will lose favor with Red bosses. Reds want you coming to them not just with problems but with solutions. They may not go along with your proposed solution, but they will be impressed by your proactive approach.

If you show competence with no confidence, then Reds may likely discount your competence. If you show confidence despite minimal competence, you might survive in the short run. Reds themselves often overshadow minimal competence with incredible confidence. But the Red looks to results so your star will eventually fade and die out if your competence doesn't justify your confidence.

The Red Subordinate

A Red subordinate may be an incredible asset or a major problem. They can be an asset when they're given the opportunity to exercise "power" and they have the competence to use it wisely. Power may be in the form of delegated responsibilities, leadership over a certain aspect of a team project or control over an aspect of the day to day duties and responsibilities of the group you lead; or it may be offering a challenge to achieve certain results with some leeway over how they're achieved.

Red subordinates can be a major problem if put in the position of "flunky" or "gopher" ("Go for this, go for that") with little opportunity to exercise power or distinguish themselves from the pack. In those circumstances, they may often challenge your authority privately and openly. These Reds may create their own leadership role among their co-workers, the purpose of which may be to advance a different agenda than your own. Again, Reds do well with win/lose (they win and you lose) but they refuse to abide by lose/win (they lose and you win). If they feel your authority over them is a net "loss" for them when it comes to what they want to achieve, then they'll either want to make it lose/lose hoping your loss will ultimately open a door for them to go through so they ultimately "win" or quit and work somewhere else where they can win.

Speak to them with clarity and conciseness. Give them responsibilities and the payoff for solid performance. Red subordinates will interpret whatever you ask within the context of what is in it for them, or in other words, what is the payoff for doing what you tell them to do. Telling them they will keep their job and salary may look to you like a payoff. In the long term, these motivators will fall short if the Reds' needs (namely, to lead, to be in control, to take action, to be right, to achieve results and to be recognized and respected by those who they respect) aren't met.

The Red Co-Worker or Colleague

Reds are political. They instinctively know how to further their agenda and sense where the real power is. The formal corporate hierarchy structure often doesn't match where the real power resides and Reds will quickly learn and change their focus to those who hold the real power in the company. Reds will then work through the "de facto" power structure to get their agenda achieved. This path may mean seeing who looks to be heading up the corporate ladder the quickest and developing alliances with him or her.

In the first edition of the reality television series, *Survivor*, there was a wonderful illustration of how Reds operate in a win/lose setting on a prolonged basis. Reds knocked off Yellows, Aquas and Blues until it came down to a few survivors, all of whom were Red; they didn't trust each other but they saw the benefit of setting up short term alliances far better than the rest and that skill got one of them all the way to the top. Reds are survivors. If you're not a Red, you better cover your flanks if you're in a "survival of the fittest" culture.

Reds can be an ally if you show competence and confidence. If they perceive you as a valuable asset, then they will want you to rise with them up the ladder (but they probably want to keep you one rung lower).

You can also be seen as a pawn in the Red colleague's own power struggle. If they don't like your boss, then they may solicit or influence you to join them in their challenge to that boss. Be aware that you might be used as as a pawn in their battle and become a casualty if you don't protect yourself.

A positive Red can be your champion. In one company that I worked with, the CEO and COO were lukewarm on the idea of training people about their DNA. But a Red Executive Vice President made sure my program was part of the training for new hires held every two months. At those trainings, the Executive Vice President took time to introduce me and testified of the benefits that come from what I would be teaching them. He was my strongest advocate in the company; yet, I had never solicited his support. He saw the payoff from the employees knowing their DNA color and invested his reputation and energy in the technology.

The Aqua Boss

If you have an Aqua boss, one strong advantage is that he or she is usually not political. Intimidation isn't part of their repertoire. In fact, they may absorb any political pressure they receive from their boss without passing it on to those they lead. The Aqua boss is low key, expecting that his team will perform their duties independently without daily pressure for the numbers or results. This can be liberating to a team who has felt squeezed by the tremendous pressure and intensity of a Red or Blue boss. The question is whether the Aqua boss can be visibly passionate enough to inspire his or her team to perform at a higher level.

The Aqua boss will be diplomatic and logical in carrying out his responsibilities. On the positive side, anger will be largely absent unless the pressure becomes too great and steam has to escape. On the negative side, the Aqua boss likely won't try to develop team spirit and camaraderie. Furthermore, you may not know where you stand with the Aqua boss because he or she feels no need to tell you. (In fact, the Aqua boss may not even have considered where you stand.)

Strong relationships aren't critical to the Aqua boss; the focus tends to be meeting the objectives that are set. When you seek to influence the Aqua boss, remember, you may not get a lot of feedback to your overtures. I had an Aqua boss and on several occasions I went in his office to report on certain projects or assignments and make recommendations. Rarely did my boss say anything more than a few sentences; the meetings lasted less than a minute once I finished giving my report. It was hard to get a sense of where I stood. On the other hand, he wasn't critical or rude; my boss just took in the information and either acted on it or did nothing.

Big decisions with the Aqua boss may be delayed. The tendency for Aquas is to deal with big problems by hoping that they get resolved on their own. Capable underlings can often make such hopes achievable. However, when no direction is given, such problems may fester and harm morale and ultimately undermine the success of the company.

During the entire time I worked for the Aqua boss, I rarely saw him have lunch with anyone. He took a walk and read while he was walking. He rarely greeted most of the employees by name and often his greeting was so soft, you could barely detect it other than a slight movement of his lips.

The strength of an Aqua boss is his or her ability to view the issues objectively and weigh all the relevant factors rather than be emotionally swayed to overreact or make impulsive decisions. Aqua bosses are open to feedback. They don't think they have all the answers. When they receive feedback, however, you may not get an immediate response. Aquas want the time and space to reflect on what you've told them. So you may be absolutely convinced the Aqua boss ignored or rejected your suggestions, but a week later you could be shocked to read a memo to the team adopting your suggestions. Be patient. Aquas work under a different decision making process and timetable.

The Aqua Subordinate

The Aqua subordinate likes to work independently. Tell them what to do and when it needs to be done and they will usually get it done. They will often not seek help from other team members if issues or problems arise so take the time to see how they're progressing and ask them questions to see if they're on track.

The Aqua subordinate won't be high maintenance. They get along with their co-workers but their quiet nature may bother those who need feedback or social conversation (Blues and Yellows). It just depends on how well the Aquas have developed their communication skills.

The Aqua subordinate won't respond well to direct pressure. He may seem cooperative but his way of getting back at those who are pushing too hard is procrastination or passive aggressive conduct— not doing what you want or doing it in a way that makes the "aggressor" pay for it in some way.

Aquas like to please and they like space. Giving them the responsibilities with some target deadlines and expressing confidence in their ability to perform will go a long way, particularly if communications are low key and kindly. Remember, Aquas need space and time to reflect so let them participate to the extent possible in setting the progress deadlines and give them a little time to give feedback. Don't put them on the spot or they might say whatever they think you want to hear regardless of whether they mean it or whether it is true. That is part of their passive aggressive reaction to those who cross over their boundaries or who pressure them intensely.

My experience with Aquas in the work place is steadiness. They go about their work without interrupting others or creating morale problems among co-workers.

The Aqua Colleague or Co-Worker

The Aqua colleague can be a great asset. One Blue trainee told me that when he hits the downside of one of those emotional roller coasters, he would sit down next to his Aqua colleague and after about a half an hour, he felt calm again. Aquas have a natural ability not to get too disturbed about the rough seas around them.

This talent, however, does have its limits because the stress isn't always repelled like water off of a duck, but often is absorbed without release. Ultimately all of that absorbed stress or anger or anxiety needs to be released. You may remember periodic news reports of the quiet and friendly employee who brings a gun into work and starts shooting his co-workers. When interviewed, his neighbors say he was a quiet man who never really bothered anybody. Elton John wrote a song about this—*Ticking*—equating it to a ticking time bomb. The passivity on the surface didn't mean he was at peace inside. He was just dealing with all the turmoil and stress in an Aqua way by stuffing it. But ultimately, the internal negatives built up so strong that the Aqua had to blow off steam like a geyser.

The Aqua co-worker will work independently but enjoys being a help to his or her colleagues if asked, unless he or she is under too much pressure or time stress. At that point they may agree to help but never get around to it. Aquas are quick to apologize but not so quick to change the behavior that warranted the apology. Aquas aren't concerned about losing any face by apologizing, unlike the Red. But often they aren't committed to changing their behavior either. Change brings unknown turbulence, which the Aquas want to avoid.

Aquas like routines. Jobs with routines are fine with them because it allows them to do their work while thinking about other things. However, they don't have the same attention to detail unless they have a secondary Blue need for order or they were trained early in life to attend to details.

Aquas will work with you in teams but aren't inclined to speak up in team meetings or to voice objections even though they have them. The key is to draw them out and develop rapport.

Developing rapport with an Aqua isn't like what you do with a Blue or Yellow. You can develop as much rapport with Aquas by just sitting next to them in silence as you can with a Blue or Yellow by talking to them. A father spent a couple of hours fishing with his Aqua son. During the two hours, there may have been a few minutes of conversation, but the Aqua son told his father while driving home that he really enjoyed the time together. So if you can be (not just act) comfortable in tranquil settings and with minimal dialogue, then you can earn the trust of the Aqua. With that trust, your influence will likely be strong.

The Yellow Boss

The Yellow boss can generate great camaraderie among his or her team because they're social. They enjoy communication and attention. Yellow bosses such as Herb Kelleher of Southwest Airlines or Richard Branson of Virgin have had phenomenal success using their natural Yellow strengths not only to define the culture of the company but also to make it fun for customers to do business with their companies.

Yellow bosses are innovative and tend to embrace rather than resist change. When such natural talents are woven into the way their companies do business, they can stay ahead of the curve, because they will generate and implement new ideas while competitors take baby steps forward.

The Yellow boss can also eschew formalities and structure, which might undermine the company's sustained success. Yellows tend to be disorganized because it interferes with their enjoyment of the present. If that passes down into the culture of the company, they may initiate wonderful strategies but have horrible execution. The Yellow boss may likely be weak when attending to details in the execution phase, so Yellow bosses need to have other members of their team fill this gap.

The advantage of a Yellow boss is their openness to new ideas and ways of doing things. They don't want heaviness in their organization. They love banter and high energy—working together to generate breakthrough concepts and strategies.

When working with a Yellow boss, be willing to listen to their stories. They tend to be great story tellers. Don't bog them down with too many details. Yellows are quick to decide; rarely are they too cautious and deliberate unless that comes from a secondary Blue or Aqua need. Impulsive decision making is a much bigger risk, because there's more emotion than logic tied to the decision making process.

Yellow and Aqua bosses are more fluid in approaching their responsibilities whereas Blue and Red bosses rely more on planning and structure.

The Yellow Subordinate

The Yellow subordinates can be great for a team if allowed to bring their natural strengths to the table on a project that stimulates their interest. They can also be a great distraction if they're bored or otherwise uncommitted to the team's objective. They won't be wallflowers. They will be noticed either positively or negatively so it is best to get them fully engaged by giving them the space and freedom to let them do their part.

They can be a great spark for creative group thinking. They'll often come up with "off the wall" ideas that turn out to get the group out of a rut thinking approach. They have a natural talent to view the problem from a variety of perspectives and not just the same linear approach that other temperaments might have. If such creativity is encouraged and rewarded in some way, then the Yellow can generate great results. If, on the other hand, the Yellows' ideas are spurned, ridiculed or flatly rejected because they're too far out there or if the Yellow is viewed as too shallow or superficial in addressing the real challenges the company faces, then you'll lose the Yellow. They'll want to go where they and their ideas are more accepted.

Yellows aren't afraid to quit their jobs if they don't like what they do anymore. So if you're a Blue, don't expect the same level of loyalty that you would give to your company. The Yellow needs to be cheered, acknowledged and enjoyed. Minimal or no feedback to their efforts will drive the Yellow away.

The Yellows tend not to be time based. They can spend vast amounts of time interacting with others on a variety of topics, many of which are irrelevant to their job. Teaching skills through lecture type instruction falls on deaf Yellow ears. Yellows love to bounce their thoughts and ideas off of others and so interactive learning is by far the most effective. Having them take things home to study or memorize won't get the same results as they would with the Red, Blue or Aqua.

Yellows tend to interrupt. When a thought jumps into their head, it usually finds its way quickly to the mouth. Finding a way not to shoot down creative ideas that pop up while minimizing the interruption of other team members speaking is the challenge.

Yellows aren't long term planners. Again their view of long term may be a lot shorter than that of Reds and Blues. Keep rewards out there to shoot for in the near term so that Yellows will feel motivated to go after them. Otherwise, they will be non-starters because Yellows recognize that a host of things can happen before the term is up, including their leaving the company.

The Yellow Colleague or Co-Worker

The Yellow can be great to have around. They will make things more fun and livelier. They exude energy and generally it is positive. Yellows are naturally optimistic people so they can lift your spirits when you're down. Take advantage of that strength because it can make you much more productive and effective in your life.

Bounce ideas off of Yellows; be more spontaneous; look at problems from a host of perspectives. You're creative too; you may have just squelched it more than the Yellows. The world of children is the world of Yellows. As children, you saw a variety of possibilities to get what you wanted or to get away from what you didn't want. You weren't linear, but were very open to new ideas and to making new connections.

The Yellow co-worker can come up with activities and rewards for achieving goals. He or she can definitely make your day more interesting and spontaneous. Be open to the spontaneity they naturally exude.

Sometimes you'll have to keep the Yellow on task; he or she may come by constantly to talk with you and large amounts of time can go by before you can get back to your work, so let the Yellow know when you have to get back to work or when you don't have time to talk to them. Remind them of the time because they can lose track and miss deadlines, meetings, appointments etc.

Recognize and pay attention to the Yellow co-worker. Ignoring them will probably make things worse because they may look for other ways to get your attention or use humor or sarcasm with others to attack you.

The Blue Boss

The Blue boss leads more deliberately and with the input of his or her team. The Blue boss delves more into details and sets up more intricate policies and procedures to ensure things are done more orderly and fairly. Sometimes this promotes frustration and paralysis by impeding the free flow of ideas and quick strategic responses to the changing market place. Sometimes this deliberate leadership style promotes more security and trust among the work force.

When dealing with the Blue boss, contribution to team efforts and cooperation with other team members of the team by sharing skills, time and energy will establish a strong rapport with her. Building up trust with the Blue boss may be tougher than with the Red boss because it isn't just about getting the job done but how you get the job done. Being genuine and sincere with no hidden agendas will go a long way with her. Once you earn her trust, the Blue boss is inclined to be loyal to you even if performance should dissipate. The Blue boss is more inclined to be sympathetic to outside forces affecting your performance.

The Blue boss will require not only the big picture objective, but also all the small steps and milestones that get you there. You can't wing it. There must be solid support underlying your suggested alternative or position or it will be rejected.

Working with the Blue boss may often entail taking the time to connect with him as a human being and expressing interest with what is going on in his life. The Blue boss values loyalty and hard work. The

Blue boss values getting the job done right, not just getting it done and he loves the extra effort of someone who puts the team, company or objective ahead of his own self-interest.

The Blue boss may use guilt trips to motivate—sarcasm with a sting. Criticism may be indirect and subtle (unless he tries to act like a Red). The Blue boss naturally isn't inclined to embrace change but may have learned to deal with it. Again, the focus is on structure, details, order and working as a team.

The Blue Subordinate

Blues can be great members of a team. They work well in a team setting and are sensitive enough to try to see that all members get the opportunity to contribute. The challenge is that Blues tend to keep a running record of perceived unfairness or favoritism. If the Blue believes you're playing favorites, then everything you and the perceived pet do will be viewed through that biased filter, regardless of reality. It'll be very hard to turn around Blues' opinion of unfairness.

Blues tend to act out of their intuition or gut. If you ask them to do something that doesn't feel right to them, you'll have a tough time. Blues tend to avoid change so they could become a major barrier to new ideas, even if these changes will be for the better. Blues tend not to be the early adapter to a major shift in company culture, processes or policy because their natural inclination is to stick with the status quo. Change shakes their structure. If you introduce change, help the Blue to get a concrete sense of what the change will bring and that it'll make the company stronger and more stable. Don't use fear as the motivator to accept change—"adjust or be fired!" You'll likely lose the Blue with all of her strengths, talents, skills and experience.

Blues will be loyal to you if you've earned their trust. They may be critical at times because seeing the imperfections in anything, including themselves, is a natural pattern rather than seeing just the strengths. They pride themselves on being practical, realistic and grounded. Blues are very grounded but sometimes that prevents them from launching themselves or their companies to a higher level. They prefer to avoid the risk of losing what they have rather than focus on the opportunity to achieve something better.

A Blue can become your strongest ally. But if you offend them or break their trust, they can be transformed into your biggest enemy. Listening to them, appreciating their efforts and showing that you understand where they're coming from will create a friend and ally. With Blues, money can certainly be a factor but there are stronger reasons why a Blue will stay and work hard for a company. If they're emotionally tied to the company or its leaders, then they're willing to sacrifice money and perks to serve the cause or to stick with someone they know and trust.

Blues can be on emotional roller coasters at times and take offense easily, even when none was intended. They hate being treated unfairly, unappreciated or taken for granted. They expect you to value their contribution and express gratitude for it often because they tend to give their all to doing the job.

Blues gravitate to those leaders who have a bigger vision of how their company serves humanity, not just their owner or shareholders. If they catch the vision you have for the business and it blesses and enriches the lives of the customers and clients who purchase the goods and/or services your business offers, then they can become your hardest and most productive workers.

On the other hand, when a Blue feels management has been unfair or preferential to a co-worker, it tends to consume a large part of his time and energy at work. A Blue often will complain to others and if he gets a sympathetic ear, he'll come back and commiserate often. He'll rehearse in his mind what really was behind what you said, regardless of the clarity of your message was. He'll interpret how you said it and your gestures to search for what "the real message" was. Blues can see a mixed message even when none was intended.

The Blue Colleague or Co-Worker

A Blue co-worker can be your greatest ally or your worst enemy. If the Blue thinks you're a fake or have some hidden political agenda to advance, then they'll do what they can to make you fail. They don't mind if they don't get ahead, just as long as you lose. Misery loves company.

On the other hand, if you value, listen to and appreciate the Blue, they'll be with you through thick or thin. They'll plead your case and console you during harder times. They'll be your "bridge over troubled waters."

It is against Blues nature to be phony so if you have a phony Blue or one that lies repeatedly, stay away because he may likely be neurotic or psychotic. I've worked with some. They're not uncommon.

Blues value honesty, integrity, humility and dedication. Blues love to share where they're at and to know about all that is going on or at least rumored to be going on. They want the real low down, not the spin. Blues hate spin.

Blues can be non-stop talkers, always wanting to communicate. That usually is the case with a secondary Yellow or they can be brooders if they have a secondary Aqua. Blues tend to have strong moral underpinnings that they use to guide them in all things. Blues tend to hold strong to their opinions and views of the world.

The key to working well with the Blue is to be a team player who doesn't care who gets the credit for a job well done. Standing strong in moral views also goes a long way to engendering their trust, loyalty and service. Be aware that Blues often give with strings attached, so be clear on what expectations they may have of you as a colleague or co-worker.

> *"Know that although in the eternal scheme of things you are small, you are also unique and irreplaceable, as are all your fellow humans everywhere in the world."*
>
> *— Margaret Laurence*

C H A P T E R   1 2

"We do not believe in ourselves until someone reveals that what is deep inside us is valuable, worth listening to, worthy of our trust, sacred to our touch. Once we believe in ourselves, we can risk curiosity, wonder, spontaneous delight or any experience that reveals the human spirit."

— E.E. Cummings

Influencing Others Outside the Workplace

We're around all types of personalities outside the workplace. If you're looking for suggestions on how to be more influential with a friend, a neighbor, a child, a sibling or even a spouse, look no further than this chapter, although a more in depth book on DNA inside the marriage and family is planned. Some of what I suggest is repetitive to the last chapter, but remember, repetition enhances recall.

Before putting others on the "psychological couch," we better be clear of our own DNA, including our weaknesses. When we don't know who we are and try to be something we are not, we're muddled in our thinking and send mixed messages to all those with whom we interact. Others aren't clear on our motives, and therefore, are inclined to be repelled by our efforts to build a relationship or to influence their behavior or decisions. Some of their strange behavior towards us might be because we're acting strangely towards them.

That is why it is critical to "cleanse the inner vessel first"—come to know and be who you are and consciously meet your needs through your natural strengths, not your weaknesses. You then build win/win rather than win/lose, lose/win or lose/lose outcomes.

When you embrace who you are and recognize and accept the whole package—your weaknesses as well as strengths—then you're ready to communicate and relate to others in their own "language" and thereby expand your ability to lead and influence tremendously.

Here are some general suggestions for dealing with each of the four personalities outside the business setting. If we're emotionally healthy—understanding and accepting our innate personality and embracing the gifts we have been given—then we'll have little problem relating to others who share that same personality color. The key then is enhancing our people skills with the other three personality groups.

Reds

Reds are generally the easiest behavior to identify. The key is testing to ensure that the person you're dealing with is truly a Red or if she is some other color acting Red. When you speak to them as a Red and observe their responses, a non-Red will start to leak his or her color. Assuming you're dealing with a Red, here is how you maximize your ability to lead and influence that Red.

Don't take the Reds' abrupt style personally. Reds value clarity and succinct communication. They're not the "touchy/feely" type so they won't mince words. They can take, and even respect, blunt speech.

A Red spouse or friend may tell you your dress is too tight or that your hair looks lousy or that you look a little heavy in the pants you're wearing. Your first reaction may be to turn "red"—either with anger or embarrassment. How dare he be so rude! But the Red spouse or friend believes he is being clear and telling you what others are thinking but afraid to share. The Red is letting you know so you can do something about it. The Red is giving you a gift. Take in the substance of the message (for whatever it is worth) without reacting to the blunt way it was delivered. Otherwise, you may continue to wear "the ugly dress" or style your hair in an unflattering manner.

Keep your communication with a Red short and to the point. Speak staccato—sharing the highlights but leaving out the details unless asked. Show the Red brother you value his time by being brief and to the point. He'll appreciate it and come back more often to talk to you.

Recognize a Red's achievements. Reds like to be told how well they did if it is sincere. Tell your Red daughter: "Great job!!" They value themselves by what they do so recognizing them by sincerely acknowledging the excellence of their work will increase your rapport with her. Recognizing a Red son for his natural strengths such as decisiveness, boldness and leadership will bond you even more to him. Be sincere because Reds tend to see through false praise and they hate it.

When you tell a Red friend what happened at an event or meeting they missed, give her the bottom line first. She may not be listening to anything that follows it unless it is meaningful to her given the one line summary you provided.

Look Reds in the eye. Show energy. Exude confidence. Without eye contact, the Red may likely not pay attention to what you're saying.

When dealing with a Red spouse in a difficult situation, don't emote. Reds turn off when that happens. If you confront a Red husband with some wrong he has committed against you, verbalize it with clarity and without emotion. Point out the consequence of his wrongdoing and how it impacted you. Point out what will happen if he repeats his mistake. The Red will get the message.

Don't expect the Red to immediately apologize. That isn't in her nature. Often the best result is to get the Red not to do the same action again because she sees it won't be in her best interest.

Don't expect compassion or sincere sympathy from a Red. You may not get any sympathy from a Red acquaintance by pointing out the suffering and difficulty you went through on his behalf. He expects you not to complain. Just move forward.

Reds are action and future oriented so don't make a Red dwell on her past mistakes. Best just to relay the behavior that is acceptable going forward and why you're pointing out the mistakes she made.

Aquas

Aquas tend to move at their own pace. Trying always to hasten the pace with your Aqua wife may likely create stubborn resistance. Helping her to see the benefit if she increases her pace, on the other hand, may produce the desired result. Aquas like to please themselves and others. If you've patiently built rapport with an Aqua wife, then she will want to please you by increasing her pace.

Aquas are often the hardest to motivate because they give so little feedback as to where they're at. The biggest challenge is drawing it out of them without them feeling too much pressure from you. Aquas resist pressure, but they do it passively by either saying "OK" and doing nothing or simply just ignoring what you say. Rarely will they tell you they're feeling too pressured by you. If they don't give you eye contact, seek it out, but be patient.

Give Aquas few, rather than many choices. I remember once when my Aqua daughter Marisa and my oldest daughter Natalie, a Red, were with me at a local artist festival and we went up to a mobile trailer selling food. The sign listing the different food they sold was large and the options among which to choose were many. Natalie told me what she wanted to eat almost instantly but it took Marisa about ten minutes to decide. What made it even more frustrating for Natalie was that we were leaving the festival fifteen minutes earlier when Marisa looked at me hesitantly as if she wanted something but was afraid to express it. When I asked her, she said she was very hungry and wanted something to eat. But her indecisiveness was prolonging her and now our hunger. Natalie applied some subtle and then not so subtle pressure and Marisa finally told us what she wanted. We all laughed about it afterwards, seeing how well it showed them leaking their colors.

Freely give Aquas encouragement without expectation of feedback. They will take it in and it will impact them more than you know. Patience will bear good fruits because when you least expect it, the Aqua will respond positively to your encouragement.

Ask for Aquas' input. Often, they will say: "I don't know" or "It doesn't matter." Be patient and give them a few alternatives to choose from. That may make it easier for them to decide.

In a family setting, Aquas often have things to share with the rest of the family but are reluctant to share them. Your calling on them in a family meeting gives them that opportunity. If they say they have nothing to share, respect it but don't hesitate to provide them with more opportunities to contribute or share with other family members.

Compliment Aquas for doing their chores or doing well in school. Again, you may not notice the effects immediately but they're taking it in and rapport is building. They will be more prone to want to please you when another opportunity arises.

Wait to respond to an Aqua until they're completely finished. Yellows usually don't mind being interrupted because they interrupt others, but if you interrupt an Aqua, you may not get them to say anything more. Don't sabotage all your efforts to get them to talk by interrupting them in mid-sentence.

Yellows

Yellows are high energy people. The best way to connect with Yellows is to exude that same energy and enthusiasm. Enjoy the humor and excitement they bring.

Don't ignore them. Yellows may seek negative attention if you try to ignore them. They feed off interaction with others and with life. Your shutting them off will **lose** rapport with them.

Be spontaneous. Yellows love spontaneity. Unlike Blues, Yellows don't thrive with schedules and structure. They love the unexpected— the little things that are outside routine because they're not routine lovers. Break the routines with your Yellow daughter or son. The fun breaks from routine will be greatly appreciated. Give them the chance to take breaks from their homework for Instant Messaging, surfing the Web or watching TV. They do better when they're not forced to do it all at once, especially when homework will take them a couple of hours.

Give colorful details when you're sharing your experiences with a Yellow friend. Yellows don't like facts to get in the way of a good story. Yellows are good story tellers and love that same attribute in others. Yellows are connected with life, so stories bring home the principles you want them to learn.

Yellows are interactive learners. They don't like just to read and study books. Making learning fun will be a big challenge for parents of Yellow children. Reds, Blues and even Aquas can do well with independent study, but Yellows learn by interacting with the teacher or fellow students; two way communication and whole body experiences of what is being taught are critical.

Yellows love off the wall and out of the box thinking. Creativity flows freely with Yellows because they don't tend to embrace the rules and structure that stifle their creativity. Praise their creative ways of seeing life and their day to day experiences.

My daughter Natalie shared with me an experience she had at a leadership retreat where one of the participants was Yellow. In the middle of brainstorming, she would share things that were "off- the-wall", like imagining what it would be like to be a giant bug—so big that if you hit a car's windshield, you shattered it. Her visuals sparked laughter and opened up the team to new and better ideas on how to resolve the challenges they were confronting. Take in what may seem like bizarre ideas because they often can lead to breakthrough strategies. The essence of creative thinking is to look at the problem or opportunity from various perspectives. Look for the connections because Yellows are often not rut thinkers and the best solutions are outside the "rut".

Praise Yellows for their efforts. Let them know you enjoy what they contributed. Be expressive with your praise—not just a "ho-hum" thank you. The more expressive you are without going over the top, the more rapport you'll build with the Yellow.

Give them freedom and flexibility. Yellows thrive outside the structure of routines and schedules. Giving Yellows freedom and flexibility by focusing on the desired results (rather than micro-managing each step you believe they should take to get there) will enhance their performance.

Blues

Blues are deep people who desire to do their best. If you take the time and effort to build trust with a Blue child, they will want to obey you and do what's right. They're intensely loyal with those they trust. So the most important thing to do right from the outset is to be who you are and be sincere in all that you do and share.

You can't afford to start off on the wrong foot with a Blue by being something you aren't or spinning the truth. Blues see through it and they will peg you as someone not to trust.

Blues want to be good and to obey the rules. They need to feel secure and structure helps them feel safe. Don't take them out of their comfort zone without recognizing how scary it will be for them. Be there to support them and encourage them.

If you're genuine from the outset and seek earnestly to understand and appreciate the Blue for what he contributes, then he will build a bond with you that will stay strong.

Blues look for incongruity between verbal and non verbal communication. If your words don't match what you say with your body, Blues will be suspicious, cautious and reluctant to trust you. Don't lie to anyone, but particularly to a Blue. You will lose a lot more than anything you think you gain from not telling the truth.

Listen to the Blues with the intent to understand, not to fix, whatever problem they're encountering. Sharing where they're at is part of the process they go through to reach resolution. It is often not a cry for help to solve the problem but a desire to have your share and appreciate the experience they're having. Be with them emotionally and they will feel empowered to take action to move ahead.

Don't get impatient with Blues. They may take a lot longer to get to the point than Reds but being succinct in expression of feelings isn't the point to Blues. Understanding the whole context of the Blue's shared experience, no matter how protracted it may seem, meets their need and they in turn will want to meet your needs. Listen compassionately and you'll get Blues to stand by you when you need them most.

Blues like input. Give them the input they request. Asking for their input endears them to you. Blues value two being as one. Appreciate that quality and share your gratitude for their friendship.

If you want a Blue to trust you, do your part. Don't say you did great at something they asked you to do when you only did a slipshod job. Better to confess and offer to do it again.

Compassion and empathy are highly valued by Blues. If you have it and if you share it with them, Blues will submit to your influence. Be willing to laugh with your spouse in good times and cry with him or her in rough times. Be patient with his or her struggles to let go of the past.

Trust comes easily from Yellows. Trust is earned from Blues. Be patient and persistent in gaining that trust. If you betray that trust, prepare for a long ordeal to earn it back again.

Once earned, do not risk doing anything again that will breach that trust. Acknowledge errors or mistakes quickly; don't try to hide them. Be truthful and genuine in all you do and the Blues will love and support you through thick and thin.

> *"Your vision will become clear only when you look into your heart. Who looks outside, dreams. Who looks inside, awakens."*
>
> *— Carl Jung*

C H A P T E R   1 3

"They always say time changes things, but you actually have to change them yourself."

— *Andy Warhol*

Making Changes Stick

Making big changes in our lives can be tough. When we feel the need to get rid of a bad habit or behavior, we try to stretch out of our comfort zone and stay there until the changes become permanent. We often feel anxious (or at best ambivalent) about making the change and are easily inclined to head back to the comfort zone of our old habits when we face any resistance; in fact, the biggest battle often takes place in our own mind, as thoughts come to us questioning whether we can change or whether making the change is worth it.

The change that comes from learning about your DNA, however, is different. Instead of fighting to break out of a negative routine or pattern, you are returning to your true comfort zone. You're rediscovering who you are and what strengths you naturally bring to the table. You're not feeling the pressure of having to be like someone else. Instead, you're experiencing the power of authenticity and the influence it naturally generates over other people. It is that desire and passion to be the best you, you can be that will spark continued growth in how you relate with others by understanding their core drives and needs and by communicating to them in their "language."

The most powerful motivator for using DNA to make significant changes in your business or personal life is an intense and passionate desire for an outcome. Fear of negative consequences if you don't "change" won't get you there. When you feel a deep and strong desire for something—to be yourself and to strengthen your power to influence others—and you keep it in your consciousness each day, you engage your whole mind and body in the change process. Change is no longer the enemy but a byproduct of your powerful desire for a specific outcome. Change happens naturally as you forge a new path that you believe will lead you where you strongly intend and desire to go.

I know of a man I'll call Matt who had battled for years with weight problems. He tried every new fangled weight loss plan that came his way without success. A wise female friend, who I'll call Julie, then asked him what physical activity he dreamed of doing, but had been prevented by his overweight condition. Matt told her he loved watching skiing competitions on television, but never had tried it himself. Julie first told Matt to envision himself on skis at the top of a beautiful slope of fresh snow. Julie then urged Matt to "go through the motions"— pretend with his body he was skiing—hands gripping poles and legs moving in unison back and forth. Julie then encouraged Matt to follow this routine for an hour or so daily and then book a winter vacation at a ski resort three to four months down the road.

Matt first "skied" in his bedroom each day using his imagination, but later changed to exercising with a machine that simulated the skiing movements. Months later, Matt had lost over fifty pounds and was on the slopes skiing on real powder and loving it. Matt had lost weight as a byproduct of going after his dream rather than as an end in itself. Moreover, the weight reduction was permanent because he saw himself as an athletically fit skier, not as a fat person struggling to change his nature by following a diet. That's the power of pursuing something that's tied to a burning desire to create instead of trying to do something you feel like you should do or trying to avoid a negative outcome based on fear.

An intellectual decision to follow a certain course doesn't mean you'll create it; your ego can always come up with reasons not to pursue that alternative or to excuse your failure if you give it a try and then quit. An emotional commitment tied to your personal identity, however, pushes you to move forward and to overcome all obstacles and trials along the way. When your heart is committed and it resonates with who you are, you're more inclined to persist, no matter how difficult it might seem. Your heart simply is better equipped than your intellect to bring about lasting change.

If you don't want the influence or happiness that can come from better relationships or you don't see how improving your people skills will make you more valuable in the business world no matter what direction you take, then the odds are against your adopting what this book teaches. On the other hand, if you tie it to something you really want, the odds of making permanent improvements in your power to influence others jumps up dramatically.

You currently have well-established communication and relationship patterns with those you know. They're like big freeways in your brain. Looking at these relationships, however, from the "DNA" perspective opens up a whole new way of relating to these people. You're creating a small new pathway in your mind. Your heart will buy into the change if you can envision and experience the feeling of what it would be like to more effectively influence and relate to those people through DNA principles. A potent motivator for change is being the best and most influential you, you can be. Seeking a more specific positive outcome that can be measured and recognized when it is achieved is even a better change catalyst. Significant and permanent improvements will come naturally as you focus your thoughts and emotions on that outcome.

Treating others as they want to be treated because you understand their drives, needs and aptitudes will change your relationships. Making this type of change is akin to a paradigm shift. Instead of reacting to the behavior of those you know or falling into the same interaction behavioral patterns, you'll now be approaching these relationships from an entirely new perspective—looking at their behavior through the filters of their (not your) DNA colors. You'll be different in what you observe and in how you respond to what you observe. You'll see things you've missed up until now and your influence will grow. The key for now is to visualize in vivid detail what having that kind of positive influence with those you know will be like for you and for them. Then make that vision a reality.

Creating a Support Network

The key component to successful change when it comes to DNA is to solidify this new pattern of observing and responding to others from consistent observation and testing of the DNA principles. That can come when you have a support network that holds you accountable and encourages you to stay the course.

First, find someone to be accountable to for implementing this new approach. Communicate no less than weekly with this confidante and account for what you promised you would do the prior week. Set new targets and make appropriate adjustments based on the results achieved. Then account to that confidante the following week for what action steps you promised to take. Yes, this takes effort and discipline, but making yourself accountable to another for your commitment to change shows how much you really want the result. The confidante will help you to stick with it.

I'm not talking about your making small and subtle changes to how you relate to your colleagues, subordinates, bosses or clients because you probably won't notice, let alone get excited about, the subtle changes subtle efforts produce. Change how you talk to your colleagues, friends and family members and how you listen. Change how you start the conversation and how you end it. Change the conversation and relationship patterns by consciously observing what is happening and discerning what is driving the other person to act and talk the way they are.

Make notes of what you observe. Go back to and review those notes before your next encounter with that person. Decide what actions to take to implement the DNA principles and strategies you've learned. Notice the changes your new behavior causes. You're starting to construct a new highway of relating to these people in your mind and your behavior will spur them to relate to you differently. Understanding and valuing their drives and needs when you communicate with them will lead to greater influence. When your influence with them grows, you'll build the necessary emotional momentum to make such changes permanent.

You'll misidentify some people's DNA colors along the way. But the new approach will become more comfortable and more rewarding. You'll become more confident in applying what you've learned and you'll start to take bigger risks by using the principles in entirely new settings with people you've just met.

If you're not sure what someone's DNA color is, check out your conclusions and the facts that support them with someone else who has read this book. Chances are that each of you will see things that the other missed. You'll learn of more mixed signals. You'll both improve your observation skills from the interaction because each of you is now more attuned to what was missed in the last "diagnosis."

Permit me to share an example. My wife Laura and I attended an awards banquet for one of our daughters and sat next to a mother and daughter that neither of us had ever met. I'll refer to the mother as Dianne. When Dianne first started talking to us, she somehow got on the subject of how her husband "lived" before she met him. Dianne's husband used to use the same glass each day for mixing an "Instant Breakfast"; he would then do a quick rinse of the glass with water and set it on the counter to use the next day. Dianne's husband apparently never washed the glass. After Dianne met him and saw this, she told us she spent a long time scouring the glass to make it clean again from all the "instant breakfast powder" build up.

If someone told this to you about their spouse right out of the gate, what color DNA would you guess she has? Here's what I thought. The woman wanted to explain how hard she worked to restore quality and to contrast her orderliness with her husband's sloppiness. Her behavior doesn't sound like Yellow because it sure doesn't seem fun. An Aqua probably wouldn't come out and make a statement to Laura and me that might be viewed as being critical of her husband; in fact, an Aqua probably would prefer to let her husband "march to the beat of his own dirty glass" no matter where that might take him. So Aqua and Yellow are out of the picture. Blues value orderliness and cleanliness, but letting strangers know what she did to address her husband's messy habit could be Red too. So it's down to two colors.

I took a closer look at what Dianne was communicating to me about her DNA by her appearance. Dianne was impeccably dressed. Makeup and hair were perfectly in place. Eye contact was strong. Dianne was very direct in how she sat and talked. Blues like to look sharp and so do Reds. Blues have good eye contact with those they feel they can trust. Reds have strong eye contact with most everybody.

But Reds are more direct and concise in how they relay information. So neither color was eliminated by looking at what Dianne was communicating by her appearance and nonverbal gestures. But Dianne was leaking a little more Red than Blue.

Dianne then told Laura about how she left a small town of less than five thousand in Wisconsin as a teenager and traveled with a group to New York where she slept in basements of churches along the way. Dianne explained how she told her mother at age eighteen she was heading off to UCLA. UCLA, of course, is in Los Angeles, a city of millions of residents; that paints a stark contrast to her small home town in Wisconsin. Dianne didn't ask her mother back then whether it was ok to go to UCLA. She wanted the big change. Dianne indicated to us that she asked her mother recently why she hadn't tried to stop Dianne from moving away and her mother responded that Dianne seemed so determined about her decision to make the change, that her mother didn't dare try to stop her. Now one DNA color is emerging as the more likely choice.

Most of what Dianne said she did pointed to Red. Dianne's life story was the focus of the conversation and Dianne did most of the talking. That is more Red than Blue. Blues generally ask questions of and show some interest in those with whom they're talking. Dianne didn't show much interest in learning more about us.

Dianne's stories as a teenager showed she was a risk taker willing to make bold decisions and break away from secure surroundings. Furthermore, Dianne was sharing with us her accomplishments, a natural thing for Reds to do. So I concluded that Dianne was Red.

When we were walking to the car after the event, Laura commented: "Boy, was she Red!" I wasn't aware Laura was even thinking about what DNA color Dianne was or what observations led Laura to make that comment, but Laura was right. Dianne was acting Red. Dianne could have been a Blue trying to act Red but her life story conflicts with that conclusion. If I had explored it, Laura probably would have shared things I had missed and I would have shared observations that Laura missed, but we both got the gist of what Dianne was leaking—Red.

Each interaction with another is an opportunity to apply what you're learning and bounce your conclusion off of others who know the system or test it with the person you're trying to identify by addressing them according to to the drives and needs of the DNA color you think the person is. The more you do it, the better you get and the more influential you become.

It's easier to begin working on the "diagnosis" skills. There's no risk involved in observation, just conscious effort to observe and note all that they communicate, verbally and nonverbally. But don't do it alone. Get another person involved who has read this book. Then compare notes. It helps both of you to refine your observation skills.

Changing The Company For The Better

Getting your company to adopt DNA people skills as a new paradigm for communicating with and influencing others is a big challenge. It will seem like a radical change to most in your company and so you'll likely encounter active and passive resistance. Many, if not most, may go through the motions with DNA training unless they feel an emotional commitment to change because of a desired outcome or unless this type of change gains enough momentum and "converts" to become part of your company's culture. Providing incentives for change will help. An incentive that inspires change with your management team or employees may be a promotion, recognition, a raise, a bonus or a new opportunity to advance in their field. Here are a few strategies to help you achieve global change inside your business.

Identify And Reward The Early Adapters

Look for those who are most likely to respond positively and immediately to the incentives to adopt the DNA principles to lead the way. They can be any DNA color but more often than not they will be Red or Yellow. Reds like to take risks and are quick to see whether new information or skills can advance them in their careers. Reds love monetary incentives and those that will increase their power or status. Yellows also are quick to decide and take action and love the attention they would get from being openly rewarded for their efforts. When these early adapters get positive results from applying the DNA principles, set up meetings where they share their success stories and re-teach the key principles by having the early adapters tell the rest of the group how they applied these principles to achieve the desired outcomes. Co-workers are much more inclined to follow one of their own because they see it is no longer just abstract theories but principles that produce tangible results. Using the early adapters to reinforce the power of the DNA principles will increase the motivational commitment of the entire group, particularly when the similar incentives are offered for those who follow their leadership.

Role Play

One strategy we use that works very well with companies is role play. Let me share with you what we do for companies and you then can decide how you want to adapt it to your business. With management authorization, we send an e-mail to all employees who will participate in the DNA training and we ask them to come up with situations that they confront in their jobs where working with some type of person has been a problem or challenge. We tell them to send these situations to us confidentially and we tweak their descriptions of the problem person (the "antagonist") a bit to exaggerate some aspects of his or her personality.

We do this to make it a little easier for the group to identify the dominant DNA color. Our changing some of the characteristics of the antagonist also helps to protect the innocent (and the guilty). Once we teach the group in a seminar format all about the four DNA personality groups, we proceed with a series of role plays so that the principles come to life before their very eyes.

We create multiple scenarios where I or another trainer takes on the role of being the antagonist. Each scenario has an objective—to get the employee to try to influence the antagonist into doing something differently so the problem gets solved or goes away. For each scenario, we consciously select an employee participant that we know has a different DNA color than the antagonist. The participant is then told to influence the antagonist to change his or her behavior to solve the problem.

Because we, as trainers, know each of the personality groups well, we are better equipped to react to what the participant does and to "throw some curves" along the way that will stimulate even more understanding of the DNA principles.

We start the role play and let the participant try to correct the behavioral problem using the people skills she has developed thus far. After a few minutes of generally unsuccessful persuasion, the role play is stopped and everyone is asked to vote on what DNA color the antagonist is. The DNA color getting the most votes will form the basis for the influence strategy that the group will tell the participant to use. The participant and the group may go back to a PowerPoint slide on how to deal with someone with that DNA color before resuming with the role play.

If the majority's conclusion about the antagonist's DNA color is wrong, it will soon become evident, because the antagonist won't react well to the employee's efforts to resolve the problem. The participant won't be treating the antagonist as he wants to be treated. The group will then understand not only intellectually but also experientially why you can't influence people effectively if you don't understand what drives them and what their needs are.

If the majority made a mistake, then we have them vote again as to what is the antagonist's DNA color. I have never trained any group or company where the majority of participants don't get it right either the first or the second time. When the majority of the group is right in the detection of the DNA color and then tells the participant to use strategies that are congruent with the drives and needs of that DNA color, the entire group will experience first hand how the power to influence can grow almost instantaneously.

This impact is enhanced further when the participant directly seeks the advice of those from the audience who have the same DNA color as the antagonist.

Let me share an example from one of my trainings. The antagonist role that I played was an analyst in the Information Technology ("IT") department of the company. This analyst was responsible for taking electronic data received from a client and merging the data into a report using the company's proprietary software. The report was then used to help find transactions where the client had mistakenly paid more than it needed to pay its vendors.

The process of turning the data into a report was often time consuming and difficult, depending on the amount of data through which the analyst needs to wade. The participant I chose was a Red auditor, who I'll refer to as Mary; Mary needed the report from the analyst to help her find various types of overpayments that she could try to recover from the vendors on her client's behalf.

Before beginning the role play, I told Mary that the antagonist had not completed the report for her to use with her client and it was long overdue. Mary's mission was to influence me—the antagonist—-to make her report my top priority. I told Mary facts about prior experiences she and others had had with me, which created the impression that I was soft spoken, easy going and non-confrontational.

Remember, Mary was Red and the analyst was an Aqua. This particular scenario probably had occurred many times even before the role play because there were many Aquas in the client's IT department and there were many Red auditors. That made the role play even more impactful as the group saw Mary try to persuade the analyst to get her report done right away. Many had faced or were facing a similar challenge. The realistic scenario made what they learned easily applicable.

We began the role play. Mary's secondary DNA color was Yellow so she was quick to use humor and light pressure, but her Red core became more dominant as resistance built. Mary started with a warm greeting, but then pointed out to me she had waited a long time for me to complete the report. Mary explained that she really needed the report and then asked me when I'd get it to her. I said I would try to get it done within the next week. She thanked me. Mary thought she had done great.

I then stopped the role play and "threw a curve." I told Mary that it was now two weeks later and she still hadn't received the report. Mary had to meet with me again to find out why and get me to commit to a certain deadline and fulfill my commitment. The "curve" I threw wasn't outside what Aquas can do. A shallow promise to someone pressuring them followed by no fulfillment is not uncommon, especially when they don't like the person pressuring them. It's their way of getting revenge.

This time Mary sarcastically expressed her excitement to sit by the phone until she receives my call telling her the report is complete. This was followed by even more pressure to get a firm commitment for a short deadline; but I wouldn't give her one. Mary's softer Yellow side had faded and her negative Red tactics were in total display.

Everyone could see in the audience from my crossed arms and demeanor that I wasn't about to go along with Mary's agenda. I felt the tension and pressure she was putting on me and wanted to resist it and make her wait even longer. All I told her was that I would get around to it and found a way to end the meeting. Neither Mary nor the audience thought Mary had succeeded because she wasn't treating me as I wanted to be treated.

I then stopped the role play and turned to the group of auditors observing this standoff. I asked if anyone else wanted to give it a shot. One gentleman, who I'll call Dan, raised his hand. Dan came up at my request and sat down across from me where Mary once was. Mary had sat on the edge of her seat staring me straight in the eyes. Dan did it differently. Dan's casual posture and manner and limited eye contact palpably reduced the tension in the air. Dan "bled" Aqua. Dan's voice was soft and easy going. Dan first spent some time asking me about how things are going and whether I had seen a movie that had come out a few weeks ago. I literally felt the walls of my resistance start to crumble. I uncrossed my arms and slid back in my seat as Dan talked with me. I felt a desire to help him. Yes, I was playing a role but I didn't have to play it. It felt easy to be open to his influence.

Dan then asked me if I could help him help his client by finishing the report that had been on my desk for a few weeks. Dan wasn't pressuring me. Dan was asking me to help him help the client. As an Aqua, I like to please others when I'm not pressured to do so. I said I would and I meant it. It wasn't a false commitment. I felt connected to Dan by his speaking to me in my language. That role play experience taught the whole group more about the power of influence through speaking the same DNA language than days of my lecturing on all the nuances of DNA principles ever could. It was truly an "Aha" moment for those present.

Everyone at that workshop then realized that they have experts in each of the four personality groups from whom they can seek advice. Your situation is no different. Once you detect the DNA color of someone you want to have influence with, seek out a colleague who has the same DNA color. There are Reds, Aquas, Yellows and Blues in most every company, but even if there aren't, you can find them among your friends or business associates outside your business.

Those who have the same DNA as the person you want to influence can teach you how best to address the drives and needs of that person because they share their same innate core.

You can adapt this type of learning to your business. Doing role plays every couple of weeks with your employees as new situations arise can increase everyone's confidence and skill in detecting and relating to other personality colors. People really enjoy them too.

Once you get "critical mass" in your company—enough employees are sharing stories each week of new successes and doing well in the role plays, then momentum will build and the culture will change. The vast majority will incorporate the skills into their way of relating with others and can begin to see the payoffs that the early adapters enjoy. Those who won't go along will either be left behind and leave the company or they'll be a drag on the company. You could try a role play with them, but if they choose to stay stuck in their old routines, then it's best for them to find another job.

Make It Part Of The Established Process

If you have sales people that work the telephone, have a manager or co-worker listen in on the conversation and share their impressions and observations to see if they agree what DNA color the prospect, customer or client has. Have them jointly develop a strategy for increasing influence with that person by getting them to buy more of your products or services.

When you have any meeting with someone outside the company in which two or more attend from your company, make it a practice to have a debriefing where each participant shares notes on what they observed; the group then plans what steps to take next based upon what they conclude about the outsider's DNA.

Make exposure to and application of the DNA principles part of the new hire training. This increases the likelihood that successful application of the DNA principles will become part of your company's culture. People will start using the DNA lingo when they talk to each other and become more conscious of other people's and their own drives, needs and aptitudes.

Having specific goals where progress can be measured also will enhance the likelihood of success. For example, with each sales associate, have them alternate using and not using the DNA principles with prospects and monitor the results. Again the key to sustained change is making their involvement in the principles deeper and stronger through repeated application and measurement of the results. Measurable improvement from pre-existing practices will continue the momentum towards lasting change.

Schedule bi-weekly or even weekly activities where employees can apply their DNA skills and steadily build up a mastery of these proven principles for increasing the power to influence others. Participate yourself in these activities. Share your successes and even your failures with your team, telling them what you learned from both. Your humility and desire to improve your people skills will motivate them to follow in your footsteps.

It's up to you to get it started. Your commitment to helping your team master the principles of successful influence will create a valuable strategic advantage over your competitors. Your people are your company's most valuable asset. Is there any better time than now to grow your company's revenues by having your people communicate to your vendors, business partners, shareholders, clients and prospects in their DNA "language"? Is there any better time than now to decrease absenteeism, attrition, and employee disgruntlement because they feel valued for who they are and confident about what they best can contribute to enhance the company's success?

C H A P T E R   1 4

*"If a man does not keep pace with his compan-
ions, perhaps it is because he hears a different
drummer. Let him step to the music which he
hears, however measured or far away."*

— Henry David Thoreau

Valuing What Others Bring to the Table

When all is said and done, it matters little what color your DNA is but
it matters greatly what you do with it. If you're a Blue and wish you
were a Yellow, give it up. Your DNA has been and always will be Blue.
You're here for a purpose and your natural strengths can enrich not
only the lives around you but also others you don't know (including
generations to come). It also makes all the difference to being
successful when you truly value the gifts that other colors naturally
bring to you. In fact, devaluing the gifts of the other DNA colors can
lead to your downfall. For example, if you're a Red and see no value in
Aquas, you will sabotage the success that can come from them
naturally compensating for one of your natural weaknesses.

Henry David Thoreau was the quintessential Aqua. Thoreau
modeled the principle of being who he was, which is a great
achievement. But there's another level Thoreau didn't reach—truly
valuing the strengths that other DNA colors brought to the table and
stretching to learn those strengths while staying true to his own identity.

Quotes from Thoreau illustrate his Aqua DNA: *"For an
impenetrable shield, stand inside yourself."* Another reads: *"There are*

continents and seas in the moral world, to which every man is an isthmus or inlet, yet unexplored by him." Looking inside is a natural strength for an Aqua that Thoreau valued and modeled well.

However, Thoreau minimized, ignored or even rejected the great gifts that the other DNA colors brought to the table. Spurning Reds' achievements through the companies they build, the trails they blaze or the dreams they turn into reality, Thoreau commented: *"For many years I was a self appointed inspector of snowstorms and rainstorms and did my duty faithfully, though I never received payment for it."* A Red would ask how did Thoreau benefit society from doing this self-appointed task? He didn't share it with others to help them with their projects. Thoreau seems to be mocking those whose vision and hard work achieved great things to benefit society and were materially rewarded for their efforts. Thoreau then offends the Blues, who value greatly what comes from the heart, with this comment: *"The heart is forever inexperienced."* Thoreau also said: *"The pleasures of the intellect are permanent; the pleasures of the heart are transitory."*

To the Yellows who live to be happy, Thoreau writes: *"The smallest seed of faith is better than the largest fruit of happiness."* In other words, having faith in the mind in the smallest degree is better than experiencing happiness in the largest degree.

Thoreau, with the power of his pen, devalued what the Reds, Blues and Yellows value, while idealizing what the Aquas value. So what's the problem, you might ask? The problem is that he could have been more influential in the lives of others around him if he understood what mattered to them and why.

Thoreau created his own limitations. He stayed within the bounds of his Aqua DNA and deprived himself of the blessings of developing a love for all that others bring to this world from every perspective.

Mahatma Gandhi, on the other hand, exemplified through what he said, the breadth of his character. Gandhi also was an Aqua. But he magnified not only his natural talents but also learned from, appreciated and ultimately developed many of the strengths from the other DNA colors with which he was not born. As to Red, Gandhi recognized what true power can be. His unyielding commitment to non-violence became stronger than any violent resistance could have been to the British empire; Gandhi exercised the power of his personal convictions to change India and the world for generations to come.

Gandhi's compassion for people led him to do many selfless acts akin to a Blue. While boarding a moving train one day, one of Gandhi's shoes slipped off and fell upon the track. As he was unable to retrieve it, Gandhi - to the astonishment of his fellow travelers - calmly removed his other shoe and threw it down the track to where the first had landed. "The poor man who finds the shoe lying on the track," Gandhi explained, "will now have a pair he can use."

Gandhi valued the Yellow perspective. His love for people helped him to stay in the moment and welcome all that came his way. He prized the Yellow virtue of forgiveness; he forgave others easily. Gandhi loved the freedom to express oneself at every moment.

Thus Gandhi became the best and most influential "Gandhi", he could be.

The power that comes from knowing and being true to your DNA is limited. The power that comes from knowing and being true to your DNA and thereafter embracing what those with other DNAs can bring to you is not. Gandhi caught the vision; Thoreau stayed true to himself, but was not the best and most influential Thoreau he could have been. Both are remembered. One had a greater and broader impact on the history of mankind.

"Happiness is when what you think, what you say, and what you do are in harmony."

— Mahatma Gandhi

CHAPTER 15

"If we did the things we are capable of, we would astound ourselves."

— *Thomas A. Edison*

Wrap-Up

Now that you have a better idea of who you are and what makes those around you "tick", here are some concluding thoughts as you go forward in your job, business and career.

First, be yourself. Use your DNA to achieve what you're passionate about. But don't stop there. Look to those outside your DNA color to teach you their strengths and perspectives. Don't focus on your weaknesses. Find the strength in the other DNA colors that is the antidote for each such weakness and look for someone with the DNA color who naturally models that strength. By first valuing and then learning others' strengths, your natural weaknesses will fade into irrelevancy.

Second, inspire others to be who they were born to be and enjoy the fruits that come from their authentic self expression. Leadership is all about bringing out the best in others as you work toward a common goal. You bring out the best in others when you help them to see and be who they are and to bring out the best in themselves.

When you do both, winning friends and influencing people will seem effortless. Being effective in all arenas of your life will come naturally. You'll be in the flow—akin to the experience that skilled athletes tell about when they're performing beyond themselves. "I let the game come to me," they often say and that is what you'll experience at an even deeper level. By embracing and being thankful for not only the God given drives, needs and aptitudes you were born with, but also for those that others share with you along the way, your strengths will increase and expand and your weaknesses will disappear in the eyes of those that you seek to influence. You will be the best "you", you can be.

Enjoy the journey!

"Make the most of yourself for that is all there is of you."

— *Ralph Waldo Emerson*

APPENDICES

1. NATURAL TRAIT DEFINITIONS
2. DNA POINTERS IN A NUTSHELL
3. INFLUENCING OTHER DNA COLORS
   IN A NUTSHELL

APPENDIX 1

NATURAL TRAIT DEFINITIONS

Here are definitions of each of the traits listed in Section 1 of the *DNA Torque™ Personality Profile*.

1.   Animated—Full of life, lively use of hand arm and face gestures.

   Outspoken—Speaks frankly and without reserve.

   Pleasant—Easy going, easy to be around, easy to talk with.

   Sensitive—Attuned to the needs and desires of others and not wanting to offend them.

2.   Competitive—One who loves to compete and competes to win, not to enjoy the experience.

   Disciplined— Establishes and sticks to plans, assignments and schedules until completed or fulfilled.

   Easy going—Tends to go with the flow without raising objections or creating disharmony.

   Playful—Full of fun and good humor.

3.   Mediator—One who helps others resolve their differences.

   Sociable—One who sees being with others as opportunity to be entertaining rather than as a challenge or business opportunity.

   Strong-willed—One who is determined to have his or her own way.

   Well mannered—Follows proper etiquette in carrying out daily activities; adheres to and shows proper respect for established rules for behavior.

4.   Considerate—One who has regard for the needs and feelings of others.

   Patient—Unmoved by delay; remains calm and tolerant in the face of frustration.

   Persuasive—One who is skilled at motivating others to believe or act in a certain way through the charm of his or her own personality.

   Tenacious—Determined to break through any barrier, large or small, to achieve one's goal; won't let go until the goal is accomplished.

5.   Even-tempered—One who tends to take in life's experiences without experiencing emotional peaks and valleys.

   Refreshing—Stimulates others to take a fresh look at their circumstances and to enjoy life more.

   Resourceful—Able to act quickly and effectively in almost all situations.

   Respectful—Treats others with deference, honor and esteem.

6.   Analytical—Likes to examine the parts for their logical and proper relationships.

Charismatic—Draws others like a magnet to be around him or her and to enjoy the experience of being with them.

Confident—Self-assured and certain of own ability and ultimate success.

Dry humor—Exhibits "dry wit" by sharing humorous, often sarcastic one-liners without facial expressions.

7. Funny—Sparkling sense of humor that can make any story into a hilarious event.

Focused—One who is able to center one's attention and actions toward the desired objective or goal.

Nurturing—A person who is motivated to care for others and show concern about their welfare.

Self-governing—One who is adept at taking care of himself or herself without trying to govern others.

8. Adaptable—Easily adjusts to and is comfortable in a variety of situations.

Scheduled—Makes and lives according to a daily plan and dislikes disruption of such plans.

Decisive—Has no problem or hesitation in making a decision in spite of difficult and competing choices.

Spontaneous—One who change plans or activities on the spur of the moment without concern about what effect the change might have.

9. Assertive—Presents his or her views, opinions and thoughts without hesitation or reservation.

Deliberate—Considers and weighs all relevant information and opinions before deciding how to proceed.

Kind—One who has a gentle, considerate nature.

Optimistic—One who tends to see the positive side of events; brings cheer to others.

10. Planner—Prefers to work out a detailed arrangement beforehand for the accomplishment of a project or goal, and prefers involvement with the planning stages and the finished product rather than the carrying out of the project.

Promoter—Urges or compels others to go along do the desired action through charm.

Satisfied—One who accepts any person or situation.

Self-starter—One who will take initiative to move forward on own without prodding.

11. Diplomatic—Deals with people tactfully, sensitively and patiently.

Forgiving—One who finds it easy to forgive others who offend, hurt or mistreat them.

Self-reliant—One who can fully rely on his or her own capabilities, judgment and resources.

Sympathetic—Adept at feeling or trying to fees the emotions others are experiencing as a way of demonstrating that one cares for them.

12.   Cheerful—Consistently in good spirits and promoting happiness in others.

Detail-oriented—Does everything in proper order with a clear memory of all the things that happened.

Open-minded—One who is open to consider new ideas and opinions that may differ from one's own.

Risk-taker—One who is willing to risk failure or defeat to achieve one's goals or objectives.

13.   Contemplative—Enjoys pondering the mysteries of life and philosophical or scientific notions.

Independent—Self sufficient, self supporting, self confident and seems to have little need of help.

Inspiring—Encourages others to work, join or be involved and makes the whole event fun.

Intuitive—Tends to rely on and be guided by gut instincts, even though it may conflict with what seems like the most logical approach; senses what to do rather than figuring out what to do.

14.   Committed—Inclined to stick with whatever promises one makes or causes one pursues even when the going gets tough.

Consistent—Stays emotionally on an even keel, responding the same way when similar circumstances arise.

Demonstrative—Loves to gesticulate with facial expressions and use of arms, hands, feet and the entire body to express what he or she wants to communicate.

Positive—One who is confident it will turn out right if he or she is in charge.

15.   Creative—One who is talented at expression of oneself in a nonlinear way through, art, music, theater, poetry etc.

Innovative—Out of the box type thinking that is not a logistical extension of existing approaches, norms or processes; random, wild, and brilliant idea generation.

Inventive—One who comes up with ways to make the most of the resources at hand to create new devices, things or approaches.

Productive—Constantly in action to get things done and often finds it difficult to relax and do nothing.

16.   Conversationalist—Skilled at conversing with anyone on a variety of topics with little need for advance preparation.

Faithful—Consistently reliable, steadfast, and loyal to one's beliefs or relationships.

Tolerant—Easily accepts the thoughts and ways of others without the need to disagree with or change them.

Future-focused—One who focuses her time and energy on working toward future goals and objectives rather than enjoying what is in the present.

17.   Energetic—Full of life; vigorous, lively.

Leader—A natural born director, who is driven to be in charge of and make the decisions for the group.

Listener—Always seems willing to hear what you have to say.

Loyal—Faithful to a person, ideal or job even at times where it is no longer beneficial to one's well-being.

18.   Engaging—Skilled at involving others in a conversation or activity by making it interesting and fun.

Mover—Makes things happen; one who tends to lead others to move forward toward desired goals or objectives.

Orderly—One who has a thoughtful systematic approach to the arrangement of things.

Steady—Stable, not subject to sharp highs and lows; not inclined to overwork and not take time to rest and relax.

19.   Daring—Willing to take risks; fearless; bold.

Informal—Not interested in ceremony, appearance or adhering exactly to established ways of doing things; not inclined to dress up unless it is absolutely necessary.

Resilient—Readily able to recover from and adjust to change, misfortune or tragedy and to leave the past behind so they can enjoy the present moment.

Self-sacrificing—One who is willing to put others' needs or objectives ahead of his or her own.

20.   Gentle—Treating others with kindness and without harshness or cruelty.

Precise—Loves to have things conform strictly to standards set; likes things to be completely accurate.

Powerful—Taking charge; making things happen; influencing others to act.

Storyteller—Loves to share stories about themselves and others and to spice up the details to make it interesting for others to listen to.

21.   Ambivalent—Tends to hold conflicting feelings or opinions about things with neither dominating the other; wishy-washy.

Bossy—Commanding, domineering, sometimes overbearing in adult relationships.

Rebellious—One who tends to rebel against those who try to control him or her.

Overly cautious—unduly hesitant to take action, fearful of negative consequences even if the chances of such consequences occurring may be quite small.

22. Obnoxious— Showy, flashy, comes on strong, too loud.

    Distant—Tends not to interact with others because he or she is lost in own thoughts.

    Moody—Gets into mood swings that vary greatly depending on what is happening to them that day.

    Abrasive—One who often comes across as harsh and rough in dealing with others.

23. Impatient—A person who finds it difficult to endure irritation, tolerate delay or wait for others.

    Undependable—One who often does not do what he or she promises or commits to do, but offers excuses.

    Resentful—Often holds ill feelings as a result of real or imagined offenses.

    Reluctant—Unwilling to get involved if involves large effort or necessary interaction with others.

24. Fearful—Often experiences feelings of deep concern, anxiety or apprehension, especially when it requires conflicts in relationships with others.

    Distracted—One who easily loses focus or jumps from one topic, project or assignment to another without finishing what he or she started.

    Blunt—Tells it as he or she sees it without concern about how it affects or whether it offends others.

    Fussy—Insistent over petty matters or details, calling for great attention to trivial issues.

25. Absent-minded—Tending to forget what one has done or where one has placed things because one is lost in thought.

    Insecure—One who lacks confidence about his or her abilities and talents and worries about what others think of him or her.

    Haphazard—Has no consistent way of doing things.

    Headstrong—Insists on having his or her own way most all the time.

26. Indecisive—One who has a hard time reaching a decision because he or she has no strong feelings about the existing alternatives.

    Insensitive—Not concerned about what others think or whether one's words or actions will hurt or offend others.

Unpredictable—May be ecstatic one moment and down the next, or who expresses willingness to help and then disappears when the help is needed or promises to come but fails to show up.

Worrier—One who devotes large amounts of time thinking about all the negative things that might happen to them or others instead of being engaged in the present.

27. Interrupter—One who interrupts others as they are speaking.

Hard-to-please —A person whose standards are set so high that it is difficult to ever satisfy them.

Argumentative—Incites arguments generally because one is certain that one is right and that other ideas and opinions are wrong, no matter what the actual facts are.

Quiet—One who tends to stay silent even when others request their input or seek to know where they are at.

28. Indifferent—A person to whom most things don't matter one way or the other.

Arrogant—Believing one is smarter, knows more or otherwise is more competent than others with whom one interacts.

Permissive—Allows others (including children) to do as they please in order to be liked or accepted by them.

Pessimistic—One who focuses primarily on what's wrong or not working out or missing in one's life or areas where one's self or others' mistakes or weaknesses.

29. Aimless—Not a goal setter and having little desire to be one.

Inflexible—One who has a difficult time adjusting to changes in plans or doing things different than the established norm.

Selfish—One who generally looks at options from perspective of what is in it for him or her more than what may be best for the team or organization.

Cluttered—One who allows things to be unorganized and scattered because of lack of concern about order or perfection.

30. Confrontational—Has no hesitation to confront and battle others, verbally or otherwise even when he or she has little or no ground for taking the position that invites opposition and conflict.

Naïve—Simple and childlike perspective, lacking sophistication or consideration for the complexities of particular situations.

Flippant—Treating serious matters lightly or with irreverence.

Sarcastic—Making comments that carry a sting and are subtly disguised attacks towards others with whom they are displeased.

31. Self Critical— Harsh on one's own performance, ignoring what one did well and focusing on mistakes.

Impulsive—Tends to act on impulse without thinking through the consequences of one's actions ahead of time.

Silently stubborn—Resisting those who try to control by keeping quiet and not cooperating or obeying what has been requested or demanded or by agreeing to obey but silently deciding not to do so.

Merciless—One who is not inclined to be compassionate towards someone who he or she sees as a competitor, even if it is a co-worker or subordinate preferring to let them learn the lesson from "the school of hard knocks."

32.   Easily offended— Tending to get one's feelings hurt easily because of heightened sense of fairness, high expectations or hypersensitivity to others' behavior towards them.

Withdrawn—One who turns inward and becomes uncommunicative in times of conflict and turmoil.

"In your face"—One who aggressively and directly confronts someone he is talking to.

Too talkative—Compulsively talking without taking time to listen to others or to allow moments of silence.

33.   Disorganized—Diminished ability to get one's life and activities in order.

Domineering—Compulsively takes control of situations and people, usually telling others what to do.

Timid—Shrinks from difficult situations.

Fatalistic—Tendency to accept bad things happening as if that is how things were meant to be instead of trying to change circumstances to get better results.

34.   Guilt-ridden—One who uses guilt to manipulate others and whose own conduct is strongly influenced by feelings of guilt about one's behavior falling short of expectations.

Inconsistent—Erratic, contradictory, with actions based on transitory emotions rather than logic.

Apathetic—Lacking strong opinions or beliefs or passion.

Intimidating—Strong and forceful in approach.

35.   Easily bored—Prone to get frustrated unless life is filled with constant stimulating activities.

Crafty—Shrewd; lacking some or all scruples in getting what one wants.

Unforgiving—One who has difficulty releasing or forgetting a hurt or injustice done to him or her; apt to hold onto a grudge.

Passive—Stands by and lets things bad happen instead of taking action to prevent it from happening; slow to try to change what one does not like because it seems to require too much effort.

36.   Aggressive—Driven to get what one wants.

Noncommittal—Not inclined to commit one's time and efforts towards a project or cause.

Show-off—Needs to be the center of attention, wants to be noticed.

Skeptical—Disbelieving, questioning the motive behind the words.

37.   Dictatorial—Leads by own agenda, regardless of whether it is best for the group or team.

Rule driven—One who believes strongly that all rules must be followed to the letter.

Lazy—Evaluates work or activity in terms of how much work it takes and chooses to spend least amount of energy necessary.

Rule bending—One who is easily inclined to bend or break the rules when they tend to interfere or restrict what he or she wants to do.

38.   Forgetful—Lack of memory which is usually tied to lack of concern for remembering what has happened because focus is on what is now happening.

Short tempered—Quickly gets angry when others are not moving fast enough and have not completed what they have been asked to do. Impatient with mistakes.

Suspicious—Tends to suspect and/or distrust the motives and sincerity of others.

Gullible—Easily deceived or duped.

39.   Exacting—Willingness to forgive another only if one senses the person apologizing is sufficiently sincere and future actions clearly show expected change in behavior.

Rash—May act hastily, without thinking things through, in drive to move things forward.

Reticent—Unwilling to commit or to get involved , especially when requires a lot of effort.

Restless—Likes constant new activity because it is not fun to do the same things all the time.

40.   Abdicating—Inclined to give up own power or control in face of challenge or confrontation.

Changeable—Easily inclined to change or abandon plans even if already committed to be present or perform under the original plans.

Manipulative—Influences shrewdly for his or her own advantage and to get one's own way.

Alienated—Easily feels estranged from others often because of insecurity or fear that others don't really enjoy his or her company.

Appendix 2
DNA POINTERS IN A NUTSHELL

RELATIONSHIP SKILLS FOR A POWERFUL RED

DO

- Realize others may occasionally be right
- Listen with intent to understand
- Lead, don't push
- Learn to compromise and cooperate with others
- Learn to apologize
- Lighten Up
- Validate others by restating in your own words what you heard them say
- Let people offer opinions, without cutting them off
- Request (not demand) others' actions; use "please" and "thank you"
- Learn to relax so you won't become a workaholic

DON'T

- Expect everyone to do it your way
- Assume you know everything
- Assume everyone wants your advice
- Embarrass individuals in front of others
- Expect everyone to produce at the same level and with the same intensity as you do
- Intimidate others whose help or cooperation you need

RELATIONSHIP SKILLS FOR A PEACEFUL AQUA

DO

- Practice making and expressing choices
- Share opinions and ideas
- Prepare to contribute at team meetings
- Show enthusiasm with body language
- Trust your own abilities
- Take action despite perceived fears
- Set goals and achieve them
- Find your passion and pursue it
- Be willing to take a risk
- Speak more authoritatively and confidently
- Listen with interest and respond vocally to what is said
- Focus more on your strengths than your weaknesses
- Write down problems that need a decision and decide

DON'T

- Get locked into routines
- Sell yourself short
- Be a wet blanket on others' ideas or spontaneity
- Sacrifice your dreams for the sake of avoiding conflict
- Let resentment build. It can come out in a huff or as sarcasm in your "one-liner" humor
- Procrastinate and expect others to do your work
- Stay quiet when something is bothering you; share it in a kind way

RELATIONSHIP SKILLS FOR AN OPTIMISTIC YELLOW

DO

- Listen for and use other person's name
- Tone down the volume
- Draw others into conversation
- Be comfortable in silence
- Remember and keep your commitments
- Practice listening to understand, not to "one-up"
- Get a personal calendar and keep a schedule
- Find someone to help you be accountable for your goals and objectives
- If interrupted, continue a story only if asked
- Include those not speaking into the conversation
- Work out all the steps and details of what needs to be done before doing it

DON'T

- Be lax with other people's schedules
- Be self-absorbed
- Be late to appointments and meetings
- Exaggerate the facts to increase interest
- Expect others to protect you all the time
- Walk into a room "talking"
- Blurt out comments whenever there is silence
- Commit yourself to too many projects

RELATIONSHIP SKILLS FOR A PERSONABLE BLUE

DO

- Lighten up!
- Celebrate your accomplishments
- Receive compliments graciously
- Develop your artistic talent without getting paralyzed by your own internal critic (e.g. "I did lousy" or "I'm not good enough")
- Let go of perceived offenses against you
- Surround yourself with upbeat people
- Express gratitude daily for what you have
- Live fully in the present moment
- Ease up on any perfectionist standards you have for yourself and others—perfectionism can cause procrastination and ruin relationships
- Communicate needs and attend to them
- Look for and share positive observations of others

DON'T

- Get immobilized by past failures and mistakes
- Expect everyone to organize their lives like you
- Let your regimentation keep you from enjoying unanticipated opportunities
- Take things so personally and over-read what others communicate to you
- Overwhelm others with details
- Ramble on and on when you're talking to others
- Make everyone play 20 questions to find out what's going on with you
- Do yourself what you delegated others to do because you think you can do it better

Appendix 3
INFLUENCING OTHER DNA COLORS IN A NUTSHELL

Relationship Skills for Dealing **With** A Powerful Red

- Don't take abrupt style personally
- Keep communication short, to the point
- Give recognition and praise achievements
- Give bottom line first and details only if requested
- Perform competently and be accountable
- When approach with problem, offer potential solutions
- Don't emote; communicate logically what you are feeling if Red has offended or mistreated you by words or conduct
- Don't expect compassion or sensitivity; Red wants you to lift yourself up by your bootstraps and move ahead when things go bad

Relationship Skills For Dealing **With** A Peaceful Aqua

- Show respect/look for positive and freely give encouragement
- Get comfortable with silence; don't fill it with your voice
- Give a few rather than many alternatives to choose from
- Ask for their input and patiently persist with your request
- Express appreciation for their efforts
- Wait to speak until they are finished talking
- Give them space and time to reflect and decide; but set up reasonable boundaries and time limitations within which to decide
- Encourage Aqua to express opinions in writing or one-on-one with you if Aqua feels uncomfortable in group setting

Relationship Skills For Dealing **With** An Optimistic Yellow

- Be enthusiastic
- Listen to and enjoy their stories without getting hung up on complete accuracy
- Get out of the box; be open to their and your own creativity
- Give them your attention
- Praise them for their efforts
- Give them freedom and flexibility
- Offer short term incentives for getting desired performance
- Don't get locked into schedule; be willing to change plans and
- enjoy moment—Seize the day!

Relationship Skills for Dealing **With** A Personable Blue

- Don't interrupt activities or communication
- Respect their need to give and seek input
- Take care of the details
- Empathasize with them
- Prepare – think through what you will say before saying it
- Be sincere and genuine
- Be patient in earning their trust
- Listen with intent to understand, not to fix whatever problem they are encountering
- Encourage them to try new things and support them when they do

"Torque Up" the Performance of Your Business

Have you ever tried to change lanes while driving only to swerve back when you hear a loud honk from a car you hadn't seen in your rear view mirror? The car was in your blind spot. If we don't check our blind spots before changing lanes, we could suffer serious injury or even death.

Are there "blind spots" in your business that are dragging down its overall performance? Are there processes and procedures inside your company that run at odds with one another so that the harder you try to move ahead in one direction, some process beneath the radar is working just as hard to pull it back to the same place you started?

The DNA of Successful Leaders teaches you about "blind spots" you may have with your relationships inside and outside the company. However, other "blind spots" can hamper your business from growing. Faulty structural and system dynamics inside your company can cause stagnation and even insolvency despite how hard you and your team work.

Torque Solutions' mission is to **"torque up"** or optimize the performance by making sure the human and structural dynamics in your business work in harmony toward achieving the strategic objectives of your business. We identify the blind spots in your company and help you to design human and structural processes and systems that remove these blind spots.

For further information on how we can help your business take the next step to **"torque up"** its profitability, visit our web site at

TorqueSolutions.com

Dedication

Thank you to my friends and family for your feedback and critiques. They were most appreciated: Tony Arenella, Chel Cartmill, Janice Lee, Kelli Lee, Susan Powell, and Emma Lee Spencer, to name a few.

I have had many impressions, lessons, and ultimately a legacy of knowledge from my childhood for which I am thankful. Lessons learned were not always fun, nor were they easy. However, they were consistent and the messages clear. Thank you, Mom, Dad, and my extended family.

As a young person I remember a number of themes shared in our family unit. These were the memorable refrains in ours:

- **No one loves you more than your family.**
- **The early bird gets the worm.**
- **Nothing happens without a plan.**
- **Things happen for a reason** *(maybe more from Mom than Dad).*
- **Squeeze the juice.**
    - Dad always shared that you want to get the best out of life and out of a situation. "Squeeze the juice," he would say. Take in the moment and experience the very essence of the conversation, the view, the game, and so on. It means to be present. The moment is a gift.
    - I find this to be true and I can apply it to just about any situation.

a. an employee, to see that he or she is thriving and getting the most out of his or her contribution in the practice

b. a client conversation over lunch, deepening the relationship and creating an "aha" moment

c. baking a chocolate cake with my nephew Harrison

d. standing in front of the Colosseum in Rome taking in the awesome history

e. conversing with the local safari guide about his life at 5 a.m. in Botswana

f. watching my niece Emma gracefully execute her ballet routine

g. being there with niece Kate through Zoom as she makes chicken marsala by herself for the first time

h. watching Kelli teach Grayson to trust her and learn to swim

i. teaching Olivia to make pizza her way

j. having Sara for the weekend to play house

Contents

Squeeze the Juice

Live with purpose, then leave a legacy.

Written by Jennifer R. Lee, AWMA®, AIF®

The Juice in Life: Communicating Your Essence

Why you should write your family love letter, your ethical will

Writing your family love letter is an opportunity to communicate values, stories, experience, knowledge, and family history. To be given the awesome opportunity to communicate your most important messages is a *gift*. I learned this firsthand from my mentor and life's greatest influence. My dad was diagnosed with glioblastoma multiforme, the fastest-growing form of brain cancer. This was an unexpected shocking revelation. This man at 71 was athletically inclined playing tennis and golf weekly. He worked fifty-plus hours a week serving and taking care of clients. He participated in the Rotary Club, his community, and his church. He was a wonderful husband, father, grandfather, brother, and friend.

When faced with this terrible diagnosis, here is how my dad handled things:

Love letters can come in many forms. For my family they came as important discussions and notes on a yellow legal pad and in person.

Growing up, my siblings and I were met with regular messages, many times chores assigned, on our dad's beloved yellow legal pads. We had the distinct pleasure of having a father who made the effort to communicate—no pretense, straight from the heart, and straight from his moral compass.

Our father was diagnosed with an aggressive brain tumor. He knew that this was a battle he would not likely win. You see, my dad was a strategist and a realist. There's nothing like a life-threatening disease to jump-start a planner's mind. The immediate response was not to cry or feel self-pity; it was to assess the situation, review his life, develop a plan, and set that plan in motion. It was a bit of damage control, shall we say? Of course, there were tears and there was sadness. This pragmatic, family-focused Dad, involved grandparent, this incredible man had to wrap things up. He had to take care of his family. And now!

My dad was taken to the ER on a Friday evening. He was prescribed an aspirin (for fear he may be having a stroke). After an MRI he was later diagnosed with a brain mass. My mom has always been a big believer in "Things happen for a reason." I agree. You see, this simple little aspirin was a God-given gift to our family. This one aspirin would pause any potential surgery for seven to ten days. It freed our family to embark on our planned vacation. We could now travel together and spend an entire week connecting, talking, grieving, and celebrating us.

At 6:00 a.m. on the first day of our family summer vacation, my sister asked me to come upstairs to the upper deck. Our father was calling a family meeting. "Why 6:00 a.m.?" you ask. Because you see, our dad was an early riser. He had been up since 4 a.m. working on his legal pad, making notes, and to him we had slept long enough. Besides, we had been trained—"The early bird gets the worm."

In truth, he was terrified that he might not have many remaining opportunities to share all he was thinking. The disease was in his brain and was already impacting his left arm. He had no idea of how the disease or the pending surgery would impact his mind. And so— get up already!

Pause: God forbid, if something like this were to happen to you, what does your family need to know? What do you want to communicate to your spouse, kids, grandkids, business partner, best friend, spiritual counselor, neighbors, employees, and so on? If you really take a moment, this is an exceptionally important communication. Where are your passwords? How do you feel about those specific people? What does your family need to know about how to manage finances? How much life insurance do you have and with whom? Who are your trusted advisors and friends who can lend a hand? What are your favorite charities and why? Where do you want your funeral service? Who should speak at it? What do you want people to remember about you? Will it be a party or a somber event? Who should receive your jewelry and most precious possessions and what do they signify to you? Why do you want this specific person to receive them? Where did you hide jewelry, guns, or cash?

This information is in your head and your head only—so speak, write, get it out!

Our dad's love letter had little juicy tidbits with his personality attached. A favorite of mine: "When you go out to dinner, please don't let your mother pull out her Visa card—ever!" This is funny because he still has me jumping; only now I'm the one reaching for the check.

> ## This information is in your head and your head only—so speak, write, get it out!

I share this story to illustrate the wonderful man we were fortunate enough to have and to demonstrate the significance of communicating such a love letter. Our family was given the most generous gift of time and for this we are grateful.

Before he passed, our father emphasized that he had enjoyed a good life. He was blessed. He had a wonderful family and loved his wife and kids. He had strong and loving relationships with his sisters. He had enjoyed playing with and loving on his grandchildren. He had loved his work (it never felt like work) and felt that he had contributed to the lives of his clients and community. He had traveled and seen and enjoyed things he could never have imagined as a child. And he knew God.

How blessed to know that your life was well lived! I wish this kind of peace for everyone.

While we had only five months from diagnosis, we were able to "squeeze the juice out of life" with our dad. We communicated and celebrated together, shared stories, and connected. I feel privileged to have had that time.

I encourage you to communicate to those you love and to those who depend on you. Talk to your family; discuss the difficult things. Life can be short. We never know when we will leave this earth.

And we never know if we will be given the precious gift of time to share those last-minute important items.

For many this can be a daunting task to execute. Consider talking with an estate planning attorney, trusted advisor, spiritual advisor, coach, your spouse, and best friends to help iron out and consider these important discussions.

Warmly,

P.S. If you would like to use a template of a love letter to get the juices flowing, you can find it on our website: https://www.modern-wealth.com/loveletter

2015 Outer Banks Family Disney Night

2015 Annual Tie Dye Beach Night

CHAPTER 1

My Husband Handles That

When I first moved to Florida it was an adjustment. Not only was I in a new place, but this place felt like a continuous vacation. Palm trees and sunshine engulfed my daily life. I could feel the angst and stress just melt away with the sun. I ate it up. The challenge, of course, was making this a permanent gig and locating my work mojo.

Not knowing anyone but a realtor and a few local clients, I set out to find a networking group. In Maryland, where I had resided my entire life, I had a network of clients, family, friends, professional referral sources, and business owners. I had enjoyed plenty of lunch dates and solid connections. In Florida I was limited. I needed a network.

If you are the slightest bit shy or introverted, events like cocktail parties or professional networking groups can be painful. By the end of this book you will not likely think of me as shy, but I am more introverted than not. I much prefer a small dinner party or to be tucked away at a huge event having a deeper, more meaningful discussion. You will not find me dancing on tables or working the room. It's just not my thing.

As I started over in Florida, I found that I had to negotiate with myself when it came to this type of event: "When you have three meaningful conversations, you may leave. You must discuss and learn something about the other person—his or her life, business, family interests, and so on." Most times I was gone after that third conversation. After all, I had accomplished my goal.

So here I go, off to a women's networking event and off to promote myself. Honestly, I had not done this in years and maybe some people love this—maybe it feeds their extroverted nature. For others it is a bit of tickle torture and I am the latter. As time went on I became more comfortable. I knew more people and I eased into staying longer. I even came to run the very networking event where I had started in Florida.

Don't get me wrong, I love what I do for a living. Any discussion around money, strategy, business opportunity, and I'm hooked. I'm good at connecting with people and I enjoy clearing out the noise to get to the root of what drives them. After all, the financial stuff is in my blood.

Some of my first memories are of spending Saturday mornings at my dad's office in downtown Baltimore. I can still smell the old bank building; it was dark and musty. We would park in the alley outside the building. How we did not get towed is beyond me. I remember the thirty-foot ceilings of the bank's foyer, the ancient elevators, and all the wood paneling on the Connecticut Mutual floor. My dad was good at helping his clients and at developing opportunities. He worked hard, making phone calls at night and being up with the birds in the morning. Lucky for me, he was always around for our school events, camping events, Indian princess nights (yes, I did that), and softball games. We kids had a great life because he made it so. His successes provided him a corner office with a private bathroom—a luxury for any executive. And it afforded him a secretary (that was the title then; today we would use "administrative assistant" or "right hand"). Her name was Yvonne. On those Saturdays at the office I played at Yvonne's desk. I stapled things, used note pads, paperclips, tape, dividers. I basically destroyed Yvonne's desk. I would later learn that she was very particular and probably not at all amused with the destruction I left for her Monday morning. It was super fun spending the morning with my dad and having him all to myself.

Here I am in this group of professional women and I'm asked by enthusiastic networkers, "What do you do for a living?" Smiling, I reply, "I'm a financial advisor." If you're an advisor, never, ever say this. You would have thought I had the plague. Woman after woman leaned away from me, physically pulling their bodies back. This was so strange. What in the world was happening? Consistently I was met with two replies: (1) My husband handles that. (2) I have one of you.

My internal defenses screamed, and I'm sure my face may have expressed my horror. What of independence, self-reliance, education, and being personally informed? Whether your husband handles it or not, a woman of the 21st century surely has input and clarity regarding financial matters. She knows where mutual assets sit, who manages those assets, what insurance is in place (just in case), and she is a partner in the future of the family wealth and distribution. She has input. To think otherwise—wow! Was it real? Or was it simply a defense mechanism?

Either way, this "lean back and shut down" was a no-go for me. I went to contemplate what was happening. I evaluated my practice, sought to define the clients whom I loved working with, those who appreciated my counsel and who effortlessly referred their friends because they knew, liked, and trusted me. These were my people. We had meaningful conversations and an authentic relationship. We worked well together, and in fact it was enjoyable. These clients came to me with their most significant worries, and we worked through them together, sometimes adjusting the plan, other times adjusting their budgets. We discussed issues and I brought options until they made sense and were a fit.

I looked at my practice to see how people perceived their relationship with me. What sort of advice or needs were most prevalent? If I were going to start fresh with my messaging and really my brand, who do I want to attract? There are many questions to answer. Who am I trying to reach? Who do I want to work with? Who appreciates my communication style and perspective and is receptive to advice? Whose values are in alignment with mine? Who genuinely cares about their family and business? Who can I help the most and who needs me the most?

After much contemplation and review, the result—my new mantra:

Our firm focuses on the complex and sometimes urgent needs of people in financial transition. Our valued clients leverage us as a resource during these difficult and challenging times. If they are considering a move, divorce, job change, retirement, adding to their family, selling a business, are suffering the loss of a loved one, or are leaving a legacy, they call us.

Why?

Because reliable counsel is most needed at the intersection in life where finance and emotions converge—sometimes in crisis. It is in this collision zone where as advisors we triage the situation and help set the course through the chaos. A good financial advisor can cut through the noise and create a resolution that everyone feels good about.

As for those female networking events—my reply has markedly changed. Now when asked, "What do you do for a living?"—

I work with women in financial transition. I find that women going through a divorce or are recently widowed can benefit from the counsel and perspective I provide.

I help them determine what they really want in their new space in life, assess what they have as resources, and assist in carving their path forward. Women in financial transition need objective counsel and a strategy to deploy their future. Ongoing, they desire a sounding board and I provide that.

These days when I explain "what I do," people are less intimidated. They don't look at me as if I'm a thief or a saleswoman with an angle. Most feel secure in their relationship/marriage and say, "Tell me more." Often they share that they have a friend in the middle of a divorce or one who recently lost a loved one. People get to know me and how I operate my practice. *Know, like, and trust*—without these I am not able to help anyone. I have figured out how to make myself approachable. I can happily report that I have yet to receive another "lean back."

Women in Financial Transition

We have a specialization in transition. We have found that virtually all clients require financial counsel, a fiduciary, and professional coaching. Through empathy, discovery, and thoughtful conversations, we help uncover what life values and family needs are important to our clients. We seek to apply those values and objectives throughout their financial instruments.

CHAPTER 2

Financial Planning Is *Simple*

Many people think financial planning, finance, investments and insurance, trusts, wills and such items are complicated. Certainly they can be involved. And yet there is always a basic outline and application that can be overlaid on even the most complex of scenarios.

When an area is not your natural talent, it can make you pause. It can stop you in your tracks and present as too difficult. Sometimes you can brush aside important considerations. At present, this happens to me anytime I think of making an Instagram post or someone shares a Tik-Tok. It's silly really. How hard can it be? I believe I'm generally less open to the subject because I don't understand how to grasp it. Intellectually I know it cannot be that hard. Kids and teens are constantly posting. And yet . . .

Is it my resistance and fear that cause me to stay in the dark ages?

Let's make a deal. I will embark on the journey of becoming efficient with Instagram. I can't promise too much, but I'll figure out how to post and add these adorable boomerangs on occasion. Ugh—and what of hashtags? I'll ask my nieces. Promise.

Will you continue reading and find at least two things you can do for your future self?

Financial planning is simple. It is a basic formula. It boils down into two simple sets of information you must gather:

1. What do you have? List.

    a. Cash _____

    b. Investments_____

         _____

    c. Job and income_____

         _____

    d. Potential commissions or bonus_____

         _____

    e. Real estate: Home/investment property_____

         _____

f. 401(k) or like investments_____

_____

g. Cash flow, also known as discretionary money_____

_____

h. Inheritance_____

i. Business interest_____

_____

j. Other_____

_____

2. What do you want? Describe.

a. Financial freedom

b. More fun, less work

c. Fridays off

d. Travel budget

e. A specific amount of income

f. A business to feed your spirit or a business to feed your family

g. A lifetime or legacy gift to charity

h. Taking care of family (what is your definition?)

i. Giving your money and business away

j. Empowering others

k. Fully funding your 401(k)

l. Leaving a legacy and so on

m. Other_____

MODERN WEALTH

What do you have?

1.)

2.)

3.)

4.)

Download your worksheet here:
https://SqueezeTheJuiceBook.com/Resources

MODERN WEALTH

What do you want?

1.)

2.)

3.)

4.)

Download your worksheet here:
https://SqueezeTheJuiceBook.com/Resources

I have good news: If you've spent the time responding to the above questions, you're close to being done. The work of thinking through and gathering the information is all you need to do. You can now turn the translation of the material over to your advisor.

> We will work together to find balance between your desires of today and your dreams of tomorrow.

As your fiduciary advisor, we sort through and reconcile your assets with your goals and dreams. We evaluate income and expenses and then consider your discretionary income (on a monthly or annual basis) and allocate flexible money into categories toward your goals. Our job is not to design your life but to make sure that your financial sources are efficiently deployed so they may benefit your specific aspirations. We discuss next steps, cash flow changes, and sometimes concessions you may need to make to provide adequately for your plans. Could there be changes to your current lifestyle? Maybe, maybe not. We'll work together to find a balance between your desires of today and your dreams of tomorrow.

We provide ongoing coaching—also known as financial therapy. Who would not want a coach? What could you do with a personal advocate, assisting with an action plan of your dreams and desires? How nice would it be to have someone to cheer you on as you make great strides in your plans—and someone to pick you up when you feel overwhelmed? Mentorship, clarity, accountability, and motivation all in the direction of your plans: These are services we offer in addition to the technical components of financial planning.

No one grasps every angle or can foresee life's twists and turns in just one meeting. This is a partnership, a relationship. Financial therapy and coaching help get you to be clear about what you want. Understand that life and objectives are ever-changing as jobs, children, family, loves, are added or lost. Ongoing conversations clarify values, which allow your advisor to align assets for their intended purposes. Clients benefit from ongoing and deep discussions.

As advisors we must also observe how people communicate. This I have found to be a life application. It applies directly to you, your family, your friends, and for us and our clients. Many people say what they mean and mean what they say. And that makes things easy. However, most people show you what they mean. They demonstrate through their actions what is important and where their values rest. Watch what they do. And so, vital to planning are continued discussions about important topics.

A little course correction proves worthy. As a rule, and in the simplest of financial situations, clients should meet with their advisor to check in as infrequently as annually. Our clients prefer differing levels of communication, some as frequent as monthly, most quarterly, and still others reach out for annual planning. The caveat with all clients is that any large changes must be communicated immediately. There are constantly changing parts: job changes, residency moves, relationship changes, family losses, family additions, income shifts, economic impacts, and so on. As life happens we may need to amend and adjust the plan or the thought process. Being coached, encouraged, and educated over time makes for sound and well-thought-out financial decisions. Most importantly, our clients know to reach out when something is weighing on their minds.

Think of us as your partners and this process as fluid. There is no quick fix and no final answer.

> Ongoing conversations clarify values,
> which allows your advisor to align assets
> for their intended purposes.
> Clients benefit from ongoing and
> deep discussions.

CHAPTER 3

Are You an Ostrich?

Congratulations, you have made it through to chapter two. Please do not stick your head in the sand to hide like an ostrich.

Often when I begin a seminar or discussion around money, people share that they relate to the ostrich reference. They would much prefer to put their heads in the sand when the subjects of finance, retirement, insurance, income generating property, investment allocation, pension plans, and business insurance arise for discussion. For most it feels easier to avoid money conversations. It feels too scary. Is this you? It does not have to be hair-raising.

> The best advice I can give you if you're an ostrich is to find a financial collaborator with whom you can discuss your aspirations, assets, and worries and who you believe can assist you in your journey.

I recently went to see a new dentist. My spouse had generously and perhaps jokingly shared that I am a scared kitten when it comes to dentists. So here I am nervous enough for an exam and cleaning. The dentist introduces herself all geared up in mask, glasses, and light secured to her head (at least that's how I remember it). She says, "I understand you don't like coming to the dentist. Can you tell me why? This is not a daunting place."

My reply: "I think it's a matter of perspective. May I ask everyone in your office to come in and share their progress as it relates to their retirement strategy, the assets they've accumulated, their personal debt, their tax efficiency, and family security? Do they have a solid plan to replace their income in retirement? Do they have confidence that they continue to refine their financial plan regardless of the economic environment? After all, financial planning is not scary—it's really simple." With her hand on her stomach and a slight grin on her now-nervous face, she replied, "I see your point."

Life and professions are all a matter of point of view. Much like my dentist, I find my professional industry interesting, not intimidating.

Allow me to share my viewpoint about finances. I see money as a tool—a tool that is fully adaptable. I consider it a customizable vehicle that transports an average or good life to a fully satisfied lifestyle filled with adventure, peace, and memorable experiences. Money provides opportunities and experiences in which you can squeeze the juice out of life. It provides the ability to support your family, to provide education and quality time. Having a plan, a long-term vision for your family and your life, is an important step to not being an ostrich. My father proclaimed many times, "Nothing happens without a plan." It drove me mad as an adolescent as it seemed a constant refrain. And of course—it was true.

> Your plan requires thought, intention, and direction. Please do not run away from this.

Your plan does not need to be rigid. In fact, it should be nimble. Sometimes my clients get anxious or even stumped when asked, "What do you want?" They may not have given it any sizeable consideration. Perhaps no one has asked them. If it's a couple, they may not have shared and reconciled their desires. This is fundamental preplanning work.

If you want to get there, anywhere, I can drive the financial train. But please tell me where you would like to go, the views you would like to see, and the experience you would like to have. P.S.—Can you tell me how many passengers will be on the train? And what would they like or need to have in their experience? Now consider the endless possibilities of trips and experiences you can craft.

Ask yourself, "Where am I going? And who will be with me?"

Your plan requires thought, intention, and direction. Please do not run away from this. You may use pencil and you may erase. Pivoting and readjusting are normal, so don't fret over putting something on paper. You are here. This is your life, not a dress rehearsal. This is it! What will you choose to make of it? If you have no idea (Is that true? Is that really true?) of what you want or where you're going, guess what—you will never get there.

> Pivoting and readjusting are normal,
> so don't fret over putting something on paper.

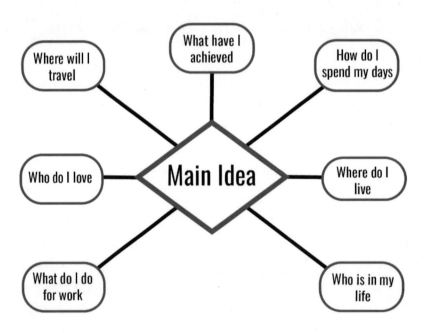

Have you ever tried "mind mapping"? It's an excellent exercise to engage your subconscious and get your creative juices flowing. Above you see a sample "mind map." You may choose to use different-colored pencils or just one. It doesn't matter. My preference is to use one writing implement and run free with my thoughts. I write quickly and try not to think. Just write. I can later refine my thinking and color-code my mind map for reference.

To get started, write your dream or goal at the center of a page, and allow yourself to go wild. Draw quickly, adding ideas off this central topic. Your map will be unique to you. Don't limit yourself—create several or combine into one big map. Try titling one: "My life in five years," "Places to travel," "My work," "My love," "My next business idea," and so on. The choices are unlimited. Don't think—just allow your stream of consciousness to flow. Putting pen to paper taps into the intuitive and creative center of the brain. Allow yourself to dream big. You can amend later. Let your mind flow.

What is a mind map anyway?

*A mind map is a diagram used to visually organize information. A mind map is **hierarchical** and shows **relationships** among pieces of the whole* (Wikipedia).

Once you've completed your mind maps, you'll be on your way to abandoning "ostrich hood." Dodging the subject of your financial future was okay in your twenties, but how long can you stay in denial before it really impacts your ability to thrive? When time was on your side, you had some additional benefits, such as compounding, employer matching (aka "free money"), and the ability to participate in a Roth IRA (tax-free growth).

As you age and approach mid-life, the importance of getting your head out of the sand becomes more and more apparent. You may need to take extra steps and focus on your financial future. Why not have your accounts work alongside you? Did you know that contributing to a 401(k), 403(b), Roth IRA, or other investment vehicle allows your money to be working while *you* work? Two on the job! And if you plan for different accounts and machines (we'll get to that later), you'll have multiple accounts working for you simultaneously.

I get it. These subjects may not be that interesting to you. But stick to it and see what happens. Did you know that ostriches are strategic when they put their heads in the sand? They are evenly rotating their eggs to ensure proper warmth for incubation.

As for financial advice, your advisor will ensure proper incubation of your financial goals and dreams. You can keep your head in the sand or raise it up and gain more knowledge. I enjoy educating my clients about my interesting industry. There are countless resources available to calculate your personal goals. Just ask Google. Sometimes what you need is an advocate and a conductor to lead the way. Come on out of the sand and schedule a call to get your burning questions answered.

Choosing where and how to use your most valuable resources of time and energy is important. Allow me to share an example. I outsource my taxes and monthly accounting to someone who is knowledgeable. I can do my taxes—or at least I still think I can. I honestly don't want to do them and I own that statement. My accountant loves tax planning and the thrill of a reconciled and organized business. I'm happy to pay my accountant for the privilege of taking that worry and headache off my plate. She is fantastic at keeping me in line, up to date on applicable tax benefits and strategies that apply to me. I don't have to sift through the tax code to see what will work for my business. We have a discussion twice a year and she shares all items applicable to my specific tax situation. If I've heard about a tax program like the PPP loan or a small business tax credit, I can ask, "Can I benefit from this?" She explains how something applies to my business or does not. She is the expert. Therefore, I pay experts.

If it's so important, why do so many procrastinate?

I think many people procrastinate financial planning because there's no defined deadline. Taxes have a deadline, signing your child up for camp has a deadline, enrolling in a course has a deadline, and so on. However, you can retire at 65, 75, or never. Wouldn't it be nice to have the option to retire at 55 or work part-time from home? What if you had a trusted advisor with whom you could discuss business strategy or whether to consider a job offer? If you had someone to volley the pros and cons of starting a business or buying an investment property, would that be valuable? It would be nice to have someone to assist you in thinking through any financial consideration. These are important discussions and topics, but they're not urgent. There's no annual tax filing deadline for retirement planning or opening a business.

Remember the quadrants that you learned in school, breaking down *urgent* and *important*? Perhaps your parents walked you through this graphic during a time of stress or management of many things on your plate. We get ourselves caught up in things that are not so urgent and perhaps not so important, and we waste our precious resources of time and energy. Take a few minutes to consider where things fall as they relate to where you spend your money and where you spend your energy in thinking about your future. Your future planning energies are important, not urgent. This is where your critical thinking comes into play.

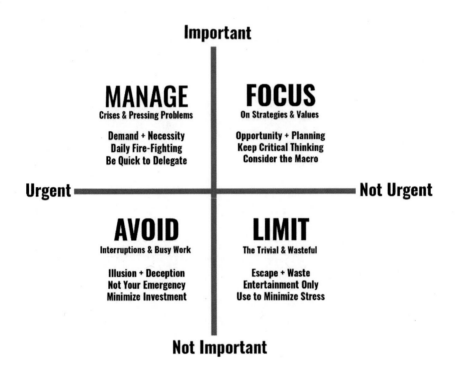

Important

MANAGE
Crises & Pressing Problems

Demand + Necessity
Daily Fire-Fighting
Be Quick to Delegate

FOCUS
On Strategies & Values

Opportunity + Planning
Keep Critical Thinking
Consider the Macro

Urgent   **Not Urgent**

AVOID
Interruptions & Busy Work

Illusion + Deception
Not Your Emergency
Minimize Investment

LIMIT
The Trivial & Wasteful

Escape + Waste
Entertainment Only
Use to Minimize Stress

Not Important

All too often once financial topics become urgent, it's too late. If you're already sick with cancer, I can't very well help you obtain life insurance to provide income replacement for your family. If you're 65 and would like to retire but you have no savings, what exactly can an advisor do? When you have health and time on your side, you have more options.

Just as you go for a physical examination annually or to the dentist, even when it makes you uncomfortable, so you must formulate a relationship with an advisor to engage and focus on your future. We promise: it won't hurt. The beauty is that you cannot un-know what you learn in those meetings. The information and perspective will sink in bit by bit over time. And you'll start to gain confidence and conviction in your plans.

Go to my website and initiate your financial collaboration: https://www.modern-wealth.com/financialcollaboration/

The best advice that I can give you if you're an ostrich is to find a financial collaborator with whom you can discuss your aspirations, assets, worries, and who you believe can assist you in your journey. I recognize that this is easier said than done. It's not as if I want to visit three dentists to make sure I have the right fit. In my experience as an advisor, it must be a match. Interview advisors and ask how they work with clients. Ask how they obtained their three most recent clients. Was it through cold calling, webinars, social media, through existing clients or professional referral? Ask about the average length of client relationships. The answers to these questions will be revealing.

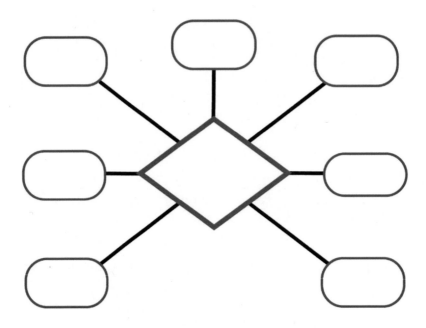

Download your worksheet here:
https://SqueezeTheJuiceBook.com/Resources

CHAPTER 4

Basic Topics to Discuss
with Your Trusted Advisor

Investment Accounts and Income Replacement

- What are the best types of investments for me?
- What type of account do you recommend for retirement planning and why?
    - o ROTH, IRA, tax-deferred annuity, tax-managed investment, taxable personal investment
- How much money do I need to have saved and invested to replace my income in retirement?
- If I draw more than four percent from my accounts for income and expenses, how long will it be before I run out of money?
- What kind of investments can create a pension-like scenario so that I may have predictability of income in retirement?

Family Protection

- I handle our finances. What does my spouse need to know?

    a. Consider writing your love letter

- My income is critical to my family. What if something happens to me prior to my funding our retirement, educating the kids, and paying off the house? How will my family survive? What will they need? How much life insurance and what kind should I have?

- If I'm hurt and can no longer work—

    o How will I replace my income?

    o Should I have disability coverage?

    a. Does your employer offer it? Paid or elective?

- When do I consider long-term care insurance? What types are there and what do they cover?

    o Traditional (old school) annual premium—use it or lose it.

    o Annuity based—park a chunk of money into a vehicle and basically forego any earnings on the cash. Those earnings go to fund the long-term care component of the contract. If you use it, it multiplies its value. If you do not need it, your beneficiaries get the return of premium or initial cash outlay.

    o Life insurance with a long-term care (LTC) rider— newest and perhaps the most cost effective. LTC if you need it and death benefit if not.

Considerations for Business Owners

- What is the best legal structure for my business?
- Should I consider bringing on a partner?
- What are the benefits and dangers?
- How can I fund the expansion of my operation?
- Help me think through and discuss my strategy for marketing and for growing into the next level of operation.
- How can I best evaluate if I have the systems and processes in place to soar?
- How can I save money on taxes?
- What type of retirement plan is best for me?
  - o Which allows for the maximum deferral personally?
  - o Do all plans allow Roth contributions?
  - o How does each plan provide for employees?
  - o What are my costs and obligations in each plan structure?
  - o Which plan will encourage employees to help themselves?
- After funding a retirement plan, I have additional funds to allocate to my future. What types of tax-efficient considerations might you suggest?
- What if my business partner or best (key) employee quit, got hurt, or suddenly died?
  - o How would my business operate without that key person?
    - a. What can I do to protect against that risk?

- o My business may suffer from a sales or cash flow perspective. The business may need a financial injection to fund the recruitment and replacement of a key employee.

- o Why should I consider a buy-sell agreement? What is the benefit of funding it with insurance?

- When I'm ready to sell or retire—

  - o Who do I consult with to discuss the tax ramifications?

  - o How should I structure the sale?

  - o Should I finance part of the deal? Or set up a longer-term buyout?

    a. What are the benefits and challenges of these strategies?

  - o How can I best evaluate an appropriate candidate?

The above are a sample of the questions to be addressed with a trusted advisor. There are many variations and more. These questions likely feel big—and they should. This is serious stuff. The way that you handle your financial instruments can determine the success or failure of your family's economic well-being. Remember that you do not have to know all the answers. And your plan will change just as life changes. Remember to squeeze the juice out of your financial advisor relationship. Be prepared and be open to the discussions to get the most out of your time. A fiduciary advisor, and one with whom you can have healthy discussions, will guide you through the process. The advisor will hold you accountable to accomplishing what you deem as important for you, your family, and your business.

When meeting with a prospective client, we conduct a discovery meeting. In this sixty-to-ninety-minute session we assess the main objectives for the relationship. And most importantly, we determine whether this will be a good working relationship. Next comes the data gathering and client homework. We usually send prospective clients home with things to consider and worksheets to complete. If we are lucky, 25% will complete it, scan it, and email it back to us. The remaining 75% must be encouraged, cajoled, and tickle-tortured to provide the information. Know your client. This is an area where we separate ourselves. Our team of coaches and financial advisors takes the time to recognize and develop what is important to your individual situation. And because we know some clients do *not* love this stuff, we sometimes schedule data-gathering calls. Our clients sit with their information (account statements, life insurance policies, employee benefits, and so on) and we will ask questions to draw out the data.

> The way that you handle your financial instruments can determine the success or failure of your family's economic well-being.

MODERN WEALTH

Notes

Download your worksheet here:
https://SqueezeTheJuiceBook.com/Resources

CHAPTER 5

Is Your Advisor What You Need?

I once had a successful professional client with great discretionary income. He lived in Pennsylvania and owned his home. He was an investment client of mine for three years. He approached me for a discussion when a large opportunity became available to him. He could be part of an IPO (initial public offering), an executive in a new company. The job would mean relocating to Chicago, receiving a large increase in salary and stock options. It was overly exciting. We discussed it and I counseled him as he weighed the opportunity. My client took the job, sold his home in Pennsylvania, relocated to Illinois, and began working for a tech start-up preparing to go public.

In Chicago he was introduced to his firm's executives and their advisory team. He was inclined to engage a local firm. And so sadly, we parted amicably.

Three years passed and I received a call from him. He asked if he had burned his bridges or if he could come back. In a bull market with most investments pointing up, his accounts had not. He had moved to the executive's advisory team; stock options stalled, and he was unhappy. He was not getting the attention and advice he had come to value.

I require all new clients to complete a financial plan, assess their discretionary funds, share with me an accurate cash flow, and be clear on their objectives—at least for that snapshot in time.

If I were to take him back as a client again, we would do as we do with all clients: start from the beginning. He knew the drill. He appreciated the drill.

I often travel to meet with clients face to face, more often pre-COVID. Now we Zoom a great deal. On a trip to Illinois I rented a car and drove into Chicago to see this client. I met him at his beautiful high-rise concierge apartment building—a one-thousand-square-foot space with a doorman, dog walkers, tiny galley kitchen, grocery delivery, and a cool view of the city. His bicycle was propped up next to the entrance. Things were compact.

We spent some time together reviewing on his laptop his current account statements, investments, and stock options. He had a few IRAs and a bunch of slow-to-vest options. He was crushing it on income. The move to Illinois had more than doubled his income. He was making well over $500,000 with options potentially worth $2.5 million. On the surface things looked fantastic.

It was lunchtime and he agreed to show me a great little place in his neighborhood where we could enjoy delicious Mediterranean food and converse. It was on our walk back from the restaurant that I broke down for him the facts as I had assessed them through our discussions. In Chicago, with no home and a non-tax-deductible apartment costing more than three times his former mortgage, a dog walker, grocery delivery, general cost of living increase in Chicago vs. back in Pennsylvania, he was making *less* money. *What?* Yes, those were the facts. He shook his head in disbelief as we walked.

If he were to become my client again, he needed to get clear on cash flow and his objectives. He was indeed "living the dream" in Illinois, but was the lifestyle all he had dreamed? Was the potential opportunity worth the short-term loss of cash flow? What was the reality of those stock options? What was the likelihood of their becoming valuable? Was it a hope and a prayer? How long could he wait it out? Was the work stimulating, the environment and culture nurturing of his career? What was important to him?

Many advisors might take this client and not necessarily solve the problem. They may be happy to open new accounts and invest his funds. They may hope that the client's stock options provide a large windfall when and if they became valuable. They may ignore or pay little attention to the significant cash flow issue of this client's daily grind. We, however, seek clients beyond the account opening. Let's be honest—his boat had a leak. The boat would eventually sink unless we plugged the leak and shored up the ride.

I left Illinois after having disrupted my client's mindset. We agreed that he would clarify so that we could strategize and consider the next steps.

He could not "un-know" what he had learned. This was an extremely intelligent man, whose mind never slowed down. He was always thinking and considering options. How could he pay $5,000 a month after tax dollars for this Chicago apartment? He may as well have been paying for an $8,000 mortgage pretax. The dog walking and other services now were less of a luxury and more of a drain. He recognized that for every year in his current situation, he was losing over $100,000 of his net worth—unless, of course, the options grew. And that was a big if.

Fast-forward one year. My client called me from Illinois and asked to discuss a position he has been offered in San Antonio. You see, after our lunch he had done some soul searching and job hunting. This opportunity sounded like a dream. The job provided a slight bump in current income and a 30% signing bonus. The new company would buy out a portion of his stock options. The technology was exciting and the opportunity curious and engaging. He would be positioned with a respected former colleague and this was a real consideration. We both recognized that he would embrace the change in lifestyle, climate, and environment. It was radically different. We assessed the cost of living and discussed whether the work would provide the engagement he desired. Last, was there anything he would be leaving behind in Illinois? What else was there to think about?

The outcome: he would have a welcome lifestyle shift in Texas. This move allowed my client to stop the bleeding of his net worth. He would purchase a home in a neighborhood where he could run with his dogs and shop at a local market. His buyout allowed for a large down payment on a new home. The list of advantages went on.

If you have an existing relationship with an advisor, consider exploring the question of whether you have in fact squeezed the juice. How do you show up in the relationship? How does your advisor show up? Do you have the right kind of advisor for you? Do you know too much now?

There is more to an advisory relationship than the technical components of managing the money. Many competent advisors can provide sound financial advice to their clients. They can offer products and strategies to move them on their paths. In addition, must-haves for a desired advisor relationship include core competencies and the fiduciary standard. And yet it is the soft skills that make for a prosperous and lifelong trusted relationship.

The relationship between me and my client continues today, and financial considerations shift as a wife and family enter the picture—more passengers on the train and perhaps a few additional stops along the way. Our ongoing discussions include his lifelong passion of starting his own business. I coach to his strengths. I encourage development of a solid marketing strategy as he builds his business platform and prepares to leave his current employment.

When interviewing advisors, be sure to read between the lines, ask the right questions, and tease out the truth. Make sure that your advisory team is focused on you. Make sure that you get the juice.

> And yet it is the soft skills that make for a prosperous and lifelong trusted relationship.

CHAPTER 6

What Does Money Mean to You?

I find it helpful to ask clients to reflect on their very first memories of money. These recollections or messages received through experience, observation, and direct communication can prove to enlighten us to our mindset and habits. Messages come from many places: parents, grandparents, teachers, employers, and other important people, especially during those formative years. These perspectives formulate the lens through which we see work and money.

Were your early experiences those of fear or of lack? Or were they of opportunity, excitement, and challenge?

I have many memorable and perhaps telling experiences with money. For me, money created circumstances, even as a small child, to thrive. I did not fear it. I played with it and leveraged it. This, I have found, is not true for most people.

I remember the excitement I felt the day that physical coins—real money—were introduced to me by Mrs. Pfeffercorn and Mrs. Doyle in kindergarten. Traditionally we worked on paper worksheets learning about currency, the different sizes and values. On this day there was legit legal tender right in the palm of my little hands. It was cool to the touch and a thrill for me. I remember it as if it were yesterday. Those currency lessons had never been so much fun as until then. My relationship with money was never the same again!

At age ten I sold enough greeting cards and earned just enough points needed to select a red skateboard from a catalogue of options. I started to see money as a tool. It helped me facilitate what I wanted, and I did not have to ask my parents for it. I could dream of all I wanted of cool red skateboards and other things kids desire. I had figured out a way to translate effort into fulfillment of stuff. It was a life lesson in how to accomplish goals through thought, effort, and ingenuity.

> What did you dream of in your early years?
> How did money make or break that from
> happening? Can you remember your first
> purchase with money you earned?

My grandfather owned a restaurant in Baltimore. He had emigrated to the United States from China as a young man. On Sunday evenings we would often go to my grandparents' restaurant for dinner and a visit. We snacked on chow mein noodles in little wax bags. We would run about, in and out of the kitchen while my grandfather prepared a family meal. One evening at my grandparents' restaurant I spotted wads of cash in the rafters above my head. I could not believe my eyes. In my enthusiasm to identify this treasure, my arm shot straight into the air. My father quietly pulled my arm down and explained that not everyone was trusting of banks. Pop-Pop Wing, having been born in Communist China, had a lens of mistrust when it came to money. His experience and relationship were quite different from mine. Everyone has a story, a history that is woven through their viewpoint. I find it valuable to have clients reflect and consider theirs.

As a curious adolescent, I asked my maternal grandmother about how she and my grandfather managed their money. They were blue collar folks with regular jobs and not a lot of extra money. As a kid, I remembered she had a Christmas club account that she would add to from every paycheck. She always seemed to have cash. Her generosity at Christmas was sizeable and disproportionate. We were her heart, and it made her super happy to give us money and buy us things. Gift giving was my Nana's "love language." In hindsight, I believe she spent too much of her small retirement on us and things we could have done without.

She shared that when she and my grandfather were first married and my mom was little, they would divide their paychecks up on Fridays. They would split the proportional amount of monthly bills into separate envelopes. This budgeting system was organized, and it worked. I was pleasantly reminded of this when I was introduced to a client some twenty-five years later. She too used the envelope budgeting system.

Money as a tool

My mom likes to tell the story about how I used to sell candy bars in the back of the school bus. I like this story too. I attended a school in Baltimore that involved a forty-five-minute bus ride. My mom would drop me at the bus stop, at a shopping center, at 7:00 a.m. in the morning. Ever entrepreneurial, I would head into the CVS or

Safeway to buy a six-pack of Snickers and a bag of Blow Pops. I realized and anticipated the demand for snacks on the ride home. At 3:45 I boarded a bus full of starving adolescents and I rocked the Snickers sales—again, money as a tool. It was not about the cash in my pocket. It was about what it accomplished. I simply wanted to fund my hunger and I did so through my sales.

Contemplate your early memories of money:

- What kinds of things did you observe as a child?
- What did your parents or grandparents communicate around the subject of money?
- How do those experiences present themselves in your life now?
- What lasting impressions create gifts or challenges today as they relate to your relationship with money?

MODERN WEALTH

Notes

CHAPTER 7

Discretionary Number: What's Yours?

We cannot truly serve our clients unless we get to know and understand them. We begin each relationship with a foundational discovery session. We learn about their family, business, generally about their resources and experiences. And then we talk with them about how they feel we can help.

A key part of the financial planning process is understanding what resources clients have at their disposal. Often clients have no awareness of where their money goes. Paychecks come in and money is spent. I call this "unconscious living" or "unconscious spending." Together we help clients determine their "discretionary number." This is the money they can apply to aspirations, goals, and plans. This knowledge allows for more thoughtful spending and purchases.

> Knowing your discretionary number is fundamental to planning. We are calculating the amount of money you and your family may spend now or will spend on your future. Freedom of choice—conscious or unconscious.

We inventory, considering existing resources, and investigate to uncover inefficiencies. In comes the homework—yes, homework. As your advisors, we need to know what we have to maneuver. What resources do you or will you have available to assist in meeting your goals? Together we grasp your spending patterns and decipher want from need. Knowing your discretionary number is fundamental to planning. We are calculating the amount of money you and your family may spend now or will spend on your future. Freedom of choice—conscious or unconscious.

Let's assume that you conducted the discretionary exercise on paper and found your household discretionary number to be $2,500 a month. So why does it not feel that you have an extra $2,500 each month? We must assess where that money is going. Is it disappearing on meals out? Is it going to excess purchases at Costco, impulse buys? Are you giving money away to your grown children? This is the hard work. It is a reckoning with your money now and your money for the future. It may not necessarily feel fun, but you must complete it. You must look at it to consider how you wish to spend your money. Not knowing where your money goes and simply realizing it has gone is living by default.

Are you living by design or by default?

Google this topic or check out the following succinct explanation and make your own determination: https://www.lifeoptimizer.org/2015/03/03/live-by-design/

Let's calculate your discretionary number.

Webster's definition of *discretionary*

1: left to individual choice or judgment: exercised at one's own *discretion*

How much money comes into the household?

Income, alimony, rental income, pension, disability, Social Security, inheritance, commission, bonus, and so on

(Less) How much leaves the household?

Fixed (must pay) expenses: mortgage, rent, health insurance, kids' tuition, utilities, car payment, car insurance, credit card payments

Variable (choose to spend): streaming services, trips to Costco, movies, meals out, boating excursions, renovations, excess clothing expenditures, Amazon

Can any of these expenses be trimmed? Should they?

Equals: discretionary number

Download your worksheet here:
https://SqueezeTheJuiceBook.com/Resources

A few months ago I met with prospective clients and good friends to discuss money. There is always the concern of mixing friends with money. Conceptually, this can be dangerous. For us it was not. I am not the best advocate for myself. I love and often communicate my profession. I delight in talking strategy or answering questions at social gatherings; however, I do not often directly ask people to do business with me. It's not my thing. I prefer to demonstrate who I am and allow situations to present themselves. I network and it drives referrals and business that are a fit for my practice. My potential client relationships flower over time when people or circumstances shift, and it becomes appropriate to have an initial discussion about working together. This is just one of those cases.

Here we have a husband and wife—dual income, no kids: aka DINK. They are earning reasonably significant money, saving some and spending most. As they approach their retirement timeline, the "money spouse" realizes that maybe it's time to take inventory, reign in the spending, and discuss their future. He would like assistance in communicating and calibrating his "non-moneyed spouse" into the conversation with ownership of their future.

We have discussions about "Chapter 1: Financial Planning Is Simple" and about their discretionary number. I send them on their way to review and determine their number. Truly they had not ever completed an exercise like this and were unaware of their spending. They realized it was a lot but did not have a real number. After the exercise, unconscious spending is more difficult. It is as simple as a shift in mindset, awareness, and perspective.

Now when this couple considers refinishing a bathroom, planting a garden, or buying a new grill they are less likely to do it all in one month. They consider and discuss desires, plan, and balance their travel and future second home plans with their daily lifestyle. Often this makes for a happier couple, more thoughtful spending, less credit card debt, and more cash accumulating for a long-term dream: a retirement villa in France. And it is especially nice to be on the same page as your spouse.

> Check in on yourself and see how your
> spending is reflected in your values.

We spend more than one third of our life at work—shouldn't it bring a high level of joy and satisfaction? I feel fortunate. Getting up in the morning is easy and work fulfills me. As we age in life and gain experiences, we ask ourselves, "What is the point of my being here?" "What are the reasons for my existence?" "What is my role in life?" "How and to whom am I contributing?" "What am I leaving as my legacy?" Have you ever read *Intentional Living,* by John Maxwell? He reminds us that we have it in our power to make our life one of significance, that we wake up each day and have one of three intentions and mindsets—success, survival, or significance. What will you choose?

If getting up for your day is a drag and you have no plan or purpose, dig deeply and consider what makes you most happy. What brings you joy? Ask yourself the 25-million-dollar question. Then find a way to incorporate those things into your daily life.

> Being miserable and being without purpose
> are synonymous.

Exercise: The 25-million-dollar question

What if you had 25 million dollars and you no longer had to work to pay your bills? Imagine for a moment that you have already enjoyed a great deal of traveling, paid your bills, purchased a luxury vehicle, and savored gourmet meals. Imagine that you have helped a friend or two, family, and others. Now ask yourself—

- Where do you live?
    a. Are you near the water or the mountains?
    b. Is your climate cold?
- Who are your friends?
- What do you do with your time?
    a. How do you spend your day?
- Do you work and if so, what do you do?
    a. Whom do you serve?
- What feeds you and fills your soul?
- What makes you grin from ear to ear?
- Who are the people with whom you surround yourself?
- How do you squeeze the juice?

These questions often stump people. There's no right answer. How frequently do you consider your passion and your most important interests? How do your habits and lifestyle stack up to your aspirations? This exercise permits you to assess your life, your work, how you spend your spare time, and with whom you spend it. Try it now and return to it often. Reflecting and considering what fills you will bring joy to your life.

Here is where the rubber meets the road, where the hard part ultimately becomes easy. You now know the amount of money that you and your family have at your discretion each month. You can choose intelligently how to spend it. Wow—there it is: *simple.*

Once you've clarified your values and have your discretionary number, you're unstoppable! Here's the beautiful part, and this is when it gets empowering and fun: you get to choose how you'll spend it.

- Will you save your discretionary $2,500 (mentioned previously) for two months and eat in so that you can plan a trip to South Africa?
- Will you save $500 more each month in your Roth IRA to take advantage of tax-free growth in your future retirement bucket?
- Will you pay a little more of your mortgage each month so you're mortgage free when you retire?
- Will you continue spending your $2,500 on things without being cognizant about your spending? I don't think you will.

For most of us there is a little voice of reason inside our head that knows you were educated and that you now know too much. This is an exceptionally good thing. Listen to that little voice.

Time for your financial advisors to get back to work. We have knowledge of your discretionary number, and you have reconciled your values and know what you want. As your advisors, we will work with you to most efficiently deploy this monthly resource of excess funds to allow for maximum opportunity to accomplish your desired outcome. Maybe you would love to have a second home. Maybe it's important for you to have an annual travel budget. Maybe you want to have savings for down payments on your children's first homes. Perhaps early retirement or opening a small wine shop thrills you. Your bucket list is yours. Remember that money is simply a tool. It should be respected, not feared; leveraged, not wasted. Ask yourself, "What do I want my money to do for me?" In three pages you will find a bucket list worksheet. Jot down a few things that quickly come to mind and let's work together to make it happen.

> Money should be respected,
> not feared; leveraged, not wasted.

In quarantine and with COVID-19 the three things I miss most: lunch out with clients (a true time to connect and share a meal), hugs, and travel. Travel is now at the top of my bucket list.

I have been humbled into reducing my expectations. Being open minded, setting fewer rigid expectations yields more joy and less disappointment in life. I still expect the best from anyone and everyone but recognize now that it is "their" best. I have found that when you let life reveal itself, you will be wildly impressed and awed. In 2018 I had the opportunity and adventure to travel to South Africa. For me, this trip was life changing. I went with zero expectations. This is not at all typical of me, but I literally blanked out my mind. I looked at this as an adventure. In advance of the trip people would suggest that the travel time would be exhausting, I simply said, "There's only one way to get there, and I'm going— so it will just be what it is." After all, I could not change the flight path. I will say that once on the fifteen-plus-hour flight, after eight hours I found myself attempting to obtain work from a flight attendant. *"Please, may I hand out water, hot towels, or do something productive?"* I needed an activity. I just couldn't watch another movie. This is how I get at a party if I stay more than two hours, like a Super Bowl party. Will someone please ask me a financial question?

> Being open minded, setting fewer rigid expectations yields more joy and less disappointment in life.

Traveling with a friend, soon to become a close friend, we set the course to see and experience life, culture, and Mother Nature. I found myself in the middle of the movie *The Lion King.* "Hakuna Matata"—it means 'no worries.'" I could not wait to Facetime the littles (my nieces and nephews) and share how I saw Timon and Pumbaa and was on the prowl for Simba. This place and its profound beauty opens your heart and melts all the drama and mediocrity away. Quite literally having no expectations of what I would experience, see, or feel blew me away. The connection to the earth, the animals, the food—I loved it all.

In hindsight, why wouldn't I have felt unstoppable? For two weeks I went to bed early (9 p.m.), drank less wine than usual (only one glass), and awoke at 4 a.m. to go on an adventure and see new and beautiful things. I had decaffeinated tea, not coffee, and ate farm-to-table at every meal. It was sensational and I never felt better. And the people—they were amazing, generous, and authentic. The animals: just wow! Majestic. We did crazy things like ride up close to a white rhinoceros and her calf while on horseback. Somehow the animals were not afraid. They knew the horses and seemed not to notice their passengers. My friend Sally wanted to, and I obliged a trip to the Republic of Zambia to take a dip in the Devil's Pool. Getting there was a little sketchy: two drivers, relinquish your passport, and take a walk across the border. Never mind lying across the actual falls with only a slick slab of rock between you and the 354-foot falls. Yes, a tour guide held my feet, but really? What was I thinking? It was only when my feet hit U.S. soil that I realized the insanity of that adventure. Suddenly I felt conservative again. We were crazy to lie on the edge of the falls after having traveled alone between provinces. I think it's safe to say that I squeezed the juice out of this experience. And I'm ready to go again! A second trip to Africa is on my bucket list.

What's on *your* bucket list?

MODERN WEALTH

My Bucket List

CHAPTER 8

Build Your Machine

Long ago at a 401(k) enrollment meeting my dad shared the following story with the employee participants. I've used this story many times and most effectively with my nephew Jacob when he was 9. When you're investing either monthly or annually a portion of your income, think of it as if you're buying nuts and bolts and sheet metal for your machine. The more money you invest, the more parts you can purchase and the bigger the machine. The general rule of thumb when starting to invest in your 20s is that you invest between 10% to 12% of your income to be able to have adequate replacement of that income in retirement. Now many of you would like to live on more income than you currently make. And in that case, you'll need to save more, 10% to 12%, of your *desired* income. We'll discuss this topic later in the building blocks to consider when saving and investing.

When I shared this story with young Jacob, he was pumped. He said, "Aunt Jenn, can I put more money away? I'm going to put like 40% away—I want a big machine!" Jacob was ambitious and an opportunist. It was a proud aunt moment. While his siblings preferred to chill in our house on a Saturday watching movies or playing video games, Jacob requested chores for cash—or as life would have it, a trip to the store. He would ask, "Are there papers to shred? Can I scoop the cat litter?" "Seriously? Yes, of course! I'll find you things to do." If you teach kids good habits when they're young, they can take ownership of their financial future as they become young adults. The hope is that pieces and parts of our communications will stick and serve them in their lives.

> The general rule of thumb when starting to invest in your 20s is that you invest between 10% to 12% of your income to be able to have adequate replacement of that income in retirement.

We have determined that the more you save, the larger the machine you'll be able to build. Think of your investment account as your machine. You want to add to it, maintain it, and not steal sheet metal and parts from it. If you take from your machine before you're ready to use it, it will not function as well and as desired. Or it may produce less. When placing money into a retirement plan, do your best to leave those funds invested for your long-term goals. Time will be on your side and your account can work alongside you. If possible, don't steal from your future retirement. Remember: the idea is that when you retire you'll leave your office or place of work. You'll flip off the light switch of your working life and you go home and turn on your machine. If properly established, maintained, and not tampered with, your machine will generate income to replace what you no longer have from your job. This is the goal: income replacement!

One of the objectives in working with an advisor is to devise a plan to have sufficient income replacement for your retirement years. We consider the possible contributing sources or streams of future income and develop a plan to supplement what may be missing. Most people will have a variety of components that comprise their replacement income. Some items may include 401(k), pension, Social Security, personally accumulated assets, dividends from stocks, bond interest, proceeds from a business sale, inheritance, residual business income, or rental property income. Everyone's situation is different; you want to meet with an advisor to get on track to living the future you desire. As things shift in your personal, professional, and financial life, it may impact your financial plan. There are so many subjects that can derail or enhance your financial picture. It's critical to involve your financial partner with major life events such as those listed below:

- Marriage
- Divorce
- Addition of children or grandchildren
- Business purchase or sale
- Adding a business partner
- Starting a new business
- Inheritance
- Retirement
- Relocation

You'll want to leverage the experience of your advisory team by bringing them into the loop as life happens. They will help you integrate additional resources into your plans.

Remember: the idea is that when you retire you'll leave your office or place of work. You'll flip off the light switch of your working life and you go home and turn on your machine.

CHAPTER 9

Financial Building Blocks

Don't let your building tumble with a weak foundation.

		Financial Independence			
		Vacation Home Other Personal Preferences	Extensive Travel Charitable Giving		
	Fully Funded Retirement Plan/ Permanent Insurance	LTC Insurance Disability Roth IRA	529 Plans/ Personal Taxable Investments	Free Money Matching 401k/403b	
Will Love Letter	Family Protection Term Insurance	Financial Strategy Partnership in Planning	Reserves Savings/ Emergency Money	Own a Home Primary Residence	Know Your Discretionary #

You would not build your financial picture the way a toddler builds his or her block tower, would you—super tall and straight up into the air? It would topple over too easily. You would start with a solid footing. You might have three to six blocks on the bottom to serve as a base. Your financial picture is the same. Start with the crucial and primary components; then build your complexity on top.

1. Bottom layer includes

   a. Will and other legal documents, such as advanced healthcare directives, medical and financial power of attorney

   b. Life insurance (family protection: replacement of income, pay debts, kids' education, fund retirement)

   c. Emergency money (three to six months of income replacement)

   d. Home (solid living situation whether you rent or own)

   e. Partnering with a financial professional: goals and dreams, initial plan or strategy, and get rolling

   f. Knowledge of your discretionary number

2. Second layer includes

   a. Free money from your work retirement plan. I love free money. If your employer offers you a match in exchange for your helping yourself through participation, jump on it. This is free money. Please do not leave it on the table. It is not a trick. It is an incentive by your employer to help you help yourself. Matches may be dollar for dollar or perhaps twenty-five cents on the dollar. It doesn't matter: money is money, so leverage it.

b. Participate in a Roth IRA if you're eligible. This vehicle allows your investments to grow tax free. You will never pay tax on the gain if you use it for retirement. Presently restrictions allow for access at age 59½ or later. One of the simplest (and my favorite) strategies is the Roth IRA. As your income increases you may be phased out of the ability to contribute. Check with your advisor or accountant to see if you're eligible. If you're 50 or older, you may contribute a bit more as a catch-up contribution.

c. Personal savings for mid-term goals (this may include cash savings, mutual funds, stocks, and bonds)

d. Education accounts for kids (prepaid, 529 plans)

e. Permanent life insurance: family protection, cash accumulation, fund estate tax, leverage life with long-term care

f. Annuities as a tax deferred investment

g. Long-term care insurance—this is insurance to protect assets for your spouse and beneficiaries. The need for long-term care services can be exceedingly expensive and can wipe out your financial resources with its cost. Many couples in retirement are at risk of depleting assets when one spouse gets sick. Long-term care insurance provides a daily benefit that pays for custodial care. Custodial care is the care not covered by your medical insurance. If you have assets, want to remain home if you get sick, or are single and have no family to care for you, long-term care insurance is something to consider. It is not for the ultra-wealthy or for those whose assets will be depleted—it's for everyone in the middle. If you have assets and a spouse who will need those assets to live, you must consider the need for long-term care insurance.

h. Disability insurance—this is insurance that covers the replacement of your income. Let's say you make $50,000 a year; you're 30 years old and plan to work to age 60. To calculate your income needing protection, we multiply the remaining working years by the amount of annual income (30 x $50,000 = $1,500,000). If you were no longer able to get up and go to work every day, disability insurance would protect your income. If you're the primary breadwinner, please evaluate your disability options. Your employer may offer a program, or you may need to consider obtaining coverage individually through an agent. Disability insurance is the hardest kind of insurance to obtain. People tend to want to purchase it after they have a documented medical issue. Consider buying this type of insurance while you're young and healthy to get the best available premium. If you're thinking that you'll get Social Security disability, think again. The qualifications are challenging at best. It's a long and arduous process that will likely end in multiple denials of claims; your disability must be severe and permanent.

3. Third layer (when you reach the third layer you can start to be super creative)—

    a. Starting and owning a business

    b. Owning investment property

    c. Vacation or second home

    d. Charitable giving

    e. Extensive travel

4. Top layer includes—

    a. Financial freedom—do what you want, when you want, and with whom you want.

    b. World travel

    c. Tithing

    d. Legacy planning or whatever you deem to be at the top of the heap

Everyone's financial picture is personalized, but the foundation and the order in which you address those topics is important to the strength of your plan.

> Start with the foundational components and build your complexity from there.

CHAPTER 10

When Aunt Jenn Asks You to Dinner

When Aunt Jenn asks you to dinner it is more than a social call. She's going to ask a lot of questions about your hopes and dreams, your plans, how you're taking advantage of opportunities, what your plan is for the next few years, and how you're spending time. Are you being your best self? Post grilling, this can be a time of self-reflection.

Is it that bad? When I was a kid, I guess it *was* a little bad. Conversations with my Dad were intense, to say the least. There was not a lot of idle chatter. My father was sometimes playful and he was definitely a loving father. Most communications, however, had a point and perhaps a scribble on a yellow legal pad. Today I realize I certainly did not fall far from the tree. This gift presents challenges in life and relationships. If you want to know, I'll tell you more. Please realize that you cannot un-know what you hear or learn. In reflecting on my childhood with my dad, I would kill to have another conversation in which he pushed me to consider choices and outcomes and to stretch to be my best. After all, that's all he wanted. And it's all I want for my family, friends, and clients.

I have inquired of the older nieces and nephews. They have assured me that they know what they're in for when they're asked for dinner. They know I'm not one for idle chit-chat. I want the real deal, the whole story with all the juicy tidbits. They recognize that I'm interested in them and in their being their best selves. My interest is in what feeds their soul and how they can squeeze the juice. They know I love them unconditionally; they also know they cannot pull the wool over my eyes as they can their friends or even their parents. That will not fly. Meaningful conversation that has impact is my "jam."

For me one of the best parts of my life is seeing and being part of a client's, friend's, niece's/nephew's (I have nine, so I identify as "AJ" or Aunt Jenn), or child's awakening to his or her potential. Seeing the development of a child's inner confidence, feeling of validation, and self-worth is priceless. This type of connection goes beneath the surface and impacts the child's character and soul. This carries me and goes a long way to deepen our special relationship.

I ask that you do your best—whatever that means. Maybe I have high expectations of myself and of everyone else. But maybe we could all just put out a little more effort. I'm not asking for the moon and the stars—just *your* best. So ask yourself—"Is this my best?" If yes, awesome! If no, dig deeply, ask, research, look, learn, and try harder.

> I'm not asking for the moon and the stars—
> just your best. So ask yourself—
> "Is this my best?"

CHAPTER 11

Values and Connection

The sweet spot in my practice has been clients in transition—men and women in financial transition (divorcing, widowed, involved in a business sale, retiring), couples retiring or dealing with spousal illness, and ultimately legacy planning. These are clients who need to take care of themselves financially and desire to provide for their families as well.

Remember: It's at the intersection in life where finances and emotions converge that reliable counsel is most needed.

We have clients in all stages of life. It's just that in transition a support team is needed more urgently. This is where many of our client relationships initiate. Later, clients are remarried, have kids, and enjoy their happy long and well-deserved retirement trekking about the country and enjoying their people.

More important than the stage of transition are one's values and connection. Trust and confidence are vital to the advisory relationship. It is essential that clients know, like, and trust us. Trust cannot be commanded, requested, or required. It can be demonstrated and earned only through discovery, referral, and conversation. Our model at its core is an honest and respectful partnership.

A partnership is an arrangement in which parties, known as business partners, agree to cooperate to advance their mutual interests. The partners in a partnership may be individuals, businesses, interest-based organizations, schools, governments, or combinations. Organizations may partner to increase the likelihood of each achieving his or her mission and to amplify his or her reach. (Wikipedia, com, adapted)

So how does this apply to financial planning? As I see it, money is a tool, an energy, something that affords your dreams and goals. For me it provides the ability to feel fulfilled. This is not to say the actual money fulfills me. The money, remember, is the device that allows you to live, contribute, enjoy, travel, and afford your life. Money concepts, fears about having enough, fears about the future can be intimidating. If I can take some of that burden, help with a healthy perspective to leverage a client's individual gifts, I've done my job and hence feel fulfilled.

As an advisor you need to know your client base and to whom you're easiest to relate to, whom you can best serve. I'm clear on who values my services and to whom I can contribute the most. And I know that making money comfortable, accessible, and understandable is one of my most important roles.

> Trust cannot be commanded, requested, or required. It can be demonstrated and earned only through discovery, referral, and conversation.

I've mentioned previously that many of our clients find money and financial topics formidable, tedious, or not interesting. And that's okay. There's no requirement that you love numbers, have an aptitude for strategy, or are interested in portfolio asset allocation. You need only to be able to communicate the resources you have, your values as they relate to your desires, dreams, and goals. Your advisor can translate the data into an appropriate basket of solutions to facilitate those plans.

In our practice we have three client pathways:

The first pathway subject matter is wide. Everyone can benefit from a chat, from using a sounding board, or enjoying a strategy session as clients reach for their personal, career, family, and financial aspirations. We offer both triage and discovery coaching sessions. Whether a discussion involves a business opportunity or specific life event, this option can address the times when you need some advice, perspective, and help thinking through decisions. As clients stretch, they may ask for an assist. The assist may be a one-time financial plan, or it may involve a small package of coaching sessions. Challenges large and small are welcome for exploration and solution-driven advice.

The second pathway is our primary offering. It is comprehensive financial planning and education and includes the client's desire to delegate. Many clients desire to pass on the facilitation of their financial plans and management of their resources. They value counsel as it relates to decisions impacting their family and their businesses. They may understand that their expertise is in other areas. These clients are our advisory clients and our relationships with them are deep, wide, and ongoing. Regular communication, including portfolio reviews, tax strategy, income planning, business transition, with access to the advisory team is pivotal to the relationship. Clients leverage the team regularly for direction or assistance as they consider life and money decisions. These are often the clients with whom we negotiate cars, conduct legacy planning, discuss career opportunities, or host love letter family meetings.

The final pathway encompasses a little of both categories above. These clients may still be in the growth or accumulation stage, requiring an annual planning session to line up their plans and set a course. We start with a financial plan and our foundational process. Clients may or may not have assets at the advisory level. They are focused and dedicated to being their best selves, personally and fiscally. These clients may be starting a business, growing a business, or aspiring to be fully financially independent. They may desire a plan and maintenance of that plan as they move through life. Regular communications and access to the advisory team are available through the coaching suite. These clients leverage technology to manage their cash flow, assets, goals, and savings. They use us for strategy, validity, and direction as they move through their plan. We often meet with them twice annually and they know to reach out as events occur in their lives: new relationship, home sale or purchase, change of job, inheritance, loss of spouse, starting a business. These clients pay a flat fee or a percentage of their income annually.

All relationships start with a financial assessment and a foundational deep dive into values, resources, and objectives. During this discovery session we can help determine the relationship fit and appropriateness of your path.

> There is no requirement that you love numbers, have an aptitude for strategy, or are interested in portfolio asset allocation.

As advisors we understand that to maintain your attention, certainly we must be relatable. We must be able to educate and provide value. This relationship is a layering affect.

Topics include a very long list: resources, goals, cash flow, awareness of discretionary money, intentional application of resources, tax strategy, educating children and spouse about financial plans, investment risk tolerance, gifting strategies, family protection, love letter, review of investments, review of economy, review of your specific plan as it relates to objectives—rinse and repeat. And the list grows.

In my life and practice it has been an ongoing quest to be relatable. I am human and yes, an ongoing work in progress. A few years ago, almost ten, I was working with a long-time insurance and 401(k) client to facilitate the sale, running of, and ultimate closing of his business. During that time I was asked to join the team in what I would consider a heavy-duty meeting in New York City with executives from American Express. We arrived downtown at Three World Financial Center. We were processed through security with picture IDs and authorization passes for the executive level of the building. Once cleared, we were sent upstairs. I am generally confident, but I'll admit that it was slightly intimidating to be on the executive level of American Express meeting with top-level people. This was American Express after all. We conducted the meeting and things seemed to go well.

"Shew! It's over!" Back in the cab on the ride to the hotel, I received a call from my wife. She said, "I just wanted to wish you good luck on your meeting and to remind you to smile, honey!" Oh, no! I don't think I smiled once! Ahhh! I too am a work in progress. "Remember to smile." So simple and yet . . .

CHAPTER 12

Sudden Money

Sudden money comes unexpectedly and as such, most people are ill prepared for it. Immediately you're thrust into a realm that's unknown. How are you expected to know what type of advisor will be helpful, what questions to ask, and how these funds will impact your life? No one prepared you for this.

Windfalls come in many different forms: inheritance, divorce settlement, lawsuit payout, lottery win. Receiving a windfall is a financial gift. However, you did not have the experience to slowly become acclimated to the challenges and responsibility of wealth. It was simply dumped into your lap.

There can be several downsides to receiving sudden money and it's important to get prepared and be cautious. You may have friends or family who seek to ask you for a loan or a handout. You may wish to go on a spending spree. There's no harm in treating yourself, but understand that people in receipt of sudden money are at a high risk of overspending. It's best to set a plan and consider how much of the money you'll spend today and how much you'll invest for your future.

> My job is not to project my values onto you. It is to assist you as you discover, uncover, and understand what money means to you.

It can be both exciting and overwhelming. Data on lottery winners indicates that 70% of winners revert to their prior economic level in five years or less (Theresa Dixon Murray, *cleveland.com,* January 1, 2019). Let's not be wasteful. Let's use sudden money as a tool to enhance your life.

My job is not to project my values onto you. It is to assist you as you discover, uncover, and understand what money means to you. Please consider how it can impact your life and the lives of your loved ones with this financial windfall. Make an effort to protect it, generate lifestyle, and grow it.

Inheritance

I have a client who came to me after inheriting a large sum of money. She and her brother each inherited $3 million from their parents. As the siblings were growing up, their parents impressed upon them the value of hard work, education, and saving money. Their parents' values surrounding money were strong and consistent. They earned a decent income and saved a large portion of their earnings, modeling good stewardship. They were mindful of their resources and still able to afford their kids the occasional luxury in life.

For my client, her values, although not front of mind, impacted her deeply when she realized that she and her husband thought differently about money. He desired to pay off the mortgage, renovate the kitchen, and buy new cars. She preferred minor repairs to the home and the purchase of a used car. She was obviously more prudent with her spending. As with many couples, money can become an issue. Both she and her husband had decent jobs but were young in their careers. Those jobs did not yet provide excess funds for lifestyle and discretionary spending. Their jobs basically paid for their life with their daughter and not much extra. This influx of inheritance could be a welcomed addition.

As advisors we must educate and caution our clients from making impulsive and unconscious decisions. And sometimes we must protect them from their spouses' desired spending habits. In this instance my job was to uncover the values of my client and help her to situate them into her financial plan. We resolved to complete a budget for the family. Rather than pay off the house, they would live on their salaries and leverage the inheritance to add spice to their life. The income generated from the inheritance machine would provide a variety of discretionary items ongoing. As a result of our partnership, my client had clarity of her values and an education regarding what this wealth could provide for her and her family—a financial plan aligned with her values and the choice of how to spend the income.

Five years later, the inheritance provides for some much-appreciated extras in their life: private school, annual family vacations, plus stabling and veterinarian costs for her horse. Horseback riding has been a long-time passion for my client. Her inheritance, if kept in this manner, will provide a lifetime supply of supplemental life experiences. If my client spends only the earnings from her investments, this gift will continue for her lifetime. More importantly, the legacy of her parent's values will continue. This same asset, aka "machine," could generate future lifestyle for her daughter and her family. Time will tell.

> ## Inheritances should always be kept separate.

My hope is that by understanding my client's values and including them in the planning, this sudden money and the strategies employed will empower joy in her life and make a continued legacy out of the gift of inheritance.

Note: Inheritances should always be kept separate. No one desires a divorce, a lawsuit, or a failed business venture, but things happen. Inherited money should be kept separate of all joint assets to protect the ultimate transition to children. Never comingle inherited money.

Taking from the principal or tapping into the nuts and bolts of the machine will render it less able to provide. Since money is a sensitive issue, careful consideration and communication are necessary when discussing such topics.

Divorce

Divorce is a legal process with financial implications, guided primarily by emotions.

Inevitably, whenever I meet someone new and share what I do, they respond by saying, "Where were you when I needed you?" And they proceed to share their horror story about their divorce, all the things they did wrong, what their attorney did not know or ask or consider. And they share the loneliness during the exhaustive process. Many clients confess that they gave up too easily—they just wanted it over. And so they took what was offered rather than standing up for what they were entitled to receive. In short, they wished they had had an advocate, a confidant, a trusted advisor, and a coach.

One of the longest divorce processes I have experienced was five years and $80,000-plus in legal fees. Three attorneys later, my client had a completed divorce. What was missed: alimony of a heightened level during that five-year process (aka "spousal maintenance"), the consideration of "collaborative divorce" since this should have been a simple uncontested split of assets—ultimately less money spent on legal fees and much less aggravation. But who knew? The client trusted her attorneys and the fact that this was a process. Surely the experienced legal team knew what they were doing.

These attorneys did not implement immediately the maximum alimony allowed during the process. Spousal maintenance is a standard by which the dependent spouse receives support during the divorce process. My client had to continually reach out to her estranged spouse and request money to pay the household bills. This standard is intended to eliminate the power play many clients experience.

My client could have had a simplified divorce process as she lived in a no-fault state. Given the length of the marriage, the divorce settlement would have been relatively simple. Their daughter was an adult and there was no contention over the properties they owned jointly. They needed only to divide everything in half: IRAs, 401(k)s, cash, stocks, homes (sell, buy out, and divide), and determine alimony based on a mandated formula, as they should have been.

These attorneys did not understand or discuss that perhaps my client would have liked to have some life insurance on her soon-to-be ex-husband to guarantee that her alimony would be paid in full for the agreed-upon term. This is a consideration that can be negotiated and implemented in cases in which you are dependent on someone's ability to earn income and be alive to pay. I brought this up to my client and her attorney. We obtained a life insurance policy that would cover the health care and alimony obligation should something unforeseen occur prior to the completion of the obligation. We required an irrevocable beneficiary designation. *Irrevocable beneficiary* means that the beneficiary named may not be changed by the policy owner. The beneficiary is irrevocable. The client remains protected.

My client and I communicated throughout this messy process—she as the client, expressing anxiety regarding attorney issues, timing, and discovery of financial documents; and me as a sounding board and rational thinker. As an advocate I am unattached to the divorce process and less influenced by the emotion. Although sometimes I felt frustrated for my client, I did my best to reflect and simplify the next steps from the sea of emotions that can overwhelm. My interest was my client's interest. As her advocate, I helped her to stay focused during this long-distance run.

The scariest part and perhaps the most common is how divorce can exhaust you. As women, we are caregivers and we like things generally to be smoother than not. We are not interested in fighting to the death—we want peace, decision, and for this thing to be over. So—often women quit, give up, or give in to the exhaustion of the process. That leaves money, property, values, beneficiaries, pensions, and sometimes arrangements regarding children on the table. And personally, that makes me crazy.

My client was divorced. One would assume that the legal process was over, right? Oh, wait—the attorney failed to request a QDRO from the judge.

A QDRO is a *qualified domestic relations order*. This legal document tells the custodian of any assets what to do. For example, if the client is entitled to 50% of the ex-spouse's 401(k), the document instructs the custodian to split the account into two and register the assets separately.

Without this document we cannot access the values in the account, the money cannot be moved, and we are stuck again in a stalemate awaiting the appropriate document and the courts' signature. What a mess! If the attorney had known how to handle a QDRO, this would have been expeditious. Instead, it was another six months before we were able to open new accounts and start to have assets moved. During this time the client was in the dark regarding asset values and positions in those accounts. The timing was fortunate; it was during an upswing in the last bull market.

In an ideal situation your advisory team is involved from the start. We are present to support client thought processes, strategy, and details regarding the many disentanglements of divorce. We work together with your attorney to support and facilitate this process to its completion. Often divorce coaches are involved to support the emotions and assist in the advancement of tasks.

If conducting a collaborative, there is a financial intermediary as well as a social worker present for all discussions. These professionals are trained in "collaborative divorce." They maintain cool heads and advocate productive discussions.

There are many financial considerations as clients enter into divorce agreements. It is imperative that clients understand the lifestyle adjustments that may need to be made post-divorce. The division of assets often necessitates clients to adjust their thinking. They may emotionally be attached to their family residence; however, it may not be the best move for them financially. Their spending may also need to be curbed.

> In short, they wished they had had an advocate, a confidant, a trusted advisor, and a coach.

Business Transition

My client of many years was a husband, father, and businessman. He was one of two blue-collar guys who built a thriving business by carving out an untapped niche—one the "idea" guy and the other the "manager of the idea" guy. They worked well together dividing and conquering. Each partner knew his role.

My primary relationship was with the management partner. He ran the day-to-day operations of the business. Early in my relationship I helped the company with standard business items such as 401(k), group health insurance, group life, and disability.

As the relationship deepened and trust grew, our conversations expanded. We discussed their spouses and the consideration of business continuation. What would happen if, God forbid, something happened to one of them? Would they want to be in business with the other's spouse? The adamant response I received directly communicated the need for a solution. And so we constructed a buy-sell agreement funded by insurance. In this case, it provided cash for the remaining business owner to buy out his partner's spouse.

An agreement between partners called a "buy-sell" indicates what will happen in the situations of retirement, death, or disability of a partner. It is the agreement between partners in advance of a future circumstance. It is recommended that these agreements be funded by life and disability insurance. It is often the most affordable manner to fund the agreement.

This business was easily worth $4 million. We funded insurance ($2 million each) and through coordination with my client's attorney, we structured the corresponding buy-sell agreement. $2 million of insurance would be owned by each one of the business partners on the life of the other. In the event the first business partner died, they agreed, the remaining business partner would buy out (for the shares of the business at the agreed-upon $2 million) the deceased partner's spouse. The transaction would be clean. The widow would be in possession of cash proceeds for the families' share of the business and the remaining partner would own the business one hundred percent.

Additionally, we installed a "key person" policy. This policy would provide money as a financial injection to the corporation. You see, the executive running the business was a key person, key to the ongoing operation and success of the business. Without him the business continuation would suffer. This money would allow for payroll to continue uninterrupted and would provide cash flow and time to hire an executive to step into the business.

My client was a smoker and as such, his premiums were five times those of his nonsmoker business partner. After the policies were in place for several years, I learned that my client had quit smoking. Two years from the last cigarette, I could rewrite his insurance policies and obtain significantly reduced premiums for him as a nonsmoker. It made fiscal sense to redo his insurance contracts.

The life insurance underwriting process can take a good bit of time; blood work is taken, and information is requested of physicians. In the case of any insurance, there must be a qualified need for the insurance. There is evaluation of what is referred to as an "insurable interest." The insurance company wants to be sure that it makes sense that one business owner would have insurance on the other. They verify whether the insurance amount is appropriate as a buyout for the insured's ownership of the business. And they confirm the value of the business. It is a process, sometimes six to eight weeks long.

Two months later we approached the finish line. My non-smoking client had been approved for the replacement of those insurance policies. The company and his business partner would save thousands annually. It was a good day.

I called my client and let him know he was approved. I had his policies in hand and shared that we had accomplished our goal. The insurance company required only two signatures: (1) a signature accepting the policy and (2) a signature indicating there had been no change in his health since applying for the coverage.

My client replied, "I can't do that. I have a pulmonary embolism and I may have lung cancer." This changed everything. Never mind the policy replacements—those applications were toast. The savings on business continuation solutions—gone. There were more important items now. Understandably, my client's focus moved to his non-moneyed wife and his son.

His son was not yet an adult and still emotionally immature. He was a bright young man, but he was young. He still needed his dad. I learned quickly and clearly that his wife did not handle any part of the finances. She ran the house, she took care of the family, and volunteered. Prior to raising their son, she had worked also. Finances were not her interest or her aptitude. She always had access to money, credit cards, and necessary and discretionary funds. However, her husband handled the finances, refinances, car negotiations, mortgages, and business deals.

The conversation with my business-owner client swiftly changed gears and his question then became "Can you take care of my wife?" His wife would soon oversee sizeable assets, life insurance proceeds, and the livelihood of her son plus the next fifty years or so for herself. She was not financially inclined, had never needed to budget, and would soon be responsible for everything. The non-moneyed spouse! My reply: "When can I meet your wife?"

> "Non-moneyed" are clients who are less inclined to be focused on the financial aspects of life and the relationship.

Business owners often enter in business, focus on the development and growth of business, implement tax saving strategies—yet fail to plan for the end game. The death of an owner is certainly disruptive, both personally and professionally.

It is important to consider the application and need of key person insurance and buy-sell disability and life insurance. This applies to both a single business owner and a partnership. A 100% business owner needs a contingency plan so his or her spouse is not left in an untenable situation: the loss of his or her spouse as well as a business in free fall. A responsible owner will consider different types of insurance to fill in the gaps. In the situation of my client, he purchased buy-sell and key person insurance. The buy-sell had a dual purpose: It provided for the deceased partner's wife and also allowed the remaining partner to become 100% owner of the company. The key person policy provided a cash infusion to allow the company the funds to hire an interim CEO. The minimal cost of insurance provided valuable facilitation at the death of the owner.

A significant amount of coaching goes along with the wealth management, portfolio construction, and cash flow planning considerations of a high-net-worth client. There are budgeting discussions, tax implications of taking income from personal assets vs IRAs, stretch IRA options, trusts, legacy planning, and so on. Education, patience, and review are required. Our firm has many non-moneyed clients. "Non-moneyed" are clients who are less inclined to be focused on the financial aspects of life and the relationship. Money is not typically their natural interest or aptitude. These are our most enjoyable client relationships and as such, we now focus our practice on transition and coaching.

Loss of Spouse

Enter my newly widowed client. Losing a spouse, your confidant, is one of the most disruptive things you will ever experience in life. Couple it with a lack of interest in handling finances and you have a perfect storm. Things need to be addressed, yet they appear relatively insignificant when everything is emotionally charged after losing a trusted partner.

As intelligent people, we recognize there are things we do not wish to contend with and yet plenty that we must. Financial decisions should not be made quickly, especially when there is a significant relationship loss. It is recommended that you wait a minimum of six months after losing a spouse to make major decisions. You can discuss and assess what you have, maybe turn on some income or liquidate a small amount of cash to cover bills and expenses. But during those first six months, please do not move, buy, or sell property or assets if possible. Generally, it is just too soon to have clarity about what you desire and need in your life without your loved one.

After my client passed, his wife and I began meeting weekly. We would review mail, process life insurance claims, change beneficiaries, change bank accounts, and discuss her love of a lifetime. Over time we would be able to spread our meetings out a bit. We had established an initial budget and a cash distribution into her checking account monthly. We would need to revise and refresh these a few times. We had rolled over her IRAs and purchased new vehicles for both her and her son. She was directly listed as the beneficiary on the IRA assets. IRAs pass directly to the designated beneficiary. They do not require facilitation through a will or trust. For this client these assets passed outside the trust and were available to access without restriction.

> Financial decisions should not be made quickly, especially when there is a significant relationship loss.

We hired a computer guru to crack her husband's computer and brought someone in to unlock a gun safe. We suspected there was cash inside the safe. We reviewed documents, plans, and assets. There was an irrevocable trust providing lifestyle for both wife and son. The trust intended to provide for income to the family as well as preservation of principal. We conducted numerous calls with the trustee, my role often as translator for my client. Attorneys have the awesome responsibility of working on solutions and leveraging the law to accomplish client objectives. However, they sometimes miss the glazed-over look or the silence of our mutual clients. As the advisor, I sometimes reword the statements made so that the client can absorb their meaning. I encouraged her to consider some questions: "How does the trust impact my day-to-day life?" "What does the trust provide on an annual basis?" Clients desire the impact of the legal documents, not necessarily the detailed comprehensive disclosure of facts and explanation of processes. I found myself rephrasing what the attorney just communicated so our mutual client could understand the tax or trust impact.

Our relationship developed into one of deep trust and reliance. After all, I became her main resource and go-to for difficult life and financial decisions. For over thirteen years now, my role has been to act as a sounding board, investment advisor, and financial coach. As ideas and decisions come up, she reaches out and we consider the desires and merits—the pros and cons of helping her son with a home purchase, investing in a beach place, downsizing her home, refinancing her home, helping family with money, acquiring a new vehicle (lease or purchase), and so on. We review her investment accounts and performance and the economy. Her comfort level managing and communicating about her finances has increased. She recognizes and is curious regarding what her money can provide for her: lifetime of income, legacy for future grandchildren, and lifestyle today. She has a small beach house she enjoys in the summer. She does not yet take Social Security. She has a grown child who is now married and starting his own business. She stays mostly within her budget and volunteers her time. Life has adjusted and most of her assets remain intact. She has come a long way through her grief and out the other side. Life is good.

Pivot/Life Shift

Sometimes life opens a window and shifts your perspective. Sometimes you can move things around and adjust to your view. After all, nothing in life is permanent. No one said that you must grow up, work, and retire in the same state, let alone in the same house. Remember: this is *your* life. And you get to craft your destiny in any design you can dream up. There are no set rules. It is your choosing. Choosing may take time and it will likely involve several conversations with your spouse and your advisor to flesh out options and develop an outline.

What do you want during this time in your life? Are your kids grown? Where do your siblings live? What climate do you enjoy? Surely quality of life has a value. What would life be like if you relocated to a warmer climate? You are young and you are healthy. These are you best years! Why not now?

In life you are sometimes blessed with amazing people who enter your life at just the right time with just the right set of skills and experience, fantastic values to boot.

Enter Linda Parisi. I had the good fortune of being introduced to this lovely woman through Lori, the owner of a local property and casualty insurance agency. Lori met Linda and interviewed her over lunch. At the conclusion of lunch, Lori said, "I would love to offer you a position. I love your work ethic and you have extensive experience; you're relatable and likely an asset if I hire you. But I have to say—I think you're a better fit for Jennifer Lee and Modern-Wealth. I would like to introduce you."

Oh, the gift that landed in my lap! Did I ever receive the mother of all gifts? The first time we connected, in August of 2018, Linda and I spoke by telephone, a "fifteen-minute call" that actually lasted ninety minutes. She later flew in to meet me in person. We spent another five hours talking and sharing family, values, work ethic, and experiences. A match! It's a rare find to meet someone who is your equal and yet possesses skills that are not your same strengths. We balance each another, make each other better, and compose an excellent team.

Twenty-four months later Linda is woven into the fabric of Modern Wealth as if she had been here all along. She is loved, essential, a very dear colleague, and a trusted friend. And working together is fun—two nerds (okay, maybe just *one* nerd) who love talking strategy, product solutions, client development, and experience.

> You get to craft your destiny in any design you can dream up. What will you choose?

Linda had spent most of her career in the banking environment. She was an advisor inside a bank for thirty years. And she really impacted many lives. She worked a lot, cared for her clients, trained employees, mentored new and growing team members, and was well loved. She had quite the successful and fulfilling career in Ohio. She and her husband, Tony, had raised their three children. Enter Tony (this is for Tony—he likes to be included). He is gorgeous inside and out, a family man, a business mind, and a fierce competitor. Oh, and he is super sweet if you give the sarcasm a minute to die down. All true!

Nearing the age of sixty, with a small second home in Florida, Linda and Tony found themselves not wanting to return to Ohio after a long weekend in the Sunshine State. Wheels started to turn, and they considered how they might adjust their lives, their careers, and their income to move their life to include more beach and boat time, a little less stress, and a lot more vitamin D.

As a key person in his firm, Tony was able to negotiate working from Florida with a monthly trip to Ohio. Work from home, same income, fewer taxes, better environment. Done. Linda was looking for something she could embrace with a little less responsibility than she was carrying in Ohio. Lucky for my clients, now *our* clients, and for me, she found a home with Modern Wealth. Over the last twenty-four months together we have streamlined our business. Our processes are in place, organized and strategic. We are clear on the clients we seek and the people we can best serve. We love what we do, and we love the people we serve. We will not settle for mediocrity. We are open to locating that additional advisor who, like us, is a needle in a haystack.

Our only sticking point comes on bank holidays. I work and she sends me pictures of herself on a boat. It's a bit of a regular joke—and one I'm happy to concede.

Pre-Retirement

Life happened—you raised kids, you worked, you spent money, *C'est la vie* was your mantra, and time flew. Now you look up and wonder, "When can I retire?" Well, at least you have the foresight to consider the future now.

If you're in the end zone and are serious about making plans, it's time to tighten up that strategy and get real. Typically, although not always, this is the time when you're making the most money, and your kids are out of the house and less of a financial drain. You may find yourself with a few extra dollars in your pocket. How do you allocate them?

This is crunch time because you're most likely in your top earning years. I hope you're crushing it from a cash flow or discretionary perspective. In other words, you likely have more resources to put toward your retirement goal. You probably have accumulated some monies and need to consider how things are invested. What adjustments can be made given how close you are to the proverbial finish line? Perhaps you have participated in multiple plans through the years and not recently considered how they are positioned. Are there miscellaneous former 401(k) plans and IRAs floating about? It's time to get organized and more serious.

Are the kids grown and out of the house? Are car and mortgage payments comfortable or nearing their end? This is your time. Let's roll! We're going to strategize and think through the best use of those accumulated assets and that discretionary number.

Maybe you're embarrassed about money mistakes of the past or about your delay in planning. Honestly everyone makes financial missteps or delays planning. To procrastinate on what is uncomfortable or unknown is human.

There's no value in being embarrassed. We can't change the past—all we can do is learn from it.

> Assess today, adjust, and squeeze the juice.
> You have one life. Go live it!

Let's discuss and consider the following types of questions:

- How much income will you desire in retirement?
    - o Can you afford to stop working now or in ten years?
    - o How long will your assets last at that rate of distribution?
        - a. Will you run out of money?
- What will retirement look like for you?
    - o What is important to you in retirement?
    - o How will you spend your days?
- How are you willing to allocate your discretionary money between current and future needs?
    - o Where do you focus your discretionary income?
        - a. Travel bucket, income bucket, wedding for children, kids' student loans, and so on
- Do you have old IRAs, 401(k)s, 401(b)s all over the place?
    - o Would it make sense to consolidate them?
    - o Are your accounts too aggressive, too conservative?
    - o When is the last time you reviewed your risk profile?

- Will you live in the same house?
  - o Is it paid off?
  - o Should you pay more monthly on your home to try and have it paid off?
  - o Will you downsize?
  - o If you move, will it be to another state?
  - o What is the tax situation in that state?
- Do you have a pension? If so, how much?
  - o When can you start taking it?
  - o Does it adjust for inflation?
  - o Is there an option for continuation to your spouse?
    - a. If not, do you have life insurance to replace income should you die prematurely?
- What is your expected Social Security payment?
  - o Should you take it immediately or let it grow?
  - o Do you have longevity in your family?
- Do you have outside life insurance or will it go away when you retire?
  - o Do you need life insurance?
  - o Do you need long-term care insurance?
    - a. Does it make sense to consider consolidating them?
- Who will take care of you and how will it impact your spouse if you need long-term care?

Discussing these questions and more will provide a framework for your advisor to include top-priority items. It can help to highlight and narrow your focus. Planning now will be a much easier task. You may consider consolidating any accumulated monies, organizing, and making the most of your resources. Knowing your discretionary number allows you to be more cognizant of your choices. Focus on your future desired lifestyle instead of today's *Mocha Frappuccino Grande.* Google "The Latte Factor" to see how a simple adjustment can provide thousands of future dollars.

Life can be short. Make today count!

> Focus on your future desired lifestyle
> instead of today's
> Mocha Frappuccino Grande.

The average life expectancy is 76 (27,740 days) for men and 81 (29,565 days) for women. I shared earlier that I'm 50. I just calculated that on average I have 11,315 days left on this earth. That's a small number. And now I can't un-know that number. Live each day with purpose.

As I move about in my relationships and my business, I'm acutely aware of the sand in the hourglass. Doesn't this heighten the impact of every connection or lack of connection? It affords me the opportunity to value my time and relationships and to consider how I spend and save my resources, my time being my greatest resource.

Average life expectancy in days: Male 27,740 / Female 29,565

Less: current age_____ x 365 = (_____)

# of days left to live with intention _____

# of Saturdays (divide above # by 7) _____

# of sunrises or sunsets _____

# of gourmet meals _____

MODERN WEALTH

Notes

Download your worksheet here:
https://SqueezeTheJuiceBook.com/Resources

CHAPTER 13

Teaching Legacy

Why not communicate your experience and values to the next generation or two? Isn't that a great idea? What if you started life knowing what you know now? How much more could you accomplish? Would your life have been easier, smoother? Would you have taken more risk? What if you shared your knowledge, your values, and your assets through a foundation? That's a gift that keeps on giving and a true legacy.

> A variety of solutions are available to the wealthy. They include components such as trusts, foundations, charitable remainder trusts, gifting strategies, and more. These are complex considerations and should be considered with a team of advisors, including a tax professional, a financial and insurance advisor, and an estate planning attorney.

By now you recognize that when the subject of money or business strategy presents itself, I'm completely engaged. I had a drink with a friend, recently widowed. As we visited she shared the following statement: "There's so much money. All the grandkids have education funds—there's a trust. It's all buttoned up. We did well. There's just so much." This was an actual conversation with my friend.

She and her husband had worked hard, built their careers, and provided for their families. They had enjoyed life through travel and theater and had deep connections to their community. After his death, the realization that she could never spend the money they had amassed seemed to be at the top of her mind. We agreed that this was both a luxury and a burden. To be responsible for the disposition of assets, would she leave the kids and grandkids with too much?

I asked, "Have you ever thought of a donor-advised fund or a foundation? What if you involved your kids and grandkids in a gifting strategy?"

My suggestion was to involve the children and grandchildren in the research and consideration of where to gift, to host an annual family meeting to discuss the charities and organizations the family researched. They could prepare and consider in advance the organizations for which they had conviction. These meetings would provide both a financial and personal legacy and would serve to communicate the life values and passions of the donor. These would serve as a valuable family connection with impact.

Multiple considerations should be examined with clients, from a donor-advised fund to the inclusion of a charitable remainder trust (CRT) to establishing a foundation. Appreciated assets can be leveraged, insurance can be implemented, and income and tax strategies deployed. Each of these instruments has differing levels of complexity, responsibility, and cost. Depending on the wealth of the client and his or her need for control or for income, one vehicle will certainly be a better choice than others.

For my friend, her need of income from these assets was negligible. What piqued her interest was the opportunity to share her values with her grandchildren. She could accomplish her objective more simply through the choice of a donor-advised fund. She would teach her grandkids about generosity, integrity, and responsibility through this process. Donated funds and appreciated assets would be distributed annually. Deep communication and conversation with the kids and grandkids regarding values are, of course, a desirable benefit. If desired, this legacy could go on indefinitely.

CHAPTER 14

Writing Mine

Like many couples, Kelli and I divide and conquer duties. We both cook, but very differently. If you crave authentic Italian sauce, a roast chicken, or unbelievable mashed potatoes, look to Kelli. On the other hand, if you want a cooking and eating experience in our kitchen and desire a randomly crafted meal, I am your gal. I love to cook on the fly.

In our family, I am the primary breadwinner. I absolutely love what I do for a living so mostly it's not work. Sure, there are challenging and frustrating days, but fortunately for me they are only a sliver of my work life.

In my practice and in life I have found that often there is a money spouse and a non-moneyed spouse. This is a made-up word that describes my wife and many people I encounter as clients. Kelli has little to no interest in budget; investments; savings models; financing; negotiating a car purchase; the stock market; cash flow; Roth IRAs; vehicles like 401(k)s, 403(b)s, and IRAs that provide tax deferral; life insurance; long-term care; or the benefits of paying the equivalent of one extra mortgage payment a year. She has earned a living, having run her own business, and yet has zero interest in discussing finances. Let's just say that financial topics are far from Kelli's natural disposition. For us it's a good match, since there is no competition for gardening, cooking, decorating, paying bills, or running the businesses. We simply divide and conquer. And mostly we stay in our corners—a fair deal for us.

People have differing aptitudes and they are sometimes evident as children. Kelli likely does not remember playing with real coins in kindergarten when she was small, as I do. Kelli started playing with her aunt's hair at age 2, and it stuck.

Realizing that she is more capable than me in matters of creativity, ingenuity, warmth, and socialization, I do not attempt to delve into her area of expertise. She makes everything more beautiful. She is the salt added to my life, making everything just a little better. And she sometimes gets me to pause to listen to the waves, smell the salty air, and soak up the sun.

Kelli has rarely met a person whom she could not get to be her friend and a future resource. It would seem she knows just about everyone. She has a guy for this and that, and of course you should see our dentist—she is awesome. If you were to meet Kelli you would soon be embraced with the most genuine and amazing hug. She exudes warmth. This gift I do not so naturally possess. I *am* a good hugger—but it's just not the same.

> My best recommendation in writing
> your love letter is to establish your mindset.
> Consider the conversation you would have if this
> were your last—with your spouse, child, loved one.
> Very simply, what do you need him or her to know?
> And what do you want to share?

Your love letter should include a variety of informational components as well as personal impact. I will illustrate through my love letter.

I wrote mine on the way to the airport. You see, I had taught a colleague the love letter presentation and had attended her rendition of the presentation the night before I left for a conference in California. I had not yet put pen to paper myself. Was I the shoemaker and my spouse was left barefoot? There was so much to say. If something happened to me, Kelli would be taken care of. I had a trust, life insurance, and assets, but—she really would not know whom to trust, where to start, what assets we have, how to facilitate sales of my businesses. She would worry about having enough money to pay bills, whether she could stay in our home, where my passwords could be found, what to do about life insurance claims, and so on.

She might be at risk of her finances vanishing too quickly. She might be scared and anxious about areas that were, in our relationship, my responsibility. I could make this smoother with some communication. As the self-proclaimed driver in the family, aka control freak, I asked Kelli to drive me to the airport. She was shocked and awed by the task since I *always* drive. I proceeded to write feverishly over the course of the forty-five-minute ride to the Tampa airport.

Dear Kelli,

My life with you has been full. Colorful, comforting, and joyful. You are my chosen family. I have appreciated your outgoing, extroverted, engaging, and energetic personality. Your affection is contagious. I love the way you engage and hug new people as if you have known them for years. You have a familiarity, a sweetness, and an openness that is not common.

You have made my offices, our homes, and other people's homes beautiful and functional with your creativity and style. I have always been impressed. And you designed them all ever mindful of the cost. It never ceases to amaze me when you get that curious expression as you create something new in your head. It is sure to come out beautifully.

The thing that drew me to you and always impressed, maybe intimidated, me was your connection and closeness to your family. Having the same connection, passion, and love for our nieces and nephews was just not so commonplace. And it was no surprise when you embraced my family as your own.

Thank you for the richness, affect, delight, and order you brought to my life. It would not have been so vivid without you.

As for the financial part of the love letter:

There are assets, life insurance, and there is a trust. You will have all that you need for this life and plenty to leave to the kids, all nine nieces and nephews, and possibly grandnieces and grandnephews.

The life insurance will be paid into the trust. I have two policies: one term policy as well as a variable universal life policy. The trust is set up to provide for you. You will not need to worry about being able to pay the mortgage or whether you can continue your lifestyle. You will receive a liberal income. The trust will invest and protect the principal to provide income for your lifetime and as a potential future inheritance. Additionally, should you need access to the principal for health, welfare, and maintenance, there are provisions.

I know that you have little or no interest in finances and money management, so I have set things up in my trust to provide you with cash flow, ease of management, and a little less stress. Your monthly income will cover mortgage, cars, groceries, travel, health expenses, insurance, gifts, improvements, repairs, etc. You can think of these monthly distributions like a paycheck. It is not a paycheck but will be a steady flow of money so that you can live financially as if I were still here.

Life insurance: If you are the breadwinner, you may have people depending on you. Such responsibility motivates you to take care of your people. Life insurance is a simple and cost-effective way to cover your family while you are accumulating assets, saving for retirement, paying mortgages, educating your children, and preparing to have fun in retirement. Life insurance kicks in if your time is cut short.

Young and healthy is easiest. Buy a thirty-year term policy, pay minimally for insurance, and buy yourself some time to get your ducks in a row.

Young and healthy and want to make sure that you have something to show for those insurance premiums? Consider permanent insurance, perhaps a blend of the two. There are many variations and combinations that may be appropriate. As you explore the financial building blocks and consider your resources, the appropriate choice will become clearer.

For me, I had gone with a thirty-year term policy when I was 33. I'm 50 now. My policy costs only $730 annually, a steal. I also purchased a smaller permanent policy for the purpose of cash accumulation to provide options: tax favorable, borrowing from myself, and access to funds prior to age 59½. I used a variable universal life policy to provide payment flexibility and more assertive internal policy investment options. The death benefit on this one is smaller. My intention with these policies has been to provide my family coverage as I accumulate assets. If you do as you plan and pay down mortgages, fund retirement plans, and accumulate personal assets, then term insurance will have been a viable and cost-effective option.

If you are older there is still plenty of opportunity—it is just that life and doctors happen, so there's underwriting. You need a good agent to screen you, educate you, and then guide you through the insurance and underwriting process. It's not rocket science, but it's not for your rookie nephew either.

And then there is the use of insurance for tax and charitable purposes, estate planning, business cash flow, business buyouts, continuity, and so on. Each of these topics could comprise a chapter, but you don't want to know how to do it, and you don't necessarily need to. What you need is an advocate, a trusted advisor, a fiduciary. An experienced advisor will discuss what's important to you specifically as well as the risks associated with your current situation. By the way, everything changes, and nothing is perfect. So revisit this conversation every few years.

> It's not rocket science,
> but it's not for your rookie nephew either.

To calculate your personal insurance needs, go to lifehappens.org for insurance awareness, calculators, and educational information.

Of course, I know that you'll want a new truck every few years and you can continue to buy one every five years or so. Get Eric to negotiate your vehicle or ask your advisor. Neither will be emotionally attached to the purchase.

In my practice I have negotiated a few vehicles for clients. Once during a routine check with my client when she mentioned that she would like to buy a new car, she said she wondered if it was feasible. We reviewed her investment account, its performance, scheduled income, and determined that yes, it was plausible. I asked her about the type of vehicle and its potential cost. She hesitated. She then indicated that she thought she wanted a two- or three-year-old car but one with certain features. Something in her voice made me ask, "Have you ever negotiated a car purchase before?" Her reply: "No, my dad always helped me with it." I see.

I offered to assist in the negotiation process and to alleviate some of the stressors and take out the emotion of purchasing the vehicle. You see, I was not tied to any car—not to color, model, year, or any potential sales pitch. My focus was on my client and getting her the most favorable deal I could negotiate. I took down the details of her desired general vehicle and placed a search online. My phone and email began blowing up with salespeople. I began and continued negotiations and the search for viable options meeting the criteria. I negotiated the deal and arranged for delivery. I met the client at the dealership, we test drove the car, and when she said yes, I finished with the salesman and had paperwork set up for her to purchase the car that evening. The client was happy. A fair deal had been negotiated and unnecessary stressors removed.

> *The IRA assets are paid out directly to you. You can withdraw them at once or over a period of years. The rules change, so it's best to check on your options. You may have access to stretch your distributions, which could be to your advantage. Consider your options and please wait six months before making any big decisions. Talk this through with Linda Parisi and our accountant, Karen.*

Presently the distribution laws for IRAs allow for a variety of choices and they are different for spousal beneficiaries and non-spousal beneficiaries. It's best to check the IRS.gov site to see the current options allowed.

IRAs can be added to a trust. Consult your estate planning attorney, accountant, and advisor to discuss the pros and cons to determine the best solution for you. Many people like me choose to simply allow the IRAs to pass outside the trust. In my case, their value in contrast to personally held taxable assets is 25%. This, however, may not be true for your situation.

You may have beneficiaries whose spending you would like to manage, or more specifically you may desire to control your assets from the grave. The only way to maintain control during incapacity or after death is through a trust.

A seasoned financial advisor will have relationships with trusted advisors like estate planning attorneys, tax experts, charitable giving resources, accountants, and professional money managers. Some of these professionals may be needed or important for your plan.

There's also the case of my two businesses as well as other personal assets. The businesses are a bit more complex.

If Linda is still in the financial services business, that part is a bit easier. She can take over day-to-day operations. Some might say that she already does. She can buy the business from you over time through fees/revenues that come into Modern Wealth. There is a general standard application of purchase price for our industry. Karen, portfolio management company resources, a broker dealer, or another accountant can assist in determining standard and fair purchase value. If Linda does not desire to buy it, she would ideally be able to assist in the sale. She should be compensated for finding an appropriate buyer whether through a business partner or through our network like a broker (fees paid to a broker are usually around 5%). In 2021 I am certain that the business would be purchased by her. She is amazing, integrated with clients, experienced, and more than qualified. In 2035, well, I hope to have brought on other advisors and developed an alternative buyout. In any case, the worst thing that would happen is that you would contact business partners and source an appropriate buyer. Reaching out directly to the portfolio management teams will be valuable as they can connect you to other advisors who may be an appropriate fit for my clients. Not all advisors are created equal. And my clients will recognize a disconnect. Be sure to hire an attorney to represent you. These things can get complex and sometimes emotional. And you know how I hate to leave anything on the table. Make a good deal, at least a fair one. You can always gift it to someone in need.

If PNB is still in our financial picture, any buyer will need to be approved by the franchise. I would start with "What do you want out of the business?" I know that your answer would likely be a resounding "Nothing!" However, there is a value to the business. It's paid off and generates revenue and profits. Our accountant or attorney can assist in determining.

Please be sure that you take care of Kris. She has been a valued partner. Truly she has performed like an owner and should be treated as such. She will be critical in facilitating the business transition and should be rewarded for sticking it out—a retention bonus in addition to a portion of the sale. And she may be ready to own it. Consider this as an option.

Initially I would suggest going to other franchisees, perhaps individually at first and then on a franchise call. They are the most natural fit for purchase. They know the business and can step in. Someone will want it, or he or she may know someone who will buy it. One of our clients may even be interested. Attorney, attorney, attorney. I cannot stress it enough. This deal would be less straightforward than Modern Wealth. Just have representation.

If you own a business, or two, as I do, things can get more thorny. Do you have a business succession plan? Is there a business partner or an industry partner who can take over a business? How will the value be determined? Is that person fiscally able to buy out your family/spouse? Have you agreed upon a purchase price and funded your buy-sell agreement with life insurance? Can your spouse continue to operate the business by hiring a CEO? Does he or she have the proper licenses? Is there a market for your business?

These are important considerations to make for a smooth transition should you die while still operating your business. Many business owners simply let their business die with them. This seems like a shame to me: money left on the table, a lifetime of work and creation left to fade away, employees left without a path. Such discussions must be had with business partners, with insurance and financial professionals, and ultimately with your attorney. You will want to have an agreement in place that outlines how the value of the business is determined as well as the payout structure to your beneficiaries.

There will also be a financial buffer for travel and fun stuff. Try to travel—there's nothing like exploring someplace new, examining different people and cultures, food and wine, and traditions. I had some of my most joyful memories traveling to Italy with you, traveling to China and to South Africa. Squeeze the juice out of a country, city, or experience.

Take Stephanie with you or hitch onto a trip with the family or the chamber. Steph would love it and she would look after you. She has always been a mother hen. Life is about experiences. Keep having new ones. Think of me when you travel or stretch.

And then there are the pragmatic details:

- What does your spouse need to know?
- Where are your passwords?
- Who are your trusted advisors?
- What are your values and how would you like them respected?
- Are there treasures in your home with a story that only you know about?
  - a. What do they symbolize, what is the story, and why are they important?
- What resources will your spouse have?
  - a. income, Social Security, life insurance, brokerage accounts, IRAs, real estate
- What is your greatest fear for them?
- How would you like your final services?
  - a. buried or cremated?

- Who gets what?
- Is there any money hidden? and on and on
- What do they need to know—about love, sacrifice, community, integrity, work ethic, finances, self-care, marriage?

> Have you communicated these values and lessons? If you have smaller children, even teenagers, this may create a lump in your throat. Embrace that lump and get to writing.

There are things to worry about, but not financial resources. Please know that you have enough assets to take care of you for your lifetime. Linda Parisi can certainly take care of helping you with the management of funds and making good decisions.

I will leave you with this money advice. You have heard it before—do your best not to spend the principal, live on the earnings, and you will not run out. If you decide that you are not comfortable talking about the money, take Suzanne or Rhonda with you. They will ask anything and everything. Travel, teach the nieces and nephews to fish—don't just give them money. Give them opportunities or experiences. Live your life and find love again.

Share with your loved ones whom to trust, whom not to trust, assurances about the resources at their disposal, suggestions about how to proceed, confessions of your love, and requests to share your love for the special people in your life through stories. Provide explanations and distributions of favorite and meaningful items. Ask yourself, "What are my most valuable possessions and who would most enjoy receiving them?" Write the story behind each item. And even consider gifting those items during your lifetime. You will get to see the joy they bring.

I have had the great fortune of an amazing extended family—aunties who have taught me how to be a good human as well as a beloved aunt. My Aunt Pat has always been a special person in my life. Aunts are cool like that and we have that connection. She is gorgeous inside and out; striking and elegant. Don't be fooled—she can cut you with a look if you step out of line. We have some similarities, at least the latter. Two years ago Aunt Pat began gifting pieces of her uncommon jewelry collection. As a child, teenager, and young adult, I was quick to note the unique and custom jewels she showcased at family gatherings. I would pepper her with questions about stones, metals, and the workmanship. She had collaborated with artists designing just what she had envisioned.

One of my favorite possessions is a ring she gave me last year. It is sterling silver with a citrine floating in the center between two pieces of silver riveted together. It is a looker and is stunning, like her. I wear it every day and it makes me think of her.

Consider whether it is time to share your stuff, your love, and your story with those in your life. You may find it enjoyable to see them appreciate and think of you.

Possessions that have value:

- Wedding rings
- Diamond earrings
- Miscellaneous sterling silver and gold jewelry
- Vehicles
- Real Estate

Possessions of personal significance:

- Collage created by Emma at age 7
- Silver-and-gold Tiffany bracelet from my mom and dad on my thirtieth birthday
- Nana's wedding band as my thumb ring
- Chinese bowls from Wing's restaurant given to me by Aunt Bev
- Chinese bowl from trip to China directly from our family village
- Ring from Aunt Pat
- The Seven Spiritual Laws—the dog-eared and notated copy

Kelli,

Would you please give my sister my thumb ring made from my Nana's wedding band? For thirty-five years of my life Nana was my favorite person. And for the last fifteen years, I have enjoyed having her with me. Please purchase my dearest girlfriends and nieces each a thumb ring to remember me—white gold or yellow gold depending on their preferences.

My wishes are for a celebration of life, not a mourning. Drink excellent wine! Have yummy food, maybe even a cook-off. That would be epic. Tell funny stories, a roast if you will.

Be well. Enjoy life. It can be short. Travel. Have new experiences. Fall in love again.

Epilogue

There is a specific clientele who thrive when working with our team. They are receptive, engaged, yet often anxious or disinterested when it comes to money. They have much to address when it comes to life and finance. They love their family and their businesses. They are passionate about their values, even if they do not easily articulate them. They are protectionist. Our clients understand their money mostly in the form of lifestyle: kids' private school, retirement, house paid off, reduced debt, wealth accumulation, financial freedom, legacy.

We would love the opportunity to partner with you. The role we have in our partnership with clients is to uncover, translate, and leverage resources so that you can enjoy the benefits of financial freedom. Remember: financial planning is *simple.* If you can identify what you have and what you want, we can take it from there.

In family, business, legacy, and money, clients desire to provide for something beyond themselves, today as well as in the future. They don't want to just give it away—they desire to make an impact. They love the idea of a legacy—of their persona, money, business, and values living on. These are the people of likeminded vision with whom we seek to have a financial partnership.

Our practice is structured this way so that we can maintain personal relationships with clients. We have a limited number of advisory client relationships and we selectively grow our practice. Through comprehensive planning and communication, our clients have the desired level of support to make thoughtful financial decisions. Through our discovery sessions, we educate and highlight what a partnership will look like. If it is a good fit for both parties, we proceed.

Primarily we seek to influence and support the non-moneyed party with a long-term partnership.

When the need is more strategic, we offer a discovery session often followed by a financial plan and coaching sessions. Clients who are focused and dedicated to financial freedom embrace the coaching and accountability model. They are task oriented and motivated to move their plans forward. They are focused and dedicated to being their best selves. They leverage us for strategy as they move through their plan. We meet our clients where they are. We accompany them where they desire to travel.

> If you have a group you feel would benefit from *Squeeze the Juice*, just ask.

I hope you have enjoyed this book, that it has made you think and perhaps woken you up to using money as a tool. If we can help with a book, a seminar, a workshop, or a talk, we welcome the opportunity. It is most awesome to speak with groups. The support and comradery in the room are tangible. If you have a group you feel would benefit from a talk, workshop or an excerpt of Squeeze the Juice, please reach out to us at booking@squeezethejuicebook.com. I believe that knowledge should be shared.

It is my feeling that everyone listening to or reading this book can garner at least one idea, one nugget that you can add to your family's financial plan. Which of the following did you take away? It doesn't matter what gem you found—just use it.

- How to make sure your family is protected with insurance: life, disability, or long-term care
- Considering how to work with an advisor—what to expect, what questions to ask
- Finding courage or community through story
- How you can squeeze the juice in your life
- Gaining support and strength to be patient through a divorce
- Learning never to leave money on the table
- Considering a partnership with an advisory team
- Gaining awareness of "collaborative divorce"
- Learning how you can share your financial knowledge and create a legacy of values and charity for your grandchildren that will last many lifetimes
- Learning something about inherited assets
- Considering communicating with your family about your expectations
- Writing your family love letter
- Considering converting IRA assets to a Roth
- Discovering how to protect a spendthrift child with a trust or a restricted beneficiary election
- Writing a note to your child about how you know him or her, what you hope for him or her. It is the most amazing feeling to be known.

Did you garner more than one nugget? I would love to hear about it. Contact me to discuss: www.modern-wealth.com

> It is the most amazing feeling to be known.

My wish is to continue having meaningful relationships that are deep, supportive, and impactful. Professionally, I love what I do for a living. I am truly fortunate that most of the time it does not feel like work. It has been twenty-six years since I started talking to people about money—forty-four if you count my first financial conference attending as my dad's date (Mom was pregnant with my little brother). It was a date I will never forget! I had my hair done, got to wear a pretty dress, and talked with a bunch of grown-ups. I was in heaven. In fact, I thought I was already an adult.

Dressed up for my first financial conference.

Now that I'm grown and can reflect on the lessons learned from my father, it's easy to see how to squeeze the juice. Live your life—get the best out of it. Then leave your mark as your legacy.

Life is short and I want to keep loving what I do and how I spend my time. Work and spending time with my family have always been at the top of my list. Travel has become increasingly important to me. And at age fifty, the dot on my timeline has increasing significance. As I look at my next forty years, I plan and hope for health, family connection, and deep relationships. In my life I incorporate people whom I enjoy, new experiences traveling, impactful relationships, spiritual and emotional expansion. I wish for you a life with intention. Now go *squeeze the juice!*

MODERN WEALTH

Notes